L[illegible] TO THE PRAISE OF HIS GLORY

DISCOVERING HOW TO LIVE IN THE ONLY WAY THAT MATTERS

MIKE FRISBY

British Library Cataloguing-in-Publication Data

A catalogue record for this book is available from the British Library

ISBN: 978-1-0369-3187-2

First published 2025

Cover design and typesetting by Tuuli Platner, tuuliplatner.co.uk

DEDICATED TO

My dearly loved wife and best friend,

DENISE

Our highly treasured children and their partners,

REBECCA and GAVIN

TIM and JACQUI

LYDIA and TIM

Our precious and greatly loved grandchildren,

CHARLIE SOPHIA ELLA

OLIVIA ARIANNA

ELI IMMY

Contents

Westminster Shorter Catechism - Question 35

Q: What is sanctification?

A: Sanctification is the work of God's free grace, whereby we are renewed in the whole man after the image of God, and are enabled more and more to die unto sin, and live unto righteousness.[1]

[Sanctification] is a continuing change worked by God in us, freeing us from sinful habits and forming in us Christlike affections, dispositions, and virtues. It does not mean that sin is instantly eradicated, but it is also more than a counteraction, in which sin is merely restrained or repressed without being progressively destroyed. Sanctification is a real transformation, not just the appearance of one.[2]

So, we keep on praying for you, asking our God to enable you to live a life worthy of his call. May he give you the power to accomplish all the good things your faith prompts you to do. Then the name of our Lord Jesus will be honoured because of the way you live, and you will be honoured along with him. This is all made possible because of the grace of our God and Lord, Jesus Christ.
(2 Thessalonians 1 v 11 - 12 NLT)

The power of a person is found in likeness to Jesus Christ. It is not found in brilliance, gifting, knowledge, position, verbal power, reputation or fame. It is found when a mere person, such as yourself, flings open the corridors and closets of their life so that they are full of the light and love of God. That person, full of living water, will alter any landscape in which they walk. That person will help fill the earth with God's glory.[3]

Notes

1 www.cambridgepres.org.uk/resources/app/type/westminster-shorter-catechism/resource/371/title/q35

2 The Reformation Study Bible – General Editor, R. C. Sproul, Ligonier Publishing (formerly Reformation Trust), Westminster Shorter Catechism (Q. 35)

3 Redeeming Power, Understanding Authority and Abuse in the Church, Diane Langberg, Brazos Press, 20th October 2020, Chapter 11

Preface

Some years ago, I received a letter from my son in which he expressed how the talk I gave at his wedding lived with him and his wife throughout the early years of their married life. My talk had focused on the story of Moses' reluctance to embrace God's commission to lead the Israelites out of Egypt. His first response being one of self-doubt.

Nevertheless, his doubts were swiftly counteracted by God's promise to be with him, and through a series of supernatural signs, God gave him the much-needed confidence that his commission would prosper and succeed. My main point had been how ordinary lives become extraordinary lives when we surrender ourselves to the will and call of God.

My son went on to say they would often pray that God would use their ordinariness, and do extraordinary things through them for his glory:

> *I don't really have a desire to do the 'big things' in the way that many church people think of. I just want to live my life and love the people that God brings into it as Jesus would – to be a good husband, a good father, a good son, brother, friend, a good neighbour, a good firefighter. To lay my ordinary life before God, and in so doing, see God do the extraordinary through it.*

When the Apostle Paul wrote to ordinary followers of Jesus in the church at Ephesus, he reminded them of their adoption into God's family, and how God had chosen them *"to live to the praise of God's glory"* (see Ephesians 1 v 5 - 6, 12). Writing to the saints at

Philippi, he similarly encouraged them to live their lives in a way that reflected the gospel of Christ and brought glory to God:

> Whatever happens, conduct yourselves in a manner worthy of the gospel of Christ. Then, whether I come and see you or only hear about you in my absence, I will know that you stand firm in the one Spirit, striving together as one for the faith of the gospel without being frightened in any way by those who oppose you...
> (Philippians 1 v 27 - 28)

In this book we are going to look at a selection of biblical passages to help us on our journey of becoming increasingly transformed into the likeness of God's Son. We'll consider attitudes and actions to help us follow Jesus' example, displayed throughout the entirety of his life. We'll explore biblical truths, that once grasped, will enable ordinary Christians to live together in church families in a way that shows Jesus to a watching world. It was Eugene Peterson who perceptively observed:

> *The Jesus way wedded to the Jesus truth brings about the Jesus life.*[1]

Mike Frisby
(Cambridge, 2025)

---

1 The Jesus Way: A Conversation on the Ways That Jesus Is the Way, Eerdmans, 2nd September 2011

Introduction

MAKING OUR MARK

Have you ever longed to live a life larger than yourself? A life that brings honour and glory to God as you become more and more transformed into the likeness of Jesus? A life that makes a mark and enables your 'ordinary' days to draw attention to an extraordinary God?

This desire for our lives to be significant and of consequence is a sentiment that most of us can identify with, but one which we tend to wrestle with throughout the course of our lives. For despite the encouragement and affirmation of others, our own evaluation of our lives can give credence to the thought that we have not yet, in our opinion, made the mark we had hoped for!

I remember my own struggles in my early teenage years. Having been endowed with some sporting ability, I had the privilege of representing my senior school at most sports, including football, cricket and basketball. The only problem was that in my estimation, I was simply a very ordinary player.

It may have been true that on the odd occasion I exhibited flashes of brilliance, but certainly nothing exceptional! Not like my friend Graham, who was both the outstanding captain of the school football team, and an extraordinary athlete. When competing in the 400 metres, he would run like the wind and leave all the other competitors far behind in his wake. Now that was exceptional talent! Talent that was sure to make its mark, both in the sports world and in his chosen career.

That said, it did not take me long before I came to understand that comparison is a dangerous road to travel at any age!

Listen to the testimony of Magda Murawska M Ed:

Happy and proud of my friends' accomplishments, I find myself comparing my own life to theirs. It's almost an involuntary act, one that has been honed with years of practice. My comparison begins in the calm waters of commonalities, but quickly veers into the more dangerous high tide of comparisons, as I began to negatively compare what's lacking in my life based on what is present in theirs. I soon hear the thoughts of "I should be farther ahead in my career," "I should be doing this," "I should be doing that," etc. I've entered the 'Sea of Shoulds' – an unpredictable place, like the Bermuda Triangle, where few come out unscathed.

The danger of comparing ourselves to others is that our comparisons are never fair. Each one of us is a unique individual with characteristics and life events that are unique to only us.[1]

Perhaps, we need to remind ourselves more frequently that being unique means we bring to the world things no other person can!

Comparison aside, the desire to make our mark is a worthy ambition. Particularly so, if the motivation behind it springs from a sincere desire for our life to bring honour and glory to God. Wanting to be a source of blessing to others around us, loving God with all our heart, mind, soul and strength, and loving our neighbour as ourself, are all worthy objectives for followers of Jesus (see Deuteronomy 6 v 4 - 5 and Matthew 22 v 37 - 40).

So, how do we get the ball rolling in our pursuit of a God-honouring life?

Charlie Mackesy, in his enchanting and insightful book, "The Boy, the Mole, the Fox and the Horse," comes to our aid. Mackesy reminds the reader of an important truth that, once embraced, can fortify us in the pursuit of our goal to become faithful and fruitful followers of Jesus Christ. The truth, simply put, is that we don't have to be living an extraordinary life to be loved by God, or indeed to make our mark in the world:

"Sometimes I worry you'll all realise I'm ordinary," said the boy.
"Love doesn't need you to be extraordinary," said the mole.[2]

Ordinariness is no barrier to our being loved by God. When we know this deeply, it frees us to begin exploring the measures that enable our ordinary lives to draw attention to our extraordinary God and Saviour, Jesus Christ. But, before we look at these, let me say a few words about an issue that has become a stumbling block for some people in today's church.

Playing our part

Listening to a number of voices in the church, you might be forgiven for thinking that to truly make your mark as a follower of Jesus, you must aspire to some form of leadership position. But is that really true?

One writer speaks of a "leadership phenomenon" today, with its plethora of leadership books, leadership conferences, leadership retreats and leadership dinners! He notes that one of the most frequent statements he hears in church circles today is, "We are training disciples and making leaders."[3]

Let me acknowledge straightaway that leadership in the church is vital, and the honouring of our church leaders is plainly taught in Scripture. Indeed, the Apostle Paul states that if a person sets their heart on local church leadership, then they desire a valuable and honourable task.[4]

Nevertheless, it is important to ask the following questions. Does Scripture imply a church leader has greater value, influence, prestige, opportunity and ability to make a mark in life, than other followers of Jesus? What about followers of Jesus involved in other spheres and activities of life, perhaps outside of the church? Do their lives count in the grand scheme of things?

If in our thinking we attach greater value to church leaders or church workers than being a shop worker, banker, police officer, nurse, student, politician, business person, artist, sports person, computer programmer, care worker or [fill in the blank]... then in doing so, I believe we have misunderstood the purposes of God. If we feel God is more interested in humanitarian activities or the voluntary sector than "normal" work, then we have again misunderstood God's intent for his people.

You may have also observed a current trend of attaching lower status to the unemployed or others who don't receive a wage for their efforts. Or maybe you've seen we can fail to honour and value people with various kinds of disability.

The sixteenth-century English scholar William Tyndale wrote:

> *There is no work better than another to please God; to pour water, to wash dishes, to be a cobbler, or an apostle, all is one; to wash dishes and to preach is all one, as touching the deed, to please God.*[5]

Whatever our occupation, status or role in life, as followers of Jesus we are called to go about them with the utmost integrity. The late Christian leader John Stott gave us a helpful definition of work when he said:

> *Work is the expenditure of energy, mental, manual or a mixture of both, which brings fulfilment to the worker, benefit to the community and glory to God.*[6]

It has been troubling in recent days to come across followers of Jesus who seriously think that the true pinnacle of discipleship is to one day become a notable leader within their local church community, or the wider body of Christ.

Please don't get me wrong – I believe in the vital importance of church leadership (I will explain a little more about that in a moment). However, I want to suggest that numbers of churches have been suffering from a subtle form of myopia. While legitimately focusing on raising up leaders, there has been a failure to see and encourage the potential of every true follower of Jesus in the body of Christ.

To test to what degree your own thinking may have been influenced by the prominence being given to leadership roles within current church life, think for a moment how you might answer the following question:

> *Would you rather be recognised as a leader or as a follower?*

This contribution from Randy Richards and Brandon O'Brien (particularly if you are from the West), may help you in formulating your answer:

> *For many Westerners, the term follower connotes a weakness of character, as when a person cannot resist peer pressure but "goes along with the crowd." Follower connotes a lack of creativity and ambition, portraying the average office worker as a drone dutifully churning out unimportant work under the direction of a (sometimes) talented and successful manager. By contrast, the term leader connotes a constellation of virtues. It implies that a person is efficient, creative, productive and charismatic enough to encourage others to be the same. Businesses want to hire leaders, not followers. And, perhaps ironically, so do churches. The importance of leadership among Christians is illustrated by the fact that one of the most influential magazines for church leaders in the United States is called "Leadership Journal." As much as our culture pushes us to be leaders, the Bible urges us to become followers. At a certain level we know this is true, so we talk about "servant leadership" as a way of distinguishing our position from others.*
>
> *Of course, we are to be followers of Jesus (Matthew 4 v 19). But we are also to be followers of those who follow Jesus faithfully (1 Corinthians 11 v 1). God even wants us to follow those whose station in life demands our obedience, even if they are not Christians (Romans 13 v 1 - 2; 1 Peter 2 v 13 - 14). Leadership is a Western virtue; submission is a biblical virtue.*[7]

How did you fare? Are you convinced that all lives matter to God? That everyone, including leaders, are called to be followers of Jesus? And, if that last statement is true, are you clear on the contribution leaders make to the health, vitality, growth and development of God's people?

Paul, writing to the church at Ephesus, states that the gifts of people given by the risen and ascended Christ to his church (apostles, prophets, evangelists, pastors and teachers), were given for the express purpose of preparing God's people for works of service. The end goal for Paul was the development of a unified and mature body of Christ that exhibits all His fullness (see Ephesians 4 v 7 - 13).

Later in the same chapter he underscores how the body of Christ, *"grows and builds itself up in love,* ***as each part does its work"*** (verse 16; emphasis added).

Paul uses a similar analogy in 1 Corinthians 12, when again reminding followers of Jesus that each one of them is a vital and significant part of the body of Christ. There is neither room for self-disqualification, nor independence. And, in case they are tempted towards unhelpful comparisons, he reminds them, *"God has arranged the parts in the body, every one of them, just as he wanted them to be"* (verse 18). God's grace at work in each of us, is to ensure we play our part well, and that all our lives count in making their mark for the kingdom of God.

Leaders are vital to the well-being of the church because they play a key role in equipping every follower of Jesus to play their part in God's kingdom. Every single follower of Jesus is indispensable to the cause of Christ in the world and has a vital role to play in seeing the church flourish. Together, we are to make God's glory known to every people group on the face of the earth.

My good friend Mike Betts, who heads up the Relational Mission family of churches, helpfully summarises the purpose of leaders in their discipling of others:

> *Discipleship is not primarily about him, the leader, producing people who can help fulfil his vision or goal. It is rather about him as a leader, empowering others through his exercise of the grace, gifts, and internal authority God has entrusted to him so that others can start their own calling and vision. In essence, a philosophy of increase, multiplication, and release of others with great generosity and faith in God's overall purposes and plans.*[8]

One of the key ways a church leader disciples and helps others embrace their calling, is by being an example to them of what it means to follow Jesus. Paul was able to say to the church at Corinth, *"Follow* ***my example,*** *as I follow the example of Christ"*[9] (emphasis added). And, encouraging Timothy in his leadership role, he says, *"Don't let anyone* *look down on you because you are young, but set an example for the believers in speech, in conduct, in love, in faith and in purity."* [10]

The book of Hebrews makes the same point when exhorting followers of Jesus to, *"Remember your leaders, who spoke the word of God to you. Consider the outcome of their way of life and* ***imitate their faith"*** [11] (emphasis added). Following the example of our leaders is an essential component in making our mark and playing our part in the body of Christ.

We often think a major component of discipleship is to learn about, and grasp, biblical truth. Theology, doctrine, or 'getting our beliefs sorted out,' is vital to the renewal of our minds. But, of equal importance, is learning how to apply God's truth to our daily living. The goal being that we should become doers of God's word and not simply hearers, developing as we do so, a *"way of life."* [12]

In Jesus' time, the focus of discipleship had to do with adopting the lifestyle of one's teacher or rabbi. Following a rabbi meant not simply to grow in self-discipline, but to adopt the rabbi's ways, his lifestyle, and to be transformed into his likeness. So, how did Jewish rabbis instruct and guide their disciples in Jesus' day? Perhaps, a reminder would enable us to grasp better the kind of goal God has in mind for us as we follow our master, Rabbi Jesus.

Following Our Rabbi

In the book "Sitting at the Feet of Rabbi Jesus," Ann Spangler and Lois Tverberg discuss the difference between our Western idea of instruction and the kind of instruction given by Jewish rabbis to their disciples. They start with a useful definition:

> *Talmid; plural Talmidim – disciple or student, one who dedicated himself to learning a rabbi's understanding of Scripture and his way of living it out.*
>
> *To follow a rabbi meant something other than sitting in a classroom and absorbing his lectures. Rather, it involved a literal kind of following, in which disciples often travelled with, lived with, and imitated their rabbis, learning not only from what they*

said but from what they did – from their reactions to everyday life as well as from the manner in which they lived. The task of the disciples was to become as much like the rabbi as possible.

Learning wasn't so much about retaining data as it was about gaining essential wisdom for living, absorbing it from the rabbi.[13]

A modern equivalent of discipleship might be the word 'apprenticeship' – a time of training for a trade or other activity. However, the goal in following a rabbi was not just academic learning or acquiring new skills, but personal transformation.

The Jewish historian Shmuel Safrai reminds us that in Jesus' day, great emphasis was placed on the importance of prolonged intimacy with the rabbi:

The disciple did not grasp the full significance of his teacher's learning in all its nuances except through prolonged intimacy with his teacher, through close association with his rich and profound mind.[14]

Disciples would therefore accompany their rabbi on all his daily rounds, following him everywhere. As they did so, their minds and hearts were challenged and changed.

When Jesus appointed the twelve, we are told his purpose was, *"that* ***they might be with him*** *and that he might send them out"*[15] (emphasis added).

It was through this intimacy of relationship with Jesus, and exposure to his words and actions, that their way of looking at God and others was confronted and transformed. There is little doubt Jesus' acceptance of sinners and his association with the poor and marginalised made a huge impact on their lives. As did his shocking example of servanthood when he himself took a towel and washed their feet![16]

It is important to understand the goal of personal transformation was not achieved overnight. Discipleship to a rabbi was not seen as something where transformation could be instantaneously acquired, but rather as a protracted process. A gradual change over a period of years.

The twelve disciples spent three years following Jesus, and throughout that time he dealt with their many mistakes, weaknesses and misunderstandings. The gospel record shows it was not unusual for the disciples to mess up every now and again! And even after his resurrection and ascension, they certainly weren't the finished article. There were further vital lessons for these Jewish disciples to grasp; God's acceptance of Gentiles, *"men from every nation"*[17], being one of them.

Beyond just the close bond, the disciple was meant to become a servant of their rabbi and attend to his personal needs. Disciples were expected to take turns preparing the common meal and serving the needs of the group. Note here that discipleship took place within the context of community. We shall return to that theme later in the book. Shmuel Safrai helpfully comments:

> *Some laws could not just be studied theoretically or merely discussed but could only be learned by serving the teacher.*[18]

By learning obedience to the rabbi's directions, a disciple learnt reverence for doing God's will. And by putting himself in the position of a servant, he opened himself to correction so that his character and conduct could be shaped and refined. The rabbis, perhaps reflecting on the Old Testament Scripture in Isaiah, believed that humility was an indispensable condition for learning:

> "...These are the ones I look on with favour: those who are humble and contrite in spirit, and who tremble at my word."
> (Isaiah 66 v 2b)

Jesus himself compared the relationship between disciple and rabbi to that of master and servant 'rabbi' literally meaning, 'my master'). It was the same term a slave would have used to address his owner:

> "The student is not above the teacher, nor a servant above his master. It is enough for students to be like their teachers, and servants like their master."
> (Matthew 10 v 24 - 25a)

The rabbis would model how to live by using examples from their own lives. We have already referenced the passage from John, but look again at the importance and weight placed on a rabbi's example:

> "You call me 'Teacher' and 'Lord,' and rightly so, for that is what I am. Now that I, your Lord and Teacher, have washed your feet, you also should wash one another's feet. **I have set you an example that you should do as I have done for you."**
> (John 13 v 13 - 15; emphasis added)

In our thinking, it is all too easy for us to limit Jesus' *"example"* to the three years of his public ministry. We must not forget he had some thirty years to draw on when he had lived and worked as any other ordinary person. Like all of us, he was exposed daily to the culture and worldviews of the people that surrounded him. Perhaps he drew on his past three decades in Nazareth to provide further examples for his disciples to follow?

By living and working among mostly Jewish working-class people, he would have absorbed their culture, learnt to understand them, and been able to identify with their struggles. More than that, within this context, he lived a truly righteous life that brought glory to God in every moment of every day. Luke, speaking of Jesus' upbringing and life in Nazareth, records:

> Jesus grew in wisdom and stature and in favour with God and men.
> (Luke 2 v 51 - 52)

Eugene Peterson paraphrases John's testimony in The Message:

> The Word became flesh and blood, and moved into the neighbourhood. We saw the glory with our own eyes, the one-of-a-kind glory, like Father, like Son. Generous inside and out, true from start to finish.
> (John 1 v 14 MSG)

I love the work of the late David J. Bosch. He was an influential missiologist and theologian, best known for his book, "Transforming

Mission: Paradigm Shifts in Theology of Mission." Speaking about the life and ministry of Jesus in Luke's gospel, he explored the outworking of God the Father's providence in Jesus' life as he grew up and resided in Nazareth. Jesus followed his earthly father's trade by becoming a carpenter (builder). He would have accepted that carrying out this work in an urban or semi-urban setting, was not necessarily the most obvious grounding for his future public ministry.[19]

However, Jesus would have been close to or at the heart of the community. So, consider this. By meeting and associating with people from all kinds of backgrounds, Jesus was perfectly positioned to hear the latest happenings, stories, events and incidents. Listening to a wide range of people's life issues, would have allowed him to build up a store of anecdotes, second-hand accounts, and accepted worldly wisdom rooted in everyday life. And, while there are few stories or parables about carpentry, there are plenty about the world of agriculture, hired workers, family and domestic life.

Could it have been that his time in Nazareth provided the anvil on which Jesus learnt to hammer out his understanding of, and empathy for, all in society? For as we look at his life, we find the barriers of race, social status and gender, that often cause us such difficulty today, proved no problem to him. He appeared just as much at home with the poor and prostitutes as with the rich and religious leaders, or with women as with men.

Did his life in Nazareth teach him how to deal with issues of status and social barriers in a careful and sensitive manner? Was this the training for knowing when to challenge the status quo, or when to be more accommodating to the existing culture? When we look at Jesus' interaction with the many different types of people in the Gospels, we see how the disciples were given multiple examples of handling human relationships with grace and truth. Consider:

- The rich young ruler
- Tax collectors (Matthew and Zacchaeus)
- Close friends (Mary, Martha and Lazarus)
- Children

- Social outcasts (lepers and the demonised)
- The marginalised (the blind, deaf and lame)
- Nicodemus, a senior politician in the Sanhedrin
- The Centurion, a symbol of the occupying Roman authorities

The Gospels demonstrate his example in undermining established social norms, his genuine concern for individuals and his counter-cultural courage. He spoke frequently about the kingdom of God but was nevertheless careful to avoid political themes in his ministry. Unquestionably, he evidenced a deep understanding of the society in which he lived and the socio-political, racial and religious setting of first century Palestine. And who can forget the masterly way he handled the question of paying taxes to Caesar? Or how, in the many conflicts with the Pharisees, he seemed to know where to tread and how hard?[20]

The wonderful truth about Jesus is that he is both fully God and fully man. So, as we follow his example, we have one who has entered into every aspect of human life. As the writer to the Hebrews expressed it:

> For we do not have a high priest who is unable to empathize with our weaknesses, but we have one who has been tempted in every way, just as we are—yet he did not sin. (Hebrews 4 v 15)

Dane Ortlund helpfully expresses the blessings of Jesus' humanity:

> *The reason that Jesus is in such close solidarity with us is that the difficult path we are on is not unique to us, He has journeyed on it himself. He came as a normal man to normal men, He knows what it is to be thirsty, hungry, despised, rejected, scorned, shamed, embarrassed, abandoned, misunderstood, falsely accused, suffocated, tortured, and killed. He knows what it is to be lonely. His friends abandoned him when he needed them most.*[21]

Radiating Our Light

When Paul wrote to the church at Corinth on the theme of example, he urged the followers of Jesus to become a model to others as he had been for them:

> Follow my example, as I follow the example of Christ.
> (1 Corinthians 11 v 1)

This encouragement echoed words he had written earlier in the letter, where he described the role he had come to play in their collective lives:

> For in Christ Jesus, I became your father through the gospel. Therefore, I urge you to **imitate me.** For this reason, I am sending to you Timothy, my son, whom I love, who is faithful in the Lord. He will remind you of **my way of life in Christ Jesus,** which agrees with what I teach everywhere in every church.
> (1 Corinthians 4 v 15 - 17; emphasis added)

Note the two phrases, *"my way of life in Christ Jesus"* and *"agrees with what I teach."* Paul is not only referencing the 'whole person' method of discipling, but that his lifestyle is in keeping with his teaching - he practices what he preaches!

He encourages the church at Philippi in a similar manner:

> Whatever you have learned or received or heard from me, or seen in me - put it into practice. And the God of peace will be with you.
> (Philippians 4 v 9)

Writing to the Thessalonians, he says:

> You know how we lived among you for your sake. You **became imitators of us** and of the Lord, for you welcomed the message in the midst of severe suffering with the joy given by the Holy Spirit. And so you **became a model** to all the believers in Macedonia and Achaia.
> (1 Thessalonians 1 v 4 - 7; emphasis added)

Addressing the same church on the subject of idleness, he reminds them of his own example of hard work, and how along with Silas and Timothy, they had made themselves a *"model"* for them to follow.[22]

When Paul urges followers of Jesus to *"imitate me,"* he is not only saying follow my example, but become examples yourselves! Be people who copy my behaviour and actions, and who teach others to do so. Show others how to live, teach them the way of Jesus. Or as Matthew records Jesus' words in his gospel, *"teaching them to obey everything I have commanded you"* (Matthew 28 v 20).

One writer, commenting on God's goal for followers of Jesus, rightly reminds us:

> *God's goal isn't simply to fill the world with people who believe the right things. It is to fill the world with people who shine with the brilliance of Christ.*[23]

When speaking of the role of his followers, Jesus underscores this truth that God's people collectively are the light of the world:

> "...You're here to be light, bringing out the God-colors in the world. God is not a secret to be kept. We're going public with this, as public as a city on a hill. If I make you light-bearers, you don't think I'm going to hide you under a bucket, do you? I'm putting you on a light stand. Now that I've put you there on a hilltop, on a light stand—shine! Keep open house; be generous with your lives. By opening up to others, you'll prompt people to open up with God, this generous Father in heaven."
> (Matthew 5 v 14 - 16 MSG)

Paul expresses the same thought when he reminds followers of Jesus of the amazing truth that, *"it is God who works in you to will and to act in order to fulfil his good purpose."* He then exhorts them to live pure and blameless lives in, *"a warped and crooked generation. Then you will shine among them like stars in the sky as you hold firmly to the word of life"* (Philippians 2 v 13 - 16).

So, with these opening thoughts on discipleship, let's begin exploring what it means to follow Jesus and to live for the praise of His glory. Remembering, as we begin, Jesus' promise to all of those who follow him:

> "I am the light of the world. Whoever follows me will never walk in darkness, but will have the light of life."
> (John 8 v 12)

Notes

1 The Dangers of Comparison, Magda Murawska, The Albert Ellis Institute (rebt-cbt-post 31/07/2014), https://albertellis.org/2014/07/the-dangers-of-comparison

2 The Boy, The Mole, The Fox and The Horse, Charlie Mackesy, Ebury Press, 10th October 2010, ISBN 978 1529105100

3 Who is a leader - Real leaders are real followers, Anthony Ogunbowale-Thomas, Threads UK - 17th October 2013, https://threadsuk.com/who-is-a-leader

4 1 Thessalonians 5 v 12 - 13; 1 Timothy 5 v 17; Hebrews 13 v 7; 1 Timothy 3 v 1

5 Parker Society (1841) Volume 42, William Tyndale, Cambridge University Press, Page 102

6 Issues Facing Christians Today, John Stott, Basingstoke UK: Marshalls 1984, Page 162

7 Misreading Scripture with Western Eyes: Removing Cultural Blinders to Better Understand the Bible, Randy Richards and Brandon O'Brien, IVP Kindle Edition 2012, Kindle Locations 2046-2053.

8 The Philippians 1 Principles for Making Disciples, Mike Betts, Forum of Christian Leaders, 22nd May 2019, https://foclonline.org/talk/philippians-1-principle-making-disciples

9 1 Corinthians 11 v 1

10 1 Timothy 4 v 12

11 Hebrews 13 v 7

12 Matthew 7 v 24 - 27; James 1 v 22 - 25

13 Sitting at the Feet of Rabbi Jesus: How the Jewishness of Jesus Can Transform Your Faith, Ann Spangler and Lois Tverberg, Zondervan 2009, Pages 51, 53, 54

14 The Jewish People in the First Century, Safrai and Stern, Page 964; Quoted in Sitting at the Feet of Rabbi Jesus: How the Jewishness of Jesus Can Transform Your Faith, Ann Spangler and Lois Tverberg, Zondervan 2009, Page 55

15 Mark 3 v 14

16 John 13 v 13 - 15

17 Acts 10 v 35

18 The Jewish People in the First Century, Safrai and Stern, Page 964; Quoted in Sitting at the Feet of Rabbi Jesus: How the Jewishness of Jesus Can Transform Your Faith, Ann Spangler and Lois Tverberg, Zondervan 2009, Page 60

19 Transforming Mission: Paradigm Shifts in Theology of Mission, David J. Bosch, Orbis Books (October 1991) ISBN 0-88344-719-3

20 For those wanting to think through more on Jesus' approach to the governing authorities of his day see: "Jesus and Politics: Confronting the Powers" Alan Storkey, Baker Academic (Baker Publishing Group), 2005.

21 Gentle and Lowly, The Heart of Christ for Sinners and Sufferers, by Dane Ortlund, Copyright 2020, Page 47. Used by permission of Crossway, a publishing ministry of Good News Publishers, Wheaton, IL 60187, www.crossway.org

22 2 Thessalonians 3 v 7 - 9

23 Sitting at the Feet of Rabbi Jesus: How the Jewishness of Jesus Can Transform Your Faith, Ann Spangler and Lois Tverberg, Zondervan 2009, Page 64

CHAPTER ONE

Declare His Glory Among The Nations

In some ways, the COVID-19 pandemic and those long periods of lockdown seem a long time ago. However, the feelings of isolation and separation from family and loved ones still seem very real to us, like they do for many. Missing our grandchildren, my wife and I did our best to keep in touch with them via Zoom, FaceTime and WhatsApp. Reading books together, playing games and general chit-chat became the order of the day.

Then my wife had a great idea. What a good time to teach our grandson Charlie, aged seven, how to play chess over the Internet! So, grandad was quickly dispatched to find the chess set squirrelled away in a cupboard... and the game was on!

First step was to explain the board, where pieces were placed, and what moves they could or could not make. Lots of questions and answers ensued, and moves had to be demonstrated a number of times to help explanations stick. Then came the big question, 'What is the point of the game grandad?' Good question.

I don't know about you, but I still meet followers of Jesus who appear to know lots about church, spiritual disciplines and principles of godly living, but nevertheless seem to remain unsure or ignorant of God's endgame. That is, his ultimate purpose in sending his Son into the world.

Is the end purpose of sending Jesus simply that our personal sins may be forgiven and our eternal destiny secured? To have all our physical, material and emotional needs met? To enable us to become better people and live better lives? To have a godly influence on those around us and improve society so we can all work together for the common good? To see the needs of the poor and marginalised met and the sick healed? Or perhaps, as followers of Jesus, we would see our life purpose as bringing many other people to know Christ and be added to the church; that they may also become true followers, who make other disciples?

Surely these are all good things and getting somewhere close to the purpose...

Motivation For Mission

For many today, involvement in evangelistic mission is seen as the key priority and heart of what it means to be a follower of Jesus. I certainly thought this way in the early years of my Christian life. After all, Jesus came to seek and save those who were lost, commissioning us to go and make disciples of all nations.

I came to faith in Jesus at a children's mission at the age of ten. I was baptised at fourteen and became an active member of an evangelical church birthed out of a Christian Medical Mission. Evangelism was in our blood and our top priority. But to be perfectly honest, my personal motivation for reaching out to others was something of a mixed bag!

I genuinely loved the vision in Revelation Chapter 7, of followers from every people group on the face of the earth worshipping around the throne of Jesus. Nevertheless, there were a number of different motivations driving my engagement in evangelism and mission. Perhaps, the first one was guilt. I was 'saved,' while countless thousands were on their way to hell!

A second motivating force was duty, although I would probably have called it obedience at the time! As I've said, the importance of Jesus' Great Commission was written deeply into my thinking.

Then there was the question of the lostness of the lost. Some 15–25% of the world's population still wait to hear about Jesus for the very first time. The majority of these are amongst the world's poorest, and in lands dominated by other religions such as Islam, Hinduism and Buddhism. And, what about the plight of the millions of street children, or young people trapped in the sex trade each week? Not to mention people suffering from famine, lack of sanitation, medical treatment and education. Surely, the gospel had to impact them too? And, I should play my part!

I guess it was at this point, another motivating force began to stir stronger in my heart. I increasingly felt desire to engage with people out of a genuine heart of compassion. At last, the penny dropped. The gospel was meant to not only meet the needs of people's souls, but their material needs as well. The good news, salvation and God himself was bigger than I'd imagined – there was hope, healing and restoration for the 'whole' person!

As I began to pray, God started to touch my heart with his compassion. After a number of powerful encounters with him through the person of the Holy Spirit, I began to not only understand the words of Jesus in Matthew, but also to feel something of God's heart for all the precious people created for relationship with him:

> When he saw the crowds, he had compassion on them, because they were harassed and helpless, like sheep without a shepherd.
> (Matthew 9 v 36)

I am so thankful to God our Father that in these days my response to the lost has improved. I'm now less driven by guilt, duty and needs, but more by his grace and compassion. However, I want to suggest that even though this response is important and good, it still does not provide us with an ultimate motivation. Nor does it get to the heart of what our lives are all about.

Scripture, in many places, helps us to see and understand God's ultimate plan, which Paul expresses succinctly when writing to the Ephesians:

> ...to bring unity to all things in heaven and on earth under Christ.
> (Ephesians 1 v 10)

It's a plan involving demonstration of God's words, works and wonders, and where you and I as followers of Jesus play a crucial part as his witnesses. A plan that is universal in scope, and concerns all nations and all people groups.

Sounds as though we may be moving once more towards the theme of Revelation Chapter 7!

So, let me try and describe one final motivating force. It's a motivation that needs to eclipse even the power of compassion in our lives, as we partner with God to see all things brought together under Jesus Christ. One that became clearer to me when I was confronted with the question, 'What is the ultimate goal of the church?' Note the echo back to my grandson's chess question, 'What's the point of the game...?'

I wonder what your answer to that question would be?

Ultimate Goal

John Piper, in his splendid and challenging book, "Let the nations be glad," answers the question in the following way:

> *Mission is not the ultimate goal of the church. Worship is.*
>
> *If the pursuit of God's glory is not ordered above the pursuit of man's good in the affections of the heart and the priorities of the church, man will not be well served and God will not be duly honoured.*[1]

Our main goal, our priority, our motivation in life, should be the pursuit of the glory of God, above the pursuit of man's good. Bringing glory to God, and seeing his name honoured, should be both uppermost in our prayers, and the natural outcome of our way of life as followers of Jesus.

When we examine the life of Jesus in the Gospels, we find *"glory"* is the hallmark of his time on earth. John gives testimony to this in the prologue of his gospel:

> The Word became flesh and made his dwelling among us.
> We have seen his glory, the glory of the one and only Son,
> who came from the Father, full of grace and truth.
> (John 1 v 14)

And, in Jesus' prayer to his Father in John, we find him saying:

> "I have brought you glory on earth by finishing the work you gave me to do."
> (John 17 v 4)

But we are jumping forward. We first need to see that bringing glory to God was meant to be central to the life of God's people from the very beginning.

Declaring His Glory

In Psalm 96, we find a call for God's people to declare his glory to everyone. The end result of such declaration being that God would receive the worship of all peoples:

> Declare his glory among the nations,
> his marvellous deeds among all peoples.
>
> Ascribe to the Lord, O families of nations,
> ascribe to the Lord glory and strength.
>
> (Psalm 96 v 3, 7)

This wonderful Psalm deserves repeating whole:

> Sing to the Lord a new song;
> sing to the Lord, all the earth.
> Sing to the Lord, praise his name;
> proclaim his salvation day after day.
> Declare his glory among the nations,
> his marvellous deeds among all peoples.
>
> For great is the Lord and most worthy of praise;
> he is to be feared above all gods.
> For all the gods of the nations are idols,
> but the Lord made the heavens.
> Splendour and majesty are before him;
> strength and glory are in his sanctuary.
>
> Ascribe to the Lord, all you families of nations,
> ascribe to the Lord glory and strength.
> Ascribe to the Lord the glory due his name;

bring an offering and come into his courts.
Worship the Lord in the splendour of his holiness;
tremble before him, all the earth.
Say among the nations, "The Lord reigns."
The world is firmly established, it cannot be moved;
he will judge the peoples with equity.

Let the heavens rejoice, let the earth be glad;
let the sea resound, and all that is in it.
Let the fields be jubilant, and everything in them;
let all the trees of the forest sing for joy.
Let all creation rejoice before the Lord, for he comes,
he comes to judge the earth.
He will judge the world in righteousness
and the peoples in his faithfulness.

The Glory Of God

For many of us, myself included, we find the word 'glory' hard to grasp and define. It is an easy word to use, but also to misuse. Somehow, its meaning is elusive, and almost defies definition. I have described it in the past as being like the two pet rabbits I kept for a number of years (in my adult life, not as a child!). Let me explain.

The rabbits on their arrival were normal size, but soon grew into 'monster' rabbits of enormous proportions, with very powerful kicks! Although they had a cage, and I built them an outstanding (possible exaggeration!) run, they adeptly found ways to escape and enjoy the produce of the garden. In the end we gave in. As the garden was enclosed on all sides, we eventually allowed them to roam free.

However, trouble would arrive each night when it was time to put them back into their cages. They didn't fully appreciate the need to protect them from the foxes that frequented our neighbourhood. Nightfall would often see me creeping around the garden, manoeuvring myself into a position where I could let my hands hover over their backs. Yes, you guessed it! Every time I finally got into 'capture' mode with my hand descending on the rabbit's back, it would dart off with the speed of lightning to another part of the garden.

That is how I have felt through the years about the word 'glory.' Just as I seem to have a 'hand' on the term and understand what it means, I discover fresh nuances and revelation from God's word that sets my thinking off in new directions. Perhaps only in eternity, when we are in the presence of God, will we be able to grasp the full meaning and majesty of the word 'glory!' Glory in all its glory!

That said, I believe it is important to do our best to grasp all we can about this word 'glory' and what it means for us as followers of Jesus.

Melissa Briggs, a teacher of Hebrew, makes the following statement:

> *The Hebrew word for glory (Kavod) is a complicated word to describe because it is grand and complex, rather than concrete. God's glory is impossible to put in a box, as it is endlessly abundant. It comes from the verb (kavad) meaning to be heavy, weighty, burdensome, honoured. Used figuratively it speaks about someone's reputation, that they are impressive, worthy, of high position and wealth.*[2]

In the Greek language, the word for glory is "doxa." This speaks of someone's reputation and fame, particularly the opinion held by others, and is related to the person's actions and achievements. Although, we need to remember that in Scripture, God's glory is rooted not in others' opinions of him, but in his very nature.

In the Bible, glory has often to do with the unveiling of God's loving character. For example, when Moses asks God to show him his glory, God replies:

> "I will cause all my goodness to pass in front of you, and I will proclaim my name, the Lord, in your presence. I will have mercy on whom I will have mercy, and I will have compassion on whom I will have compassion."
> (Exodus 33 v 19)

'Glory' describes his majesty and his creative power revealed in creation. It shows the amazing beauty and intricate systems he put into place, his perfect design and how he orchestrates and sustains the wonders of his created world. The visible order and beauty around us speak of God's ingenuity and wisdom, displaying his greatness for all to see. As the psalmist writes:

> The heavens declare the glory of God;
> the skies proclaim the work of his hands.
> Day after day they pour forth speech;
> night after night they reveal knowledge.
> They have no speech they use no words;
> no sound is heard from them.
> Yet their voice goes out into all the earth,
> their words to the ends of the world.
> (Psalm 19 v 1 - 4)

'Glory' also speaks of God's redemptive power, revealed in man's deliverance and salvation. Think about the Exodus and Christ's victory at the cross (see Numbers 14 v 21 - 23; John 12 v 27 - 28). His active presence among his people is also spoken of as his glory filling the tabernacle and the temple.

The late Christian theologian J. I. Packer speaks of Scripture using the word 'glory' in three different ways:[3]

'Glory' refers, first, to what God shows and what shows God to us, namely, his own active presence with self-manifestation to eye or ear or both.

Then second, 'glory' refers to what the godly give to their God, namely, praise in response to the praise-worthiness that he has shown them.

Third, by an extension of the first meaning, 'glory' points to God's continued transforming work in us. This is the glory that God bestows on his covenant children, those who have a living faith in Christ and are united to Christ, and in whom the Holy Spirit, the master mason in character building and habit forming, now dwells.

The great British preacher of the last century, Dr Martyn Lloyd-Jones, described the glory of God as, "The essential nature of God, it is that which makes God, God!"[4]

Melissa Briggs provides a helpful summary of the word when she says:

> *Glory is God's awesome greatness on display. God's glory is the public presentation of his infinite worth, majestic beauty, astounding creativity, limitless power, righteous nature, unmatched significance, and perfect holiness; he is intrinsically worthy of great honour. God is so weighty and important, that when this is shown forth publicly, it is described as his glory.*[5]

Declaring his glory to the nations is about making his name glorious, famous and full of renown in the earth. And, when we speak of his 'name,' we mean the body of truth that God has revealed about himself. We have been commissioned to call people to become worshippers of the one true living God. In doing so, his presence is recognised and he is praised for his qualities and his acts - we give God glory.

The missiologist Steven Hawthorne says:

> *The basic rationale is that God reveals his glory to all peoples so that he may receive glory from all creation.*[6]

We are not simply engaged in witnessing to people in order to see them become disciples of Jesus, but are called to declare God's glory and bring God glory.

The Evidence Of Scripture

Many years ago, I read Steven Hawthorne's article "The Story of His Glory,"[7] and this first alerted me to the theme of God's glory running throughout all of Scripture. To enforce the truth that God's purpose has always been to glorify his name among the nations, let me share a few examples, starting with the **Exodus.**

When Moses was sent by God to Pharaoh, he went with a simple message. A message that was repeated a number of times:

> 'Let my people go, so that they may worship me.'
> (See Exodus 8 v 1, 20; 9 v 1, 13; 10 v 3)

This was not a deception or ruse. God truly wanted to receive their worship, just as he wanted to receive worship from all nations. In the midst of the plagues, God sent Moses to tell Pharaoh the reason for them—namely to show him, *"there is no other like me in all the earth,"* and that *"my name might be proclaimed in all the earth."*[8]

It is useful to note where each of the ten plagues struck. They centred on the Egyptian gods or goddesses, those false gods representing the evil spiritual forces influencing the religious, economic and military powers of the nation. It was God's way of saying they were not God, and that only he was worthy of worship. God then declares that the drowning of Pharaoh and his armies in the Red Sea would be the way he would *"gain glory"* for himself over them.[9]

In the Exodus story, when the Israelites see the Egyptians advancing against them, they accuse Moses of bringing them out of Egypt to die in the desert. In fact, they complain it would have been better for them if they had stayed in Egypt and served the Egyptians! The psalmist, looking back on this incident, comments:

> When our ancestors were in Egypt,
> they gave no thought to your miracles;
> they did not remember your many kindnesses,
> and they rebelled by the sea, the Red Sea.
> Yet he saved them **for his name's sake,**
> to make his mighty power known.
> (Psalm 106 v 7 - 8; emphasis added)

Following the crossing of the Red Sea, Moses also sings his famous song of deliverance, which includes the lines:

> "Who among the gods
> is like you, Lord?
> Who is like you —
> majestic in holiness
> awesome in glory,
> working wonders?
>
> "You stretch out your right hand,
> and the earth swallows your enemies..."
>
> "The nations will hear and tremble;
> anguish will grip the people of Philistia."
>
> (Exodus 15 v 11-12, 14)

And, so it proved, starting with Moses' father-in-law Jethro, a Midianite.

> "Now I know that the Lord is greater than all other gods, for he did this to those who had treated Israel arrogantly."
> (From Exodus 18 v 9 – 11)

Rahab, when visited by the Israelite spies sent to Jericho, explained to them how her people had heard about the destruction of Pharaoh's army and declared:

> "...for the Lord your God is God in heaven above and on the earth below."
> (From Joshua 2 v 8 – 11)

Other Old Testament writers also focus on the result of the Exodus, telling how it led to God's name being glorified among the nations:

> You made a name for yourself which remains to this day.
> (From Nehemiah 9 v 9 – 10; Daniel 9 v 15)

> To gain for himself everlasting renown
> ...to make for yourself a glorious name.
> (From Isaiah 63 v 11 – 14)

The Exodus was followed by the **Conquest,** when Israel fought numerous battles and settled into the promised land. But, even here there was a greater purpose being accomplished than simply providing an inheritance for Israel. God was also seeking to bring glory to his name:

> "And who is like your people Israel—the one nation on earth that God went out to redeem as a people for himself, and **to make a name for himself,** and to perform great and awesome wonders by driving out nations and their gods from before your people, whom you redeemed from Egypt?"
> (2 Samuel 7 v 23; emphasis added)

Another Old Testament event that demonstrates God's desire to receive glory from all nations is the building of the **Temple.** On entering the land, God chose a place to dwell with his people. It was a place to put his name (see Deuteronomy 12 v 4 – 7), and a place to reveal himself and deepen his relationship with his chosen followers. Yet, this was not to be a place exclusively for Israel, but a meeting place for all nations. This is underlined beautifully in Solomon's prayer of dedication for the temple:

> "As for the foreigner who does not belong to your people Israel but has come from a distant land because of your name—for they will hear of your great name and your mighty hand and your outstretched arm—when they come and pray toward this temple, then hear from heaven, your dwelling place. Do whatever the foreigner asks of you, **so that all the peoples of the earth may know your name and fear you,** as do your own people Israel, and may know that this house I have built bears your Name."
> (1 Kings 8 v 41 - 43; emphasis added)

And later, he records the goal of his prayer:

> "...so that all the peoples of the earth may know that the Lord is God and that there is no other."
> (1 Kings 8 v 60)

A similar theme is reflected in Psalm 67, sung in the temple at the Feast of Tabernacles. It's a prophetic psalm about the conversion of the world to the worship of God. In it, Israel seeks God's blessing, so that his *"ways may be known on the earth,"* and his *"salvation among all nations"* (verse 2), and so that, *"All the ends of the earth will fear him"* (verse 7).

Solomon's prayer was partially answered when the Queen of Sheba visited him, doing so because *"of his relation to the name of the Lord"* (1 Kings 10 v 1). Later in the chapter we are told that, *"the whole world sought audience with Solomon to hear the wisdom God had put in his heart"* (verse 24).

However, Solomon's many wives turned his heart to false gods (see 1 Kings 11 v 1 - 8), and Israel then went into a time of decline and apostasy. They failed to make God's glory known among the nations, they profaned his name in the earth, the temple was destroyed, and the people were taken into exile. But thankfully that was not the end of the story.

The next stage of Israel's journey with God was the **Return** to the land. The return was the fulfilment of God's promise to them, but it was not simply about a return to a geographical place. A higher purpose was in view – the restoration of the glory of God and the honour of his name! Listen to God's message to his people as recorded for us in the book of Ezekiel:

> '...It is not for your sake, people of Israel, that I am going to do these things, but **for the sake of my holy name,** which you have profaned among the nations where you have gone. I will show the holiness of my great name, which has been profaned among the nations, the name you have profaned among them. Then the nations will know that I am the Lord, declares the Sovereign Lord, when I am proved holy through you before their eyes.'
> (Ezekiel 36 v 22 - 23; emphasis added)

Radiance Of God's Glory

Look at this contrast. In the New Testament, we see what Israel repeatedly failed to do in demonstrating God's glory on earth, Jesus did perfectly through his life, death and resurrection. In Christ, the glory of God was revealed and declared to the world. As we saw previously, John gives testimony to his glory:

> We have seen his glory, the glory of the One and Only, who came from the Father, full of grace and truth.
> (John 1 v 14)

> No one has ever seen God, but the one and only Son, who is himself God and is in closest relationship with the Father, has made him known.
> (John 1 v 18)

And the book of Hebrews speaks of the Son being, *"The radiance of God's glory and the exact representation of his being"* (Hebrews 1 v 3).

But, how was the glory of God revealed in his earthly life?

One way was **through his miraculous signs.** When Jesus turned water into wine at the wedding at Cana in Galilee, John writes, *"He thus revealed his glory"* (John 2 v 11).

Jesus, speaking of the death of Lazarus and his subsequent rising from the dead, tells his disciples that this tragic episode is ultimately for God's glory:

> "This sickness will not end in death. No, it is for God's glory so that God's Son may be glorified through it."
> (John 11 v 4)

And later in the chapter, when he addresses Lazarus' sister Martha at the graveside, he prompts, *"Did I not tell you that if you believe, you will see the glory of God?"* (John 11 v 40).

Then there was the occasion when Jesus came down from the mount of transfiguration and healed the boy with an evil spirit. Luke, speaking of the crowd's response, says:

> They were all amazed at the greatness of God.
> (Luke 9 v 43)

And note that here, *"greatness"* can also be translated *majesty* or *glory.*

Another way Jesus revealed God's glory was **through his teaching and instruction.** For example, when the disciples ask him to teach them how to pray, he answers by giving them what many see as a model prayer or pattern of how to address God. This prayer, recorded for us in Matthew, begins by turning our focus and hearts to the truth of God being our Father. However, it is followed, not by an expression of praise, but by the petition, *"Hallowed be your name"* (see Matthew 6 v 9 - 13).

We could perhaps, therefore, paraphrase it in these words:

> *Father lift up, single out, exalt, manifest and reveal your glory. Become famous for who you are. Cause all people on earth to know and adore you.*

Then there are incidents in the life of Jesus that demonstrate the glory **through his words and actions.** Jesus understood the cosmic dimension of his work and how God's glory must be declared to all nations. One such occasion was the cleansing of the temple, where Jesus echoes the words of the prophet Isaiah:

> "'My house will be called a house of prayer for all nations.'"
> (From Mark 11 v 15 - 17 and Isaiah 56 v 7)

Another occasion was the arrival of the Gentiles (non-Jewish 'God-fearers'), who had come to Jerusalem to worship at the Jewish feast and wanted to see Jesus. It seems their coming triggered both a reaction and a response from him:

> "The hour has come for the Son of Man to be glorified."
> (John 12 v 23)

It is at this point in the narrative that Jesus, speaking of his death on the cross, uses the analogy of how a kernel of wheat must fall into the ground and die in order to produce many seeds. And, although his heart is troubled by the thought of crucifixion, he is nevertheless fully committed to the Father's will. He sees the cross as the very reason he had come to that hour. His death is central to him bringing glory to the Father and declaring God's glory to the world:

> "...what shall I say? 'Father, save me from this hour'? No, it was for this very reason I came to this hour. Father, glorify your name!"
> (From John 12 v 23 - 29)

The Glory Of The Cross

For many of us, the cross is the symbol of God's love for us and the world. The place where our salvation was secured, and the consequences of our sin dealt with once and for all. Here, as sinful and rebellious human beings, we can be reconciled back to our maker. The means whereby prodigal sons and daughters can return home into the loving arms of a waiting Father. It's beautiful.

But I wonder, do we ever think about the cross also being about the glory of God?

The cross reveals, perhaps like no other single event can, the glory of almighty God. For it is at the cross that we see a demonstration of **the wisdom of God.** Who else could have thought of such a judicious plan? One that would deal with our sinful condition and all its consequences. One that would overcome sin, death and hell, defeat the power of sin and Satan, and liberate us and set us free. Yet a plan that would enable him at the same time, to declare us righteous in his sight. Such righteousness being a free gift to us. A plan that imparts life to us, in such a way that our transformation can be spoken of as newness of life or 'new birth.' What amazing wisdom! To the world, it's utter foolishness. But to us who are being saved, we see the power and the wisdom of God.[10]

When we think about the cross, we also see a demonstration of **the holiness and righteousness of God.** It's a stark reminder that a holy God cannot overlook or wink at sin, but that sin must be atoned for. Nothing less than the death of his sinless Son could satisfy the holy demands of a righteous God. Only God making *"him who had no sin, to be sin for us"*[11] could enable us to become the righteousness of God.

And, what can we say about the revelation of **the love, mercy and grace of God?** God did not spare his only Son, but gave him up freely for us. Scripture tells us, *"God was in Christ reconciling the world to himself."*[12]

What mystery is in that verse? Can we ever comprehend what pain both Father and Son suffered that day? Jesus, forsaken by his Father in the hours of darkness, and the Father turning away from the one who was daily his delight. Yet now, along with Christ he gives us all things, bestowing sonship on us as a free gift and making us joint-heirs with Jesus. What mercy, what grace, what love![13]

In light of all this, it follows that the Apostle Paul declares to the Corinthian church:

> For I resolved to know nothing while I was with you except Jesus Christ and him crucified.
> (1 Corinthians 2 v 2)

To declare the glory of God is to declare the cross. When writing to Timothy, Paul speaks of that which, *"conforms to the gospel concerning the glory of the blessed God, which he entrusted to me"*[14], or a better translation would be, *'the gospel of glory.'* As followers of Jesus, our calling is to proclaim the gospel of glory, Jesus and his cross - to declare God's glory in word and deed to a watching world.

As a Spirit-filled people, by his grace and in the power of the Holy Spirit, we can communicate God's glory to those whose lives we touch on a daily basis. As individuals and as communities of God's people we are called to be agents of God's grace, displaying his character and increasingly reflecting his glory. When we show the world how satisfied we are in him, expressing that God is more fulfilling and better than all this world has to offer, God is beautifully glorified through our lives.

Look at some of the encouragements the New Testament writers give us to fulfil our calling to declare his glory to the nations. God wants to demonstrate his presence in our lives by displaying his qualities, both in our character and in our loving works of service. He wants to glorify himself in us. Take a moment to soak these in:

> We have been chosen and predestined to live for the praise of his glory.
> (Ephesians 1 v 12)

> Through the church, the manifold wisdom of God will be made known to the rulers and authorities in the heavenly realms.
> (Ephesians 3 v 10)

> But thanks be to God, who always leads us as captives in Christ's triumphal procession and uses us to spread the aroma of the knowledge of him everywhere.
> (2 Corinthians 2 v 14)

> We are a chosen people, a royal priesthood, a holy nation, God's special possession, that we may declare the praises of him who called us out of darkness into his wonderful light.
> (1 Peter 2 v 9)

As followers of Jesus, we have the amazing honour and privilege to be included together on God's mission, *"to bring all things in heaven and on earth together under one head, even Christ"*[15]. It's a mission to declare God's glory to every people group on the face of the earth, in order for all to bring him praise and glory. We have a calling to live a life that is larger than ourselves, a life that under God's gracious providence will make an eternal difference.

Notes

1 Let the Nations be Glad: Supremacy of God in Missions, John Piper, Inter-Varsity Press ISBN 0-85111-409-1, Pages 17,18

2 Hebrew Word Study, Glory Part 1, Melissa Briggs, Christian Friends of Israel UK, In Touch Magazine, 2nd Quarter 2017, www.cfi.org.uk/downloads/Kavod-Pt1-InTouch191.pdf

3 Weakness is the Way: Life with Christ our Strength by J. I. Packer, Copyright © 2018, Pages 103–105. Used by permission of Crossway, a publishing ministry of Good News Publishers, Wheaton, IL 60187, www.crossway.org

4 MLJ Trust Audio Library, https://www.mljtrust.org/sermons/great-biblical-doctrines/

5 Hebrew Word Study, Glory Part 1, Melissa Briggs, Christian Friends of Israel UK, In Touch Magazine, 2nd Quarter 2017, www.cfi.org.uk/downloads/Kavod-Pt1-InTouch191.pdf

6 Perspectives on the World Christian Movement, A Reader, Revised Edition (1992), Edited by R. D. Winter and S. C. Hawthorne, published by William Carey Library, Page A-35

7 Perspectives on the World Christian Movement, A Reader, Revised Edition (1992), Edited by R. D. Winter and S. C. Hawthorne, published by William Carey Library, Chapter 5

8 Exodus 9 v 13 - 16; Romans 9 v 17

9 Exodus 14 v 4, 17 - 18

10 1 Corinthians 1 v 18

11 2 Corinthians 5 v 21

12 2 Corinthians 5 v 19

13 Ibid

14 1 Timothy 1 v 11

15 Ephesians 1 v 10

CHAPTER TWO

Greater Value

According to a recent CNN business report, the combined fortunes of the world's 26 richest individuals reached the same amount as the total wealth of the 3.8 billion poorest people.[1]

Take a moment to re-read that first sentence to try and grasp the magnitude of it.

It claimed that the world's billionaires are growing richer every day, while the poorest half of the global population is seeing its net worth dwindle. The gap between rich and poor is accelerating. In a similar vein, the Mail Online reported that the combined wealth of the world's top ten billionaires is greater than the total GDP of the 85 poorest countries on Earth.[2]

Again, a re-read of that statistic might be in order.

One of the richest among this group is Microsoft's Bill Gates, with a reported personal wealth of $113 billion. However, he has been widely quoted as saying he wants to give away 90% of his wealth by the time of his death! In fact, when he was in his forties, some 20-plus years ago, Gates took the decision that Microsoft would no longer be his primary activity.

What would trigger this type of decision? Not only did he begin swimming against the tide, and the prevailing culture of 'money being a measure of success,' but he opted to set up his own charitable foundation in 2000 to focus specifically on the world's poorest. After years of successful and pioneering business activity, he invested in the pursuit of human dignity and equality. The central goals of Gates Foundation are "to enhance healthcare and reduce extreme poverty across the globe, and to expand educational opportunities and access to information technology in the U.S."[3] Commentators with or without faith have noted this generosity on a staggering scale, coining the phrase 'mega-philanthropy' and encouraging others with wealth to follow his example.

Whatever the motivation behind the change, I would suggest Gates has come to a point where he has caught sight of a greater value. Clearly, the value of pursuing human dignity and equality exceeds that of running an American multinational technology company. And we pursue what we place greatest value upon.

In the last chapter, we saw how God has invited us to join him on his mission to bring all things together under one head, even Christ, and to declare his glory among the nations. But, does serving God's purpose take precedence over, or have greater value for us, than anything this world might offer? Do we make following Jesus the primary activity of our life?

When the rich young ruler came to Jesus seeking the answer as to how he could inherit eternal life, Jesus put his finger on the one thing he still lacked. Despite his comments of having lived an exemplary life from childhood, Jesus challenged him to sell everything he had, give it to the poor, and then come and follow him. However, it appears treasure on earth had a greater value for him than treasure in heaven, for we read:

> When the young man heard this, he went away sad,
> because he had great wealth.
> (From Matthew 19 v 16 - 26)

Wealth may not be a stumbling block for us in following Jesus wholeheartedly, but there are many other things that can draw our hearts away from him. Following Jesus always involves a personal cost, as he pointed out to the listening crowds:

> Then he called the crowd to him along with his disciples and said: "Whoever wants to be my disciple must deny themselves and take up their cross and follow me. For whoever wants to save their life will lose it, but whoever loses their life for me and for the gospel will save it. What good is it for someone to gain the whole world, yet forfeit their soul? Or what can anyone give in exchange for their

soul? If anyone is ashamed of me and my words in this adulterous and sinful generation, the Son of Man will be ashamed of them when he comes in his Father's glory with the holy angels."
(Mark 8 v 34 - 38)

The willingness to lose one's life for Jesus and for the gospel, centres upon the key question of where our treasure is, and what we consider to be of greatest value. Remember, Jesus' challenge:

"...where your treasure is, there your heart will be also."
(Matthew 6 v 21)

One passage of Scripture showing this is Hebrews 11. Here, we see how God's people in the past have lived their lives for something of greater value than what the world can offer; it's considered by some to be the great honours list of people of faith.

Os Guinness, author and social critic, says of these people of faith that:

They were men and women whose vision of God called them to live and work against the customs, values and priorities of their generation. People who marched to a different tune; had their sights set on a different goal; whose home was in a different country (a heavenly one) and who looked for a different city to dwell.[4]

One man of faith who stands out in this hall of fame is Moses, whose story is familiar to many. Born in Egypt to God-fearing and faith-filled parents, they hid him for three months because of the decree from Pharaoh that, *"Every Hebrew baby boy be thrown in the river Nile and left to die"* (Exodus 1 v 22). And, when they could hide him no longer, they put him in a papyrus basket in the reeds along the bank of the Nile. The same Nile that Pharaoh's daughter came down to bathe in, before finding him and taking pity on him.

It was then, in the providence of God, that Moses' mother was independently engaged to nurse Moses. Just take that turn of events in for a moment! Here he stayed until he grew older, when he was taken to the royal palace to be brought up as Pharaoh's daughter's son and part of the royal household. The writer of Hebrews gives us this insight into Moses' adult life:

> By faith Moses, when he had grown up, refused to be known as the son of Pharaoh's daughter. He chose to be mistreated along with the people of God rather than to enjoy the fleeting pleasures of sin. He regarded disgrace for the sake of Christ as of greater value than the treasures of Egypt, because he was looking ahead to his reward. By faith he left Egypt, not fearing the king's anger; he persevered because he saw him who is invisible. By faith he kept the Passover and the application of blood, so that the destroyer of the firstborn would not touch the firstborn of Israel.
> (Hebrews 11 v 24 - 28)

Note, the writer tells us here that Moses refused to be known as the son of Pharaoh's daughter, and instead chose to be identified with God's people. More than that, it says he chose to be mistreated along with the people of God, rather than enjoy the pleasures of sin for a short time. What was it that caused such a radical change in his life?

To answer that question, let me begin by reminding us of some significant things he turned his back upon. You'll see the themes are just as familiar and relevant today as they were for Moses in Egypt.

First, he was giving up his **position**. He had been born into a slave family, but was now a royal prince. Princes in Egypt possessed status and were given recognition and honour, things that in today's world are equally highly prized and sought after. Of course, we see this reflected in the craving for celebrity culture here in the West.

It seems from the dawn of time, man has had an appetite for this recognition and position. Isaiah illustrates this when he uses poetic language to describe the King of Babylon and his desire to make himself like the *"Most High"* (see Isaiah 14 v 12 - 15). Interestingly, some commentators suggest this may be an allusion to the fallen king of Babylon being likened to a fallen Satan.

It's no surprise to see this idea continuing in the New Testament. Jesus warned the people about the Pharisees and teachers of the law who sought: to receive recognition as they walked around, to have the best seats in the synagogues, the place of honour at feasts, and titles such as *"teacher."*[5] But before we applaud Jesus' censure of them, perhaps we ourselves need to heed Jesus' warning and examine our own hearts, as sadly today's church is not immune to the same desire for recognition and status.

We are not told in the text, but it may be helpful to ask these questions. Did Moses reject his royal status because he was becoming more concerned about his position before God than before men? Had he come to understand that God's way of greatness for a man or woman is the way of service, rather than being served? Had he determined in his heart, referring to a lovely modern phrase of showing devotion to God, 'to live for an audience of one?'

Os Guinness helpfully challenges us when he says:

> *Most of us, whether we are aware of it or not, do things with an eye to the approval of some audience or other. The question is not whether we have an audience, but which audience we have?* [6]

Men and women of faith are called not to be obsessed with their own status, position in society, or indeed the church. But rather, to readily give themselves in the service of others, being keenly aware they are living their lives for an audience of one – for Jesus, our saviour. After all, we are called to follow the one of whom it was said:

> He made himself of no reputation, and took upon him the form of a servant. (KJV)
>
> He made himself nothing by taking the very nature of a servant. (NIV)
>
> (Philippians 2 v 7)

Second, he was giving up his exercise of **power**. As a royal prince, Moses had the power, within certain boundaries, to order his own affairs and control his own destiny. He could direct the affairs of others and command instant obedience. There is the real possibility that some of his decisions would have impacted whole swathes of people in the palace and the nation. Independence and influence probably characterised Moses' life.

Many people today aspire to be in a similar position of power, and history is littered with accounts of those who, at any cost, have tried to grasp and exercise religious, political or social influence. We are not simply talking here about those who have looked to wield their power for national or world domination. If we are honest, at a personal level, some of us also love the feeling of being in a position of power or control over situations or other people's lives. Indeed, the ability to be able to direct (or manipulate) others for our own ends, or to exercise authority over others is still highly prized. The biblical term used to describe this attitude, is the desire to "lord it over them." Yet Jesus said, this behaviour may be true of the world, but it was not to be so among his followers.[7]

It appears that somewhere along the line, Moses had made the decision to bring an end to his independent living. Perhaps, his relationship with God had become of greater value than the influence he exerted over the men and women around him? Was he beginning to understand that submission to the will of God was more important than personal choice and personal preference?

In our own generation, independence is often expressed through the power of personal choice, both in society and in the church. Os Guinness, commenting on what he sees today, shares his conviction that:

> *Choice is no longer just a state of mind. Choice has become a value, a priority, a right. Choice for modern man is a right that overwhelms both responsibility and rationality.*[8]

When the Centurion sent word to Jesus asking him to heal his servant, he recognised that Jesus had been given power and authority.[9] Some have suggested the explanation for Jesus' own authority was the fact he himself lived his life in total submission to the authority of his Father. Certainly, throughout the Gospels we find evidence of Jesus' dependency on his Father:

> "...the Son can do nothing by himself; he can do only what he sees his Father doing, because whatever the Father does the Son also does."
> (John 5 v 19)

> "...I do nothing on my own but speak just what the Father has taught me."
> (John 8 v 28)

> "For I have come down from heaven not to do my will but to do the will of him who sent me."
> (John 6 v 38)

Men and women of faith increasingly understand that true power and influence comes from living in total dependency upon God. They seek to ensure that all their decisions and choices are governed by submission to the revealed will of the Father. They also recognise that any power and influence they may have needs to be used for the good of others and to forward the kingdom of God on the earth.

Third, he was giving up his **possessions.** The passage in Hebrews Chapter 11 speaks of *"the treasures of Egypt,"* and it was indeed a time when this nation enjoyed an abundance of gold, silver, fine clothes and jewellery. There is no doubt Moses had his own share of these things. But there was more. Egypt was also known for its fine architecture and buildings, and was considered to be the centre of art, learning, music and culture. Today, we might refer to the term 'cultural capital,' and Moses' life was definitely enriched in this way too. The New Testament tells us as such:

> "Moses was educated in all the wisdom of the Egyptians and was powerful in speech and action."
> (Acts 7 v 22)

In every sphere of life, whether physical, material, intellectual or social, it seems Moses had been endowed with much – a 'superabundance', even. Yet, he was prepared to hand it all over and put it down. Had he discovered what Jesus taught years later, namely that *"life does not consist in an abundance of possessions"* (Luke 12 v 15)? Had he wrestled with the question posed by Jesus that still challenges now, *"What good is it for someone to gain the whole world, yet forfeit their soul?"* (Mark 8 v 36)? Had he come to a realisation that God himself was the greatest treasure, and so was prepared to give up everything in order to have God? Would he have concurred with Paul's great statement in the book of Philippians?

> But whatever were gains to me I now consider loss for the sake of Christ. What is more, I consider everything a loss because of the surpassing worth of knowing Christ Jesus my Lord, for whose sake I have lost all things. I consider them garbage, that I may gain Christ and be found in him, not having a righteousness of my own that comes from the law, but that which is through faith in Christ—the righteousness that comes from God on the basis of faith.
> (Philippians 3 v 7 - 9)

Men and women of faith learn to be content in whatever circumstances they find themselves and hold their possessions lightly. They understand the truth, as expressed by the American missionary Jim Elliot, who was martyred along with others while seeking to reach the Auca Indians in Ecuador:

> *He is no fool who gives up what he cannot keep to gain what he cannot lose.*[10]

They know, like the psalmist, that God himself is their greatest treasure:

> Yet I am with you; you hold me by my right hand. You guide me with your counsel, and afterward you will take me into glory. Whom have I in heaven but you? And earth has nothing I desire besides you. My flesh and my heart may fail, but God is the strength of my heart and my portion forever.
> (Psalm 73 v 23 - 26)

Fourth, he was giving up the opportunities to enjoy the temporary **pleasures of sin**, available to him by reason of his position and privilege as the son of Pharaoh's daughter. His privilege provided him with plenty of opportunity to indulge and gratify his own appetites and desires. While some desires were no doubt legitimate and designed by God for man's good and enjoyment, others fell under the category of sinful pursuits.

Moses made a deliberate choice to end this way of living and no longer indulge in sinful behaviour, even if provided transient pleasure. His whole value system began to change. Perhaps, the long-term and eternal consequences of his actions had started to become plain to him, or simply he had decided he would no longer be governed or dominated by the immediate.

I can imagine the impact of these choices within his immediate context. How did those around him react to these changes? Were they perplexed by his changing behaviour? Did they ridicule him for no longer indulging his passions as in the past? Was he accused of being 'out of step' with their world?

To be a follower of Christ is both world affirming and world denying at the same time. Leaving all other allegiances to do what Jesus says and resolving to live as he requires, involves walking as he walked – and that costs.

Jesus, speaking to his disciples reminded them they don't belong to this world:

> "If the world hates you, keep in mind that it hated me first. If you belonged to the world, it would love you as its own. As it is, you do not belong to the world, but I have chosen you out of the world. That is why the world hates you."
> (John 15 v 18 - 19)

And in his prayers for us to the Father, he prays:

> "I have given them your word and the world has hated them, for they are not of the world any more than I am of the world. My prayer is not that you take them out of the world but that you protect them from the evil one. They are not of the world, even as I am not of it."
> (John 17 v 14 - 16)

Os Guinness helpfully reminds followers of Jesus:

> *In the gospel there is an antithesis to the world that we dare not relax, a cost to discipleship that we cannot waive, a challenge to obedience that we must not conceal, and a scandal to faith that we should never airbrush away.*[11]

Men and women of faith seek to live a holy life worthy of their calling because they know it matters. They are prepared to die to self and sinful pleasures, knowing ultimately what counts are eternal things. They live with their eyes and hope fixed on what is to come in eternity, not the immediate and that which will pass away.

Identifying With God's People

When Moses refused to be known as the son of Pharaoh's daughter, he turned his back on his status, his personal independence and influence, his possessions as a source of lasting satisfaction, and the pleasure he received from his sinful activity. At face value, this is quite a cost!

But it is important we note what he was turning to. Hebrews tells us he chose instead to identify himself with the people of God. A despised people it is true, but a people of a divinely ordained destiny. Similarly, we are not simply called to be individual men and women of faith, but men and women who are part of a 'faith community.'

Each of us is summoned individually, and therefore uniquely and personally, to follow Christ. Yet, we are not summoned to be a bunch of individual believers; we are called to be members of God's household. And more than that, to become part of God's family. We are bound together by a covenant, and are meant to live out a corporate calling that both complements and transcends our callings as individuals.

We live today in a climate of individualism that stresses personal rights, personal fulfilment and the importance of individual choice. Even in our churches, there can sometimes be an over emphasis on discovering our personal gifts and ministry. And the result of this can be that the development of our own gifting, becomes of greater importance than the health and growth of the corporate body of the local church. A consumer mentality can also creep in, making 'church hopping' a sad feature of today's church landscape, where people move around seeking to find a church that will meet their own felt needs and preferences.

Lack of commitment to the corporate body of the church is not new, despite reading that at the start of the early church, *"All the believers were one in heart and mind"* (Acts 4 v 32). Sadly, it was not long before the writer of Hebrews had to address the fact that some believers were making a habit of not meeting together (see Hebrews 10 v 25). It is vital we all identify with God's people and God's church, and are thoroughly involved in its life and ministry. After all, both Jesus and the apostle John remind us that, *"love of the brethren"* is the authenticating mark of a true disciple (see John 13 v 34 - 35 and 1 John 3 v 14).

Identifying With Their Suffering

Moses particularly identified himself with the suffering of God's people. He chose to be mistreated along with them, for they were a nation that was despised, written off, looked down on, and oppressed. But this went beyond being ready to suffer abuse, rather than enjoy the pleasures of sin for a short time. Such was his transformation, he regarded disgrace for the sake of Christ, of greater value than the treasures of Egypt. His eyes were now fixed on his eternal reward, and even more importantly, on the eternal one:

> He persevered because he saw him who is invisible.
> (See Hebrews 11 v 24 - 28)

No doubt Moses would have agreed with the words of Paul, written many centuries later. For Paul also endured suffering and hardship for the sake of the gospel, and persevered by fixing his eyes on the eternal:

> I consider that our present sufferings are not worth comparing with the glory that will be revealed in us.
> (Romans 8 v 18)

> For our light and momentary troubles are achieving for us an eternal glory that far outweighs them all. So we fix our eyes not on what is seen, but on what is unseen, since what is seen is temporary, but what is unseen is eternal.
> (2 Corinthians 4 v 17 - 18)

Men and women of faith identify fully with the people of God and the church, in every place where she manifests her life. That is why it is so important for us to support our brothers and sisters in places where they are persecuted for their faith in Jesus. Identifying with the 'persecuted' church is not an option, but a family responsibility in which we all share.

Knowing deep in our hearts that following Jesus is of greater value than anything this world can offer, enables us to live a life of radical discipleship. Like Moses, we can choose to throw off every hindrance and be willing to suffer personal hardship, discomfort or disgrace to follow Jesus and make him known.

Graham Kendrick, worship leader and songwriter, captures something of this. In his popular song, "Knowing You,"[12] he expresses the reality of coming to a place where our relationship with Jesus is of greater value than anything or anybody in our life:

All I once held dear, built my life upon
All this world reveres, and wars to own
All I once thought gain I have counted loss
Spent and worthless now, compared to this

Knowing you, Jesus
Knowing you, there is no greater thing
You're my all, you're the best,
You're my joy, my righteousness
And I love you Lord

Now my heart's desire is to know you more
To be found in you and known as yours
To possess by faith what I could not earn
All-surpassing gift of righteousness

Oh, to know the power of your risen life
And to know You in Your sufferings
To become like you in your death, my Lord
So, with you to live and never die

I urge us to take further inspiration and challenge from two of Jesus' parables. The first is about the man who found treasure in a field and sold all he had to buy that field. The second was about a merchant looking for pearls; when he found one of great value he sold everything he had and bought it. Both these parables were describing what the kingdom of heaven is like, but as Jesus is the king of the kingdom, they also speak about him (see Matthew 13 v 44 - 45).

The important point to note is that we are told the man who found the treasure did not sell all he had begrudgingly, but did it joyfully. He saw how precious the treasure was.

The American pastor, John Piper, helps us when commenting on the man's actions:

> *He knows that, whatever he pays for that field, it's a steal. Jesus is worth so much more than anything else in all the world, that every loss endured to have more of him can be endured with joy.*[13]

We can also learn from Peter. His own story of grace in laying down his burdens of fear and doubt to 'sell everything' had been hard fought. But he was left in no doubt how precious Jesus was to us who believe (see 1 Peter 2 v 7). And so it follows, that the value we attach to him will directly impact our witness to others. Or, as John Piper's commentary on this scripture continues:

> *Our power to give a compassionate witness about Jesus to unbelievers will grow in direct proportion to how precious Jesus is to us.*

We must never forget, that although Moses gave up much to identify with God's people, it does not compare with what Jesus gave up to come to our world and identify himself with sinful humanity. As Paul reminds us when he writes to the church at Corinth:

> For you know the grace of our Lord Jesus Christ, that though he was rich, yet for your sake he became poor, so that you through his poverty might become rich.
> (2 Corinthians 8 v 9)

Notes

1 CNN Business Report, 21st January 2019 by Tami Luhby

2 Mail Online News, 20th November 2020 by Tim Stickings

3 www.gatesfoundation.org

4 The Call – Finding and Fulfilling the Central Purpose of Your Life by Os Guinness, Copyright © 1998. Used by permission of HarperCollins Christian Publishing, www.harpercollinschristian.com

5 Mark 12 v 38 - 40

6 The Call – Finding and Fulfilling the Central Purpose of Your Life by Os Guinness

7 Mark 10 v 41 - 45

8 The Call – Finding and Fulfilling the Central Purpose of Your Life by Os Guinness

9 Luke 7 v 1 - 10

10 Jim Elliot Was No Fool by Tim Chester, Crossway, 8th January 2018, www.crossway.org/articles/jim-elliot-was-no-fool

11 The Call – Finding and Fulfilling the Central Purpose of Your Life by Os Guinness

12 Graham Kendrick, Copyright © 1993 Make Way Music, www.grahamkendrick.co.uk

13 Message: How Much Is Jesus Worth? (1 Peter 2 v 7). Topic: Evangelism. By John Piper, Copyright © Desiring God Foundation. Source: www.desiringgod.org, 10th January 1982

CHAPTER THREE

Position And Performance

As followers of Jesus, it is one thing to know we have been chosen and predestined to live to the praise of his glory, but it is quite another to consistently live out that truth in our daily experience. Sadly, numbers of us continue to struggle with what one friend described as the 'imposter syndrome.' By that, he meant many of us are aware of being true followers of Jesus, but recognise that our lifestyle often falls short of what it could be, and at times dishonours God. If we are truly honest with ourselves, we can live with the constant nagging fear that one day we are going to be found out. And if we're found out, our weaknesses, faults and sins will be exposed for all to see! We can question whether we truly belong.

To add to our troubles, the enemy of our souls is constantly seeking to remind us of our lack of authenticity, trying to weigh us down with feelings of condemnation, shame and guilt. His goal in sowing these false narratives is to make our witness to Christ and his kingdom null and void. Listening to his voice can quickly erode confidence in our true identity in Christ; we can easily find ourselves taking on identities rooted in our struggles and problems, not in the truth of who we are.

Think for a moment about this list of things people commonly struggle with in life:

- Being single, divorced, unemployed, stuck in a dead-end job
- Feeling unacceptable, unlovable, rejected
- Depression, addiction, battling mental health issues or long-term illness
- Marriage undergoing a long season of difficulty
- Concern for the future well-being of your children

- Being constantly weighed down by the suffering you see in the world

Ask yourself whether these or similar sorts of things have begun to dominate your own thinking? Or, do you see these things in your loved ones? What do you struggle with at present? Has something other than Jesus' complete acceptance of you begun to shape the way you see yourself?

Given a chance, this type of thinking has a tendency to mix itself into the foundations and mortar that we build our identity and sense of worth upon. The battle is real!

Pastor and author Paul David Tripp, helpfully comments:

> *The longer we struggle with a problem the more likely we are to define ourselves by that problem. We come to believe that our struggle or problem is who we are.*[1]

He goes on to say, "although the labels we give ourselves may describe particular ways we struggle in a fallen world, they are not our identity and if we allow them to define us, then we become trapped within their boundaries."[2]

Tripp suggests it is far better as followers of Christ to say for example, "I am a child of God in Christ, and I tend to struggle with (XYZ), but I am beginning to grasp how rich I really am because of my place in His family. I am learning to live out of those riches he has provided, rather than the poverty of the identities I used to assign myself."[3]

So, the key question for us is how do we live out of our identity in Christ and take hold of the riches he has provided for us? How can we increasingly experience change and transformation to become more like Jesus? What steps can we take to ensure our thinking, character and actions match our new identity?

The author Leif Hetland, in his book "Called to Reign," identifies the prevailing worldview of our generation, which is that in order to have something, you have to do something. And, it is only when you have something that you can be somebody. By contrast, the biblical worldview emphasises our being "in Christ," where we are somebody, we have everything, and can do anything on Jesus' merit, not our own.[4]

The point I believe he is making is that as children of God, our position precedes our performance. How we live flows out of our new identity, which is assured and fixed in who we have become "in Christ."

New Identity

As a result of the kindness, love and mercy of God, our new identity is rooted in our union with Christ. The following passage describes both the amazing work God has done in bringing each one of us into Christ, and the response that should naturally flow from our lives:

> At one time we too were foolish, disobedient, deceived and enslaved by all kinds of passions and pleasures. We lived in malice and envy, being hated and hating one another. **But when the kindness and love of God our Saviour appeared, he saved us, not because of righteous things we had done, but because of his mercy.** He saved us through the washing of rebirth and renewal by the Holy Spirit, whom he poured out on us generously through Jesus Christ our Saviour, so that, having been justified by his grace, we might become heirs having the hope of eternal life. This is a trustworthy saying. And I want you to stress these things, **so that those who have trusted in God may be careful to devote themselves to doing what is good.** These things are excellent and profitable for everyone.
> (Titus 3 v 3 - 8; emphasis added)

We are a new creation, born again of the Holy Spirit, the old has gone, the new has come. No longer sinners, but saints with a new heart and a new spirit. We are renewed by the Holy Spirit living in each one of us, moving us to keep God's law of love, so we can live differently. Or as the passage puts it, so we can *"be careful to devote ourselves to doing what is good."*

We may not yet fully live as we should, but we should all relate to and be encouraged by the redeemed and transformed eighteenth-century slave trader John Newton:

I am not what I ought to be,
I am not what I want to be,
I am not what I hope to be in another world,
But still I am not what I once used to be,
And by the grace of God I am what I am.[5]

The Bible is clear that a fundamental change has taken place in our lives. God the Father has lavished his love upon us and we are no longer estranged from Him, but have become his very dear children. This is who we are (see 1 John 3 v 1).

An illustration may help us understand more clearly the importance of being assured of our adoption as children of God, and the practical outcomes that flow out of that knowledge.

I am sure many of you will remember the well-known tale by Hans Christian Anderson entitled, "The Ugly Duckling." The story tells of a homely little bird born in a barnyard who suffers abuse from the other birds around him until, much to his delight (and to the surprise of others), he matures into a beautiful swan, the most beautiful bird of all.

This tale has seen many interpretations over the years, from scholars and students alike. Maybe you'll see some truth in this selection:

- The tale was based on his own life story
- The tale demonstrates the importance of nature over accomplishment
- The tale is about finding your place in society
- The tale is about not allowing yourself to be defined by those around you

And the one I like the best is:

- He became a swan, because he was always a swan!

Whatever his initial appearance and the adverse circumstances of his early life, he was bound to experience change and transformation because he possessed the DNA of a swan, he was from the very beginning an authentic swan!

We do not start life with an innate ability to live a holy life. The reality is the very opposite. Scripture reminds us that from the beginning we were in fact dead in our transgressions and sins and sought to gratify the cravings of our sinful nature. Nevertheless, God has intervened and made us alive in Christ, giving us a new nature We are now authentic children of the living God. It's written in our spiritual DNA (Ephesians 2 v 1 - 10).

Whatever future struggles and trials may come our way, we remain genuine participators in the divine nature. Therefore, not only is our future secure, but change and transformation into the likeness of Christ is gloriously possible! More than that, the New Testament demonstrates that this isn't only for a few. As those who are genuinely "in Christ" and have been united to Him, we can all be expectant of transformation.

Changed Lives

By his Spirit, God is continually working in us to bring about deep fundamental change in our lives. Where once we were callous and insensitive, he seeks to enable us to become tender hearted. In the past we may have been dominated by bitterness and anger, but we need not be any longer. No matter what our previous background, we can become a loving and generous person, like Jesus our master.

John Piper comments:

> *Christ frees us from the terrible fatalism that says change is impossible for me. It frees me from mechanistic views that make my background my destiny.*[6]

Some conclude that all we have to do now is wait patiently, like our ugly duckling friend, for the process of transformation to be accomplished in us! But the Apostle John is careful to remind us that full transformation will only be completed at the future appearing of Jesus:

> Dear friends, now we are children of God, and what we will be has not yet been made known. But we know that when he appears, we shall be like him, for we shall see him as he is.
> (1 John 3 v 2)

Despite this glorious hope, John does not end his statement there, but adds one further sentence which is of the utmost importance:

> All who have this hope in him purify themselves, just as he is pure.
> (1 John 3 v 3)

Lifestyle transformation in this life is not a matter of sitting back and letting God do his work, but requires active cooperation, effort and diligence on our part. Yes, God is at work in us, but we have our part to play.

Paul writes to the church at Philippi:

> ...continue to work out your salvation with fear and trembling, for it is God who works in you to will and to act according to his good purpose.
> (Philippians 2 v 12 - 13)

As one preacher used to say, "What God works in, we need to work out!"

Paul emphasised to the believers at Ephesus, the importance of leaving their old lives behind and pursuing the new life gifted to them in Christ. He encouraged them to apply the truth they had been taught into their everyday lives and experience:

> You were taught, with regard to your former way of life, to put off your old self, which is being corrupted by its deceitful desires; to be made new in the attitude of your minds, and to put on the new self, created to be like God in true righteousness and holiness.
> (Ephesians 4 v 22 - 32)

He rounds off his encouragement to them by asking them to follow in the footsteps of Jesus and live a life of love:

> Follow God's example, therefore, as dearly loved children and walk in the way of love, just as Christ loved us and gave himself up for us as a fragrant offering and sacrifice to God. (Ephesians 5 v 1 - 2)

Everything We Need

Another passage in the New Testament, bringing together the truth of our position in Christ and the expected outflow of a changed life, is found in Peter's second letter to Christians scattered throughout the Roman world. He speaks first of the riches we possess in Christ, and *"for this very reason,"* he goes on to implore followers of Jesus to make every effort to use this truth and become effective and productive. Once again, understanding our position in Christ precedes our performance:

> His divine power has given us everything we need for a godly life through our knowledge of him who called us by his own glory and goodness. Through these he has given us his very great and precious promises, so that through them you may participate in the divine nature, having escaped the corruption in the world caused by evil desires.
>
> For this very reason, make every effort to add to your faith goodness; and to goodness, knowledge; and to knowledge, self-control; and to self-control, perseverance; and to perseverance, godliness; and to godliness, mutual affection; and to mutual affection, love. For if you possess these qualities in increasing measure, they will keep you from being ineffective and unproductive in your knowledge of our Lord Jesus Christ. But whoever does not have them is near sighted and blind, forgetting that they have been cleansed from their past sins.
>
> Therefore, my brothers and sisters, make every effort to confirm your calling and election. For if you do these things, you will never stumble, and you will receive a rich

> welcome into the eternal kingdom of our Lord and Saviour Jesus Christ.
>
> (2 Peter 1 v 3 - 11)

Peter starts by reminding them of God's divine power that has given them everything they need to live a godly life. God the Father, supplies his children with everything they will ever need to do what he has called them to do. The question is, did they, and do we, believe this? Everything, all of it, the lot... not just some things!

Note he says, all this has been *"given"* (perfect tense), which speaks of an action in the past that has continuing results in the future. The giving has already taken place. What they need has been placed in their storehouse and credited to their spiritual bank account, so they can draw on it at any time. And, this is not the result of their own actions, but has been accomplished by the divine power of God. You and I are also recipients of this same deposit.

Provision has been made for all followers of Jesus to live God-honouring lives from the time they are born again into God's family, until the time they join him in eternity. What we think about, what we desire and what we say or do, can all be done in a manner that honours God, our Father (see Colossians 3 v 17).

But note, Peter says this is accomplished through *"our knowledge of him who called us by his own glory and goodness"* (verse 3). Divine power becomes effective in our lives, only to the extent that we grasp these truths. We are empowered by our knowledge of the truth about the God who called us through his own glory and goodness, and as we take hold of the very great and precious promises he has made to us his children. Knowing, trusting and acting on these promises activates the power of God, and results in godliness and love growing in our lives.

John Piper, speaking about the promises of God and the witness of the local church has said:

> *We are the light bulbs of our neighbourhoods; God is the distant generator of electricity; and the cables that carry the power are God's promises.*[7]

The outcome of trusting and acting on these promises is that we become progressively more and more like Jesus. God's power flows into our lives enabling us to resist and overcome temptation, escaping the corruption in the world caused by evil desires.

When Paul writes to Titus, he expresses our grace-given ability to overcome and live lives that honour our heavenly Father:

> For the grace of God has appeared that offers salvation to all people. It teaches us to say "No" to ungodliness and worldly passions, and to live self-controlled, upright and godly lives in this present age, while we wait for the blessed hope—the appearing of the glory of our great God and Saviour, Jesus Christ, who gave himself for us to redeem us from all wickedness and to purify for himself a people that are his very own, eager to do what is good.
> (Titus 2 v 11 - 14)

It is important to note in these verses that it is not simply a question of defeating sin in our lives, but that God's grace leads to the eager pursuit of all that is good, the living of an upright life, and an ability to walk in the pathway of justice and love.

God's intent is not that we simply pursue personal well-being through a satisfying job, a successful marriage, a wonderful family, a friendly church, a good neighbourhood to live in, exciting holidays, good health and financial security. Even though all those things can be valid desires. Rather, he wants to meet our deepest and most significant needs, which are spiritual, rather than external or emotional.

He wants to: free us from our slavery to God-replacements that imprison us; deliver us from self-absorption and the pursuit of self-glory; and transform our hearts through the life changing grace of Jesus Christ.

And, because God has given us power for godliness, Peter says we must strive to become godly!

Add To Your Faith

> For this very reason make every effort to add to your faith…
> (2 Peter 1 v 5)

Order is important. God first provides, and we respond by using what is provided. Because God is working in us, moving us to do his will, we can respond by acting in accordance with his good purpose.

One of the ways we should act is by adding to our faith. In the scripture quoted above (from 2 Peter 1 v 3 - 11), Peter goes on to list eight things we should be eager to add, which when added to our faith will enable us to honour God in our lives and fulfil our calling as the salt and light of the world:

- Goodness – virtue or moral excellence
- Knowledge – enlightened understanding taught by the Spirit
- Self-control – temperance; mastery over self; self-restraint
- Perseverance – patient endurance
- Godliness – reverent and devoted living
- Mutual affection – brotherly love; love for the family of God
- Love – agape love, active love, for God, each other and our enemies

I don't think Peter has it in mind for these things to be added in any precise sequence, as many of these qualities overlap. The point he is making is that true followers of Jesus do not stop pursuing growth in grace, they are always looking to apply themselves diligently to increase these qualities. They will not settle for a bit of Christlike character, to have a slightly better attitude, or marginally more honest relationships. Being "in Christ," is a precursor to growing and producing fruit that glorifies God. For them, relationships, awkward situations and even adverse circumstances, are seen as God-given opportunities to explore and experience more of what it means to be a child of God.

And notice how Peter outlines the blessing of pursuing these qualities that reflect Christ, *"For if you possess these qualities in increasing measure, they will keep you from being ineffective and unproductive in your knowledge of our Lord Jesus Christ"* (2 Peter 1 v 8). We will not end up being ineffective, inactive, or unemployed. Nor will we be unproductive, unfruitful, or barren.

But, note how Peter also gives a warning about those who do not add to their faith:

> ...whoever does not have them is near sighted and blind, forgetting that they have been cleansed from their past sins.
> (2 Peter 1 v 9)

Such people have no clarity of their future hope in Christ, rather they are taken up with the immediate, with creature comforts and worldly desires. They have forgotten their past history and the price Christ has paid to rescue them. Their sense of excitement and gratitude for the forgiveness of their many past sins has been lost. So, he exhorts them:

> Therefore, my brothers and sisters, make every effort to confirm your calling and election.
> (2 Peter 1 v 10)

Does Peter imply by this statement that lack of diligence in growing in Christlike graces, betrays the fact that someone has not after all been called, and is therefore not among the elect of God? Is he concerned that their *"cleansing from past sins"* may simply have been a mere external reformation, without their hearts being truly changed? Or is he warning a genuine follower of Jesus who has fallen into a wrong way of living by their misunderstanding of the true nature of the Christian life?

In the New Testament the new birth and a life filled with Christlike qualities appears to be inseparably linked. Lack of such qualities in our lives may challenge our personal sense of assurance of our salvation. Although these qualities and our good works do not save us, nevertheless they do provide us with evidence that our trust in God's promise of salvation in Christ is genuine. The Apostle John illustrates this point in his first letter when he says:

We know that we have passed from death into life, because we love each other.
(1 John 3 v 14)

Peter ends with a wonderful promise for those who take action and respond to his exhortation:

...For if you do these things, you will never stumble, and you will receive a rich welcome into the eternal kingdom of our Lord and Savior Jesus Christ.
(2 Peter 1 v 10 - 11)

Life of course is not just a question of what we will receive at the end, but who we become as we seek to follow Jesus on a day-to-day basis. God has made ample provision for the progressive change of our character, so that as we deal with the problems of life in a fallen world, we can do what is right and reap a harvest of good fruit. We can become effective and productive witnesses to Christ. No longer living for self, but for Him who died for us and was raised again.

There is potential for all of us to become more like Jesus as we make every effort towards moral excellence, increasing our knowledge of God's character, and strengthening our power of self-control. It is possible to enlarge our capacity for patience, to cultivate godliness, and to develop a more passionate heart for God. Love for brothers and sisters in Christ can grow warmer, and we can spur one another on toward love and good deeds.

Dane Ortlund expresses our common calling when he says:

We are called to mature into deeper levels of personal holiness as we walk with the Lord, truer consecration, new vistas of obedience.[8]

I close this chapter by reminding us that we must be careful not to see our own growth and development in Christ as an obstacle to others, but rather as something in God's providence that will release others to reach their own potential as followers of Jesus:

Our deepest fear is not that we are inadequate. Our deepest fear is that we are powerful beyond measure. It is often our light, not our darkness that most frightens us. We ask ourselves, who am I to be an example to others of what it means to follow Christ? Actually, who are you not to be? You are a child of God. You playing small does not serve the world. There is nothing enlightened about shrinking so that other people won't feel insecure around you. We are all meant to shine, as children do. We are born to make manifest the glory of God that is within us. It is not just some of us, it's everyone. And as we let our light shine, we unconsciously give other people permission to do the same. As we are liberated from our own fear, our presence automatically liberates others.[9]

Notes

1 Instruments in the Redeemer's Hands: People in Need of Change Helping People in Need of Change by Paul David Tripp, Copyright © October 2022, P&R Publishing, Phillipsburg, NJ

2 Instruments in the Redeemer's Hands: People in Need of Change Helping People in Need of Change by Paul David Tripp

3 Instruments in the Redeemer's Hands: People in Need of Change Helping People in Need of Change by Paul David Tripp

4 Called to Reign: Living and loving from a place of rest by Leif Hetland, Convergence Press, ISBN 978-1-947165-01-4

5 www.goodreads.com/author/quotes/60149.John_Newton

6 Devotional article: Change Is Possible by John Piper, Copyright © Desiring God Foundation. Source: desiringgod.org, 17th November 2012

7 Message: Confirm Your Election (2 Peter 1 v 5-11). Topic: Sanctification and Growth by John Piper, Copyright © Desiring God Foundation. Source: www.desiringgod.org, 2nd May 1982

8 Gentle and Lowly, The Heart of Christ for Sinners and Sufferers, by Dane Ortlund, Copyright © 2020, Page 92. Used by permission of Crossway, a publishing ministry of Good News Publishers, Wheaton, IL 60187, www.crossway.org

9 Adapted from A Return to Love - Reflections on the principles of a course in miracles by Marianne Williamson, Copyright © 1992, 1996. Used by permission of HarperCollins Christian Publishing, www.harpercollinschristian.com

CHAPTER FOUR

Works In Progress

I received a grown-up 'paint by numbers' set for my birthday one year from my youngest daughter and her family. Have you seen them? On this particular canvas, there was a printed outline of the heads of a lion and lioness. The image was then divided up into hundreds of varying shapes and sizes, with each tiny section carrying a printed number. The kit also included 16 small pots of paint, with each colour needing to be applied to the corresponding shape matching its number.

I got to work. Being the methodical man I am, I started filling every shape numbered one, followed by shapes designated two, and so on. In the first few weeks of working on the painting, the canvas looked like a kaleidoscope of coloured blobs on a white background. At that stage, it was hard to convince onlookers that something beautiful would finally emerge from the chaos of colour. However, I did my best to remind them throughout that it was truly a 'work in progress!'

Eventually, after many weeks and hours of painstaking work, the painting was finished. And, to my surprise, it did turn out to be really beautiful! In fact, it was not only good enough to show friends and family, but also to have framed so it can hang on our lounge wall.

I have still not had any offers from an art gallery or any follow-up commissions, but hey, you have to start somewhere!

Why share a story of my 'creative prowess' and artistry?

'Works in progress!' You may have found the previous chapter somewhat daunting when thinking about the progress you are currently making in your life as a follower of Christ. Particularly so, if you have come to see more clearly that the goal of following Jesus is to become more like him, yet consider yourself falling short. And especially, if like many, you struggle to see yourself in light of your new, fixed and secure identity as a loved, accepted child of God.

Here's the good news. All of us who are part of God's family can be classed as 'works in progress,' both individually and corporately as the church of God. This does not negate us making every effort to respond to and cooperate with God's grace, but it does underline that our development and growth is progressive.

More than that, we need to remind ourselves that God our Father is intimately and actively involved in our lives. He will finish the task of our transformation. When writing to both the church at Philippi and Ephesus, Paul shares his complete confidence in God's ability to complete what he has started. Read these verses and be encouraged:

> Being confident of this, that he who began a good work in you will carry it on to completion until the day of Christ Jesus.
> (Philippians 1 v 6)

> ...Christ loved the church and gave himself up for her to make her holy, cleansing her by the washing with water through the word, and to present her to himself as a radiant church, without stain or wrinkle or any other blemish, but holy and blameless.
> (Ephesians 5 v 25 - 27)

God's Workmanship

Paul also describes us as being God's workmanship. God not only made you, but he continues the work of crafting you:

> For we are God's handiwork, created in Christ Jesus to do good works, which God prepared in advance for us to do.
> (Ephesians 2 v 10)

Paul pictures God as the great designer, producer, artist and craftsman who is at work forming, fashioning and moulding us into his treasured possession. And, this work appears to be part of the very nature of God; it's something the Old Testament record shows was always God's desire for Israel:

> 'Now if you obey me fully and keep my covenant, then out of all nations you will be my treasured possession.'
> (Exodus 19 v 5)

Here, the word *"treasured"* speaks of the private wealth of a great king and the things kept in his private possession or private chambers. These were items of great value to him personally that brought him special delight.

Like beautiful, treasured pieces of art, we have been created to draw attention to our great artist, and to bring him fame and renown in the earth.

For each one of us there was a day when God reached down, broke into our lives, took hold of us, and began to shape and fashion us into his likeness. And, he is still actively at work in our lives today by his Spirit, transforming us from one degree of glory to another (see 2 Corinthians 3 v 18).

Paul experienced God taking hold of him when he was a rebel and persecutor of the early church. His encounter with Jesus on the Damascus Road turned his life upside down. Writing in later life, he talks about how God apprehended him, but confesses that he too is a work in progress, and has not yet been made perfect:

> Not that I have already obtained all this, or have already arrived at my goal, but I press on to take hold of that for which Christ Jesus took hold of me.
> (Philippians 3 v 12)

When Paul uses the term *"created in Christ Jesus,"* we see the idea of something being made out of nothing – something that was not there before, but is now brought into being. It's the same for us. God, by his grace, has brought something into being in our lives that was not there before. By a creative act, he has reshaped us from within. Look at how Dr. Martyn Lloyd-Jones expresses it:

> *By an act of God, a principle of new life has been implanted in me so that the governing disposition of my soul has been made*

holy. God has initiated something within me, so new that only the image of a new birth or new creation can adequately describe it.[1]

A radical change has taken place, affecting our natural tendencies and the inclinations of our hearts. We no longer have a disposition, a bias, a tendency to sin, nor are our lives dominated by the world, our flesh and the devil. Instead, there is a new governing principle at work in our lives steering us towards holiness, so that our focus in life is centred on God. The power that raised Jesus from the dead is now at work in us by the person of the Holy Spirit, empowering us, influencing us, moulding us, guiding us, convicting us, and freeing us to do the will of God. We may have the same intelligence, the same physical features, the same abilities, but there is a new power guiding them all. This truth is why John can write of followers of Jesus:

> No one who is born of God will continue to sin, because God's seed remains in them; they cannot go on sinning, because they have been born of God.
> (1 John 3 v 9)

Paul does not simply say we are *"created,"* but says we are *"created in Christ Jesus."* He is reminding us that our identification with Christ's atoning death, and all the benefits that flow from it, has brought about our radical transformation. *"In Christ,"* also shows that Jesus is the pattern into which we are all being shaped and moulded. As Paul points out to the church at Rome, Christlikeness is our destiny:

> For those God foreknew he also predestined to be conformed to the image of his Son, that he might be the firstborn among many brothers and sisters.
> (Romans 8 v 29)

Created To Do Good Works

We are not saved by our good works. However, Paul does say we are saved to do good works that God has prepared in advance for us. Hence, we see his encouragement to the church at Ephesus to be imitators of Christ:

> Follow God's example, therefore, as dearly loved children and walk in the way of love, just as Christ loved us and gave himself up for us as a fragrant offering and sacrifice to God. (Ephesians 5 v 1 - 2)

Scripture says Jesus was anointed with the Holy Spirit and power - God was with him. He acted in this power, doing good and healing all who were under the power of the devil. God is with us also, so it should not surprise us that Scripture teaches us to be *"eager to do what is good,"* and to *"be careful to devote ourselves to doing what is good"* (see Acts 10 v 38; Titus 2 v 14).

When commenting on these good works, C H Spurgeon (1834–1892) says:

> *They are not the root, but the fruit of a Christian's salvation. They are not the way of the believer's salvation; they are his walk in the way of salvation. Where there is healthy life in a tree, the tree will bear fruit according to its kind; so, if God has made our nature good, the fruit will be good.*[2]

If you are thinking there is little evidence of good works in your life, or that you are on the potter's wheel but so far there appears to be little form or shape taking place, then be encouraged! God is not a workman who will knock-off early and leave the job half-done! He is fully committed to you, and there is nothing outside of you or inside of you that can prevent him completing his masterpiece.

Remind yourself of the truth. He is *"able to keep you from stumbling and to present you before his glorious presence without fault and with great joy!"* (Jude v 24).

In Galatians, Paul talks about the spiritual growth of the believers in the church. He likens the pain he felt, that Christ had not yet been formed in them, to childbirth; he is desperate for the fruit of their new life and identity to appear. And, when writing to the Colossians, he speaks of his labour and how he struggles with all the energy that powerfully works within him, to present everyone perfect in Christ. Clearly, among the churches he served, he was dealing with many 'works in progress!' (See Galatians 4 v 19; Colossians 1 v 28 - 29.)

Case Study At Corinth

Are you a work in progress? If so, you're in good company.

It is both informative and encouraging to see the way Paul interacted with the churches under his fatherly care. Take for example his dealings with the church at Corinth.

These are the opening words of his first letter to them:

> To the church of God in Corinth, to those sanctified in Christ Jesus and called to be his holy people, together with all those everywhere who call on the name of our Lord Jesus Christ – their Lord and ours:
>
> Grace and peace to you from God our Father and the Lord Jesus Christ.
>
> I always thank my God for you because of his grace given you in Christ Jesus. For in him you have been enriched in every way—with all kinds of speech and with all knowledge— God thus confirming our testimony about Christ among you. Therefore you do not lack any spiritual gift as you eagerly wait for our Lord Jesus Christ to be revealed. He will also keep you firm to the end, so that you will be blameless on the day of our Lord Jesus Christ. God is faithful, who has called you into fellowship with his Son, Jesus Christ our Lord.
>
> (1 Corinthians 1 v 2 - 9)

We know from later in the letter, following Jesus wasn't simple for the Corinthian church. In Chapter 6, Paul lists the kinds of people who will not inherit the kingdom of God, including the sexually immoral, idolaters, adulterers, male prostitutes, homosexual offenders, thieves, the greedy, drunkards, slanderers, and swindlers (verses 9 - 10). It was clear that a number of the people at Corinth came from just those kinds of backgrounds.

But, by the mercy of God they had been washed, sanctified, and justified in the name of the Lord Jesus Christ and by the Spirit of God. As a result of the sacrificial death and resurrection of Jesus Christ, all their past sins had been forgiven and blotted out. Born again of the Spirit, their lives were now heading in an entirely new direction.

However, all was not well. Any look at Paul's two letters to them reveals the great need for further transformation in their lives. There were divisions and cliques that had grown up around individual leaders. Immorality, incest and prostitution occurred and was not addressed. Litigation took place between church members (taking each other to court). Idolatry was rife, as worship of God was mixed with pagan practices. Gender issues emerged and people sought to abolish gender distinctions. There was abuse of the Lord's supper, with a lack of consideration for others and overeating or getting drunk. And, last but not least, Paul was aware of chaotic church meetings involving the misuse of spiritual gifts.

Despite being far from maturity in Christ, listen to how Paul addresses them.

He starts, not by tackling their faults and failings, but by reminding them of who they are in God. He addresses them as, *"the church of God in Corinth"* (verse 1). Despite their many weaknesses, failings and immaturity, he underscores their position as God's people. They remain sons and daughters of the one true living God – the 'ekklesia' or the 'called out' ones.

And, because of their union with Christ they had been sanctified. They were set apart as holy to God, devoted to his purposes and made members of God's household and worldwide family. Older versions described them as, *"called to be saints,"* showing them as those appointed to live holy (morally pure) Christlike lives. The Apostle Peter was keen to encourage the same in his letter to believers.

> But just as he who called you is holy, so be holy in all you do;
> for it is written: "Be holy, because I am holy."
> (1 Peter 1 v 15 - 16)

Paul affirms this calling, while swiftly emphasising it is not exclusive to the believers at Corinth. He freely acknowledges their solidarity with the worldwide body of Christ by saying, *"together with all those everywhere who call on the name of our Lord"* (verse 2). Therefore, we see that all who call on Christ as Lord are called to live holy lives. It's a call and challenge common to all believers across the world, throughout all history, and includes us today.

Also, notice the way he expresses thanks for them; *"I always thank God for you"* (verse 4). This may appear strange in the light of their current behaviour, which to say the least was pretty appalling, and certainly not a good advert for what the church of Jesus Christ was meant to look like!

I guess if you or I were writing to them, we may have started with something like, 'I am thoroughly ashamed of the way you are living, and it's about time you cleaned up your act. Don't you guys know your behaviour casts a slur on my ministry and brings the gospel into disrepute?'

But he doesn't. Instead, he gives thanks for them and affirms them as believers; later in the letter he even says:

> For you are the seal of my apostleship in the Lord.
> (1 Corinthians 9 v 2)

In other words - Church at Corinth, even with all your failings as works in progress, you authenticate the fact that I am a true apostle!

Enriched In Every Way

The reason he gives thanks for them is they have been recipients of God's saving grace. Their salvation had not been attained through their own merit or achievement, but through God's kindness and mercy. They had felt the divine influence on their hearts. While they were dead in sin - objects of God's wrath - God had made them alive with Christ. They were no longer God's enemies, for they had been reconciled to God through the death of Jesus. More than that, Paul says they had been, *"enriched in every way"* (verse 5), by their union with Christ. Not only had they been given an ability to understand and communicate God's word, but also as a church they did not lack any spiritual gift.

At this point a question might arise in our minds. We have said the Corinthians were immature and their lives were somewhat in a mess. How then could they excel in spiritual gifts? The simple answer is that spiritual gifts are not given on the basis of merit, maturity, or the length of time we have been a believer - praise God! They are gifts of God's grace (charisma), freely given for the building up of the church. And, notice he puts the reason for their enrichment down to the fact, *"our testimony about Christ was confirmed in you"* (verse 6).

No doubt Paul's testimony focused on Jesus' life, death and resurrection, and included the signs and miracles that normally accompanied his preaching. But perhaps more importantly in this context, we need to note he speaks of their testimony being confirmed in the Corinthians. He was no doubt speaking of their response of repentance, baptism and faith in Christ as Lord, which had led to their receiving of the Holy Spirit. For on the day of Pentecost, Peter had outlined God's promise to all who would receive Christ as Saviour and Lord:

> 'Repent and be baptised, every one of you, in the name of Jesus Christ for the forgiveness of your sins. **And you will receive the gift of the Holy Spirit.** The promise is for you and your children and for all who are far off – for all whom the Lord our God will call.'
> (Acts 2 v 38 - 39 NIVUK; emphasis added)

The Corinthians are enriched because, despite their struggles with sin and weakness, the Holy Spirit has imparted new life to them. And, it is that same Spirit who now lives and works in them to will and to act according to God's good purpose, who also endows them with spiritual gifts.

Bright Future – Faithful God

Paul is upbeat about their future. They are not only eagerly waiting for the revealing of the Lord Jesus Christ, but he is convinced God will keep them strong to the end. When Christ comes again, they will stand blameless before him. The reason Paul is so confident things will turn out right for them, is that his confidence is not in the Corinthians themselves, but in a faithful God:

> God is faithful, who has called you into fellowship with his Son, Jesus Christ our Lord.
> (1 Corinthians 1 v 9)

The Apostle Paul knew their **past** reality; God, fully aware of all their sins and weaknesses, had called them, saved them and set them apart for himself. Paul could relate to this more than anyone. Their **present** reality put them in fellowship with Christ and they were, therefore, enriched in every way and had everything they needed for life and godliness through their knowledge of him. And their ultimate **future** reality would see them stand blameless (irreproachable) in God's presence, because of God's own faithfulness.

Future hope is based on God's thorough work with our past so, no doubt, Paul would have concurred with Jude's doxology:

> To him who is able to keep you from stumbling and to present you before his glorious presence without fault and with great joy — to the only God our Saviour be glory, majesty, power and authority, through Jesus Christ our Lord, before all ages, now and forevermore! Amen.
> (Jude v 24 - 25)

Only after Paul has reminded the Corinthians of their identity and destiny in Christ, does he go on to tackle the many issues hindering (and damaging) their individual and corporate lives.

Knowing that God has determined to bring us into a glorious future with him, should energise us to pursue deeper levels of personal holiness in our lives. If we do sin, forsaking our true identity as children of God, and grieving our heavenly Father, then we have one who speaks to the Father on our behalf - Jesus Christ. Jesus, the Righteous One, who always lives to intercede for us. Jesus, who by one sacrifice, has made perfect, forever, those who are being made holy (see 1 John 2 v 1; Hebrews 7 v 25; Hebrews 10 v 14).

Jesus is not repelled or put off by our weaknesses and sins. His heart and longing is for us to succeed, to grow and become more like him. More than that, the writer of Hebrews tells us that having experienced and overcome every temptation and trial we will ever have to face, he is able to sympathise or suffer with us. His heart is drawn to our distress and he longs to bring relief and resolution to our condition. Hence, the encouragement to come boldly to him, in the confidence that we will receive mercy and grace in our time of need:

> For we do not have a high priest who is unable to empathise with our weaknesses, but we have one who has been tempted in every way, just as we are—yet he did not sin. Let us then approach God's throne of grace with confidence, so that we may receive mercy and find grace to help us in our time of need.
> (Hebrews 4 v 15 - 16)

Dane Ortlund helpfully reminds us of Christ's solidarity with us in these times of testing when he says:

> *When the relationship goes sour, when feelings of futility come flooding in, when it feels like life is passing us by, when it seems that our one shot at significance has slipped through our fingers, when we can't sort our emotions, when the longtime friend lets us down, when a family member betrays us, when we feel deeply misunderstood, when we are laughed at by the impressive - in short, when the fallenness of the world closes in on us and makes us want to throw in the towel - there, right there, we have a Friend who knows exactly what such testing feels like, and sits close to us, embraces us. With us. Solidarity.*
>
> *The risen Lord alive and well in heaven today is not somehow less approachable and less compassionate than he was when he walked the earth.*[3]

So, let's keep pressing on day by day to become more like Jesus, keeping our eyes on Him as the author and perfector of our faith. For when we see him, we shall be like him (see Hebrews 12 v 1 - 3; 1 John 3 v 1 - 3)!

Notes

1 God's Way of Reconciliation: Studies in Ephesians (2) by Dr Martyn Lloyd-Jones, Copyright © 1978, Published by The Banner of Truth Trust

2 The Agreement of Salvation by Grace with Walking in Good Works, Metropolitan Tabernacle Pulpit sermon 2210 in The Complete Works of C H Spurgeon, vol 37, www.spurgeongems.org

3 Gentle and Lowly, The Heart of Christ for Sinners and Sufferers, Dane Ortlund, Copyright © 2020, Pages 44, 48. Used by permission of Crossway, a publishing ministry of Good News Publishers, Wheaton, IL 60187, www.crossway.org

CHAPTER FIVE

Living By Grace

"... that saved a wretch like me!"

They say John Newton's song, "Amazing Grace," is the most recorded of all time. Its impact has endured for more than two centuries, offering hope to those grieving or searching for meaning in life. With its simple melody and message of salvation, "Amazing Grace" continues to resonate with people across the globe, reaching those with much faith, some or none.

For many, the word 'grace' speaks of something unmerited – something that cannot be earned. It reflects favour or kindness being extended to one who doesn't deserve it, simply out of the goodness of the giver. But for the followers of Jesus, grace has a still deeper and more profound meaning.

For the believer, grace means being accepted by and put right with God, opening a living relationship with him. This position is undeserved; we haven't earned it through our good works or by keeping religious rules and traditions. Rather, it is given to us, because Jesus offered up his own perfect life on the cross as a sacrifice and substitute in our place, taking the punishment for our sin. And, by rising again, he opened the way for us to become sons and daughters of God in a loving and eternal relationship.

This wonderful truth is why many Jesus followers hold Paul's words to the Ephesians so centrally in their hearts. Jesus has achieved fully and completely what we were powerless to do:

> For it is by grace you have been saved, through faith—and this is not from yourselves, it is the gift of God—not by works, so that no one can boast.
> (Ephesians 2 v 8 - 9)

For followers of Jesus, grace speaks of God's resources being made freely available to us, in order that we may live each day in a way that pleases him. Having put our trust in Christ to save us, and been given God's Spirit to live within us, the Holy Spirit enables us to freely enjoy God's rich resources in Christ. Paul is convinced the power of grace in a believer's life enables us to overcome ungodliness and worldly passions. The believer is not only saved by God's grace but is enabled to reign in life by constantly drawing upon it:

> For the grace of God has appeared that offers salvation to all people. It teaches us to say "No" to ungodliness and worldly passions, and to live self-controlled, upright and godly lives in this present age, while we wait for the blessed hope—the appearing of the glory of our great God and Saviour, Jesus Christ, who gave himself for us to redeem us from all wickedness and to purify for himself a people that are his very own, eager to do what is good.
> (Titus 2 v 11 - 14)

Grace equips us to live the upright and godly life that matches our new secure identity as a forgiven and accepted child of God. Let's look at its transformative power in a believer's life by exploring five common challenges.

Insecurity

People are often concerned about their image; what others may think or say about them. Some suffer from the reoccurring thought, 'If they really knew the real me, they wouldn't like me.' For those battling such thoughts, modern technology provides them with an opportunity to build an online persona grata, airbrushed and manicured to make themselves more acceptable. But let's be honest, no-one is completely immune to the negative impact of comparison this can create.

Similarly, it is not unusual to find people spending large amounts of time and energy trying to please others in pursuit of acceptance and a sense of belonging. Whether conscious of these attempts or not, the result is often continued insecurity, fear of rejection, and reluctance at being who they really are.

It's interesting to look at this bold statement made by Paul in 1 Corinthians:

> But by the grace of God I am what I am, and his grace to me was not without effect. No, I worked harder than all of them—yet not I, but the grace of God that was with me.
> (1 Corinthians 15 v 10)

In the preceding verses, Paul talks about those who had been apostles before him and were eyewitnesses to the resurrection of Jesus. He then reflects on his own journey. By comparison, his previous persecution of the church made it easy for him to view himself as completely unfit to be an apostle. Yet God had awakened him. His powerful grace changed Paul's life and his whole perspective on himself. Despite his dubious past, God's grace made him what he was, gave him courage to be *who he was,* and energised him to accomplish *what he did.* Paul knew this at his core.

The realisation he did not deserve, nor could ever earn, the privileges given him, freed Paul to be exactly who he was and do what he was called to do. Grace was his silent companion and invisible security. He no longer had cause to compare himself to others or compete with his peers.

God gives us grace to be who we are in Jesus.

Weakness

Many of us are only too aware of our human frailty and weakness, whether physical, emotional, or intellectual. We also know our weaknesses often cause us to mess up and regularly leave us feeling bad about ourselves. At times we suffer hurt and get beaten up by life itself, often by circumstances or events outside our control.

Weakness is common to all people, as we read in 2 Corinthians Chapter 12. Here, Paul speaks of his battle with, *"a thorn in his flesh – a messenger of Satan to torment me"* (verse 7). While people disagree about the exact nature of the thorn, the context gives us a clue. It may have been the hardships, insults, difficulties, persecutions, beatings and imprisonments he suffered as an ambassador of Jesus Christ, and these things left him feeling weak, helpless and vulnerable.

Three times he prays to God to take the thorn away from him, but God's answer to him is, *"My grace is sufficient for you, for my power is perfected in weakness"* (verse 9). God's grace not only gave him the ability to be content with his weaknesses, but also gave him strength (power) to persevere despite them. The impact of this grace in his life is so great that he's able to say:

> Therefore, I will boast all the more gladly about my weaknesses, so that Christ's power may rest on me. That is why, for Christ's sake, I delight in weaknesses, in insults, in hardships, in persecutions, in difficulties. For when I am weak, then I am strong.
> (2 Corinthians 12 v 9 - 10)

Grace enables us to be vulnerable, so that we do not have to hide or deny our weaknesses or imperfections. It lets us admit our struggles and let the cracks in our life show; it frees us to be real. Admitting our own weaknesses invites other people in, helping them identify with and feel comfortable around us. It enables us to become instruments of power in God's hands.

God gives us grace to bear, and then learn, from our weaknesses.

Sensitivity

Have you ever noticed that life is a series of responses? We constantly interact with our spouse, children, parents, friends, work colleagues, fellow students, those in authority, those in need, other drivers on the road, or those in the supermarket queue. This list can go on and on.

Therefore, it is good to ask ourselves the question, "Do we always respond to others in a sensitive, helpful and godly way?" I am thinking here, particularly, of our speech and our spoken responses.

Jesus said, *"For the mouth speaks what the heart is full of"* (Matthew 12 v 34), while James reminds us our tongue is a powerful instrument, with the power to both build up and destroy. He likens the tongue to a tiny spark that sets on fire a whole forest (see James 3 v 5 - 9). Sadly, it is not uncommon to find people today who have been damaged by, and are still struggling with, words spoken to them many years ago.

Here again, God's grace in our life helps us cement the instinct to build others up rather than knock them down. The true nature of our new identity in Christ can become our first response, so our speech becomes an expression of God's grace at work in our life. We respond out of a place of our own security.

Paul speaks of this very thing when instructing the church at Colossae:

> Let your conversation be always full of grace, seasoned with salt, so that you may know how to answer everyone.
> (Colossians 4 v 6)

Salt carries with it the idea of good taste, tactfulness, and well-timed words. Grace involves being sincere and open in communication, while at the same time showing respect for the other person's feelings and taking care not to hurt them unnecessarily. Grace helps us cushion our words so that truth can be received without needless (or unwanted) offence.

It is said of those in Jesus' hometown of Nazareth where he grew up that:

> All spoke well of him and were **amazed at the gracious words** that came from his lips.
> (Luke 4 v 22; emphasis added)

God's grace also helps us to speak well to those we encounter.

Compromise

Truth has become relative today. Truth for an individual appears to be whatever you want it to be and, 'Living *your* truth' is heralded as a sign of success or personal strength. There are no longer clear moral boundaries of what is 'wrong' or 'right,' but rather the common value of tolerance for everything and everybody. Therefore, if you come along with strong opinions of a moral or spiritual nature, you can face difficulty. Clear ideas about what is wrong and right, or firmly held religious or spiritual convictions will often be met with opposition, harassment, social exclusion, marginalisation, hostility, and even hate. This can be further compounded when you not only hold such views but seek to live them out, letting them impact every area of your life, both public and private.

In the face of such hostility, it is all too easy to back down or back away from any confrontation – to stay quiet when the subject of faith surfaces, or to lose one's distinctiveness and mingle with the crowd. In such a climate we can stop fighting for the truth, throw in the towel and compromise our faith, erring towards the seemingly calm waters of worldly acceptance or a sense of belonging.

Paul forewarns the early followers of Jesus:

> But mark this: There will be terrible times in the last days. People will be lovers of themselves, lovers of money, boastful, proud, abusive, disobedient to their parents, ungrateful, unholy, without love, unforgiving, slanderous, without self-control, brutal, not lovers of the good, treacherous, rash, conceited, lovers of pleasure rather than lovers of God—having a form of godliness but denying its power.
> (2 Timothy 3 v 1 - 5)

He makes them aware that, *"everyone who wants to live a godly life in Christ Jesus will be persecuted"* (2 Timothy 3 v 12).

This turned out to be the case for many followers of Jesus in the first-century church, particularly the recipients of the letter to the Hebrews. These Jewish Christians were undergoing severe harassment and persecution; some were in the process of turning away from the faith and lapsing back into Judaism. Listen to what the writer says to them:

> Do not be carried away by all kinds of strange teachings. It is good for our hearts to be **strengthened by grace,** not by eating ceremonial foods, which is of no benefit to those who do so.
> (Hebrews 13 v 9; emphasis added)

Grace awakens in us the courage to stand firm and stand up for what we believe. It prompts within us the authenticity of who we really are as sons and daughters of the living God. It imparts power to live passionate and uncompromising lives in the face of opposition and ridicule.

Grace lets us live out our new identity in Christ, secure in our position and who we are.

Pride

Pride is something most of us struggle with yet find hard to admit to! It is always present and ready to defend itself, has the ability to 'go underground,' and masks its ugliness in subtle quiet ways.

We're not just talking about pride in respect to the power and influence we may wield. Nor the possessions we might own or the status we might occupy in social circles. We're also talking about the exaggerated opinion of our own qualities, merits, and abilities. We often value ourselves too highly, feeling we are better or more important than others. Such pride can reveal itself in an arrogant attitude or conceited conduct!

Let's not, even for one second, forget the value God places on us. We are precious. But problems arise when the focus of our confidence becomes us—our skills, our achievements and what we can do—and not who Jesus is.

There is a tendency in most of us to do things on our terms, thinking our way is best and right! We can think we can handle life and eternity on our own terms without any outside help, either from other people or God. Sometimes life, circumstances or misguided (but sometimes well-meaning) logic has taught us this false narrative. But the truth is, we all have needs in life we cannot meet ourselves. Even with our best efforts, we cannot turn ourselves into 'a better person,' and certainly none of us has the power to secure our own immortality.

Grace is how we can receive all we need for life and eternity! Look at these verses from Scripture – there's a reason they are often repeated:

> God opposes the proud, but shows favour to the humble.
> (From James 4 v 6 - 7; 1 Peter 5 v 5)

It's a promise as much as it is a challenge. If we will humble ourselves, admit our needs and submit to God, drawing near to him with a humble and penitent heart, then the promise is he will come near to us. His grace, freely given, will lift us up to become a people who increasingly reflect God's glory.

God gives us grace to submit our lives to his sovereign will and purposes.

Reigning In Life

Across all areas of our lives, we need to draw daily on the strengthening and empowering grace of God. In everything we encounter, it is important to remain confident in God's freely given and abundant provision of grace, so that we might reign in life.

> For if, by the trespass of the one man, death reigned through that one man, how much more will those who receive God's abundant provision of grace and the gift of righteousness reign in life through the one man, Jesus Christ.
> (Romans 5 v 17)

Sadly, many of us fail to draw fully on God's grace. Even though we are encouraged to confidently approach God's throne to receive mercy and find grace to help us in our time of need (see Hebrews 4 v 16), we can still remain reluctant to do so. I've seen this among my family and friends, in my role as a church leader and, at times, have had to confront it in my own life.

Why do we see this apparent disconnect between the truth of God's grace and us readily drawing from it? Often, we can be burdened by a sense of shame about our sin, failure or weakness. This barrier can be coupled with an incorrect and unhelpful view of God. It's not uncommon to find people harbouring the thought of a perfect and holy God meeting us with a frown of disapproval, dressing down, or even disdain. But nothing could be further from the truth!

This kind of thinking about God is nothing new among believers. For example, listen to the old English pastor Thomas Goodwin reflecting (in old English) on Matthew Chapter 11, verses 28 - 30.

> *Men are apt to have contrary conceits of Christ, but he tells them his disposition there, by preventing such hard thoughts of him, to allure them unto him the more. We are apt to think that he, being so holy, is therefore of a severe and sour disposition against sinners, and not able to bear them. "No," says he; "I am meek; gentleness is my nature and temper."*[1]

When we look at Jesus' life in the Gospels, we find that rather than being of a "severe and sour disposition," he is instead filled with joy, love and mercy. It is not the righteous he is drawn to. Jesus constantly reaches out to the overtly undeserving, those weighed down by their sin, those suffering from sickness, the social outcasts, those troubled by demonic powers, and the harassed and helpless. To them, he was fully approachable and compassionate, so it is no wonder he earned the title, 'friend of sinners' among the religious people of the day! What was meant disparagingly at the time, remains a wonderful hope for all who see their own need (see Matthew 9 v 10 - 13, 35 - 36).

Jesus didn't find his joy in pronouncing judgement and condemnation on people. He did so by bringing them God's mercy and forgiveness, and by teaching, healing, delivering, comforting and restoring them to their true relationship with God the Father. And the risen Jesus is still doing the same today; he has not changed and he is still fully approachable and compassionate. Even more so, to those of us who have accepted Jesus and are God's own beloved children.

We forget too easily that it was while we were still powerless, ungodly and sinners, Jesus died for us. Too easily, the world, worry or doubt can shout louder than the truth that the God who did not spare his own Son, but gave him up for us, graciously has given us all things along with him. Paul's words probably need to echo more frequently in our ears – that God is for us, and not against us! Indeed, King David's famous psalm reminds us that because of our great shepherd Jesus, we can also say, *"surely goodness and mercy will follow me all the days of my life"* (Psalm 23 ESV). Try replacing the word *"follow,"* with the word 'pursue.' Now consider that, more than just being available to us, we actually can't even evade God's goodness or escape his mercy (see Romans 5 v 6 - 8; Romans 8 v 31 - 32).

Members Of His Own Body

One of the reasons why Jesus is so ready to come to our aid with his abundant grace, is that we are members of his own body. As Paul pointed out:

> After all, no one ever hated their own body, but they feed and care for their body, just as Christ does the church — for we are members of his body.
> (Ephesians 5 v 29)

Dane Ortlund, commenting on the words of Thomas Goodwin, underscores this wonderful truth:

> *If you are part of Christ's own body, your sins evoke his deepest heart, his compassion and pity. He "takes part" with you – that is, he's on your side. He sides with you against your sin, not against you because of your sin. He hates sin. But he loves you.*[2]

Advocate And Intercessor

In his writings, John tells us of Jesus' faithfulness when met with our sin:

"But if anybody does sin, we have an advocate with the Father — Jesus Christ, the Righteous One."
(1 John 2 v 1)

He will defend our cause because of the merits of his suffering and death.

Jesus is fully qualified to appear on our behalf in the courts of heaven. But he doesn't do so in some detached manner; he stands in solidarity with us, feeling what we feel, fully aware of the specific sin we have fallen into or that has entangled us. He does not leave us alone to fend for ourselves but comes alongside us as a true friend to speak on our behalf.

Wonderfully, we also read in Hebrews that Jesus is our high priest who meets our needs and, *"always lives to intercede for us"* (Hebrews 7 v 25). Similarly, Paul reminds us that, *"Christ Jesus who died - more than that, who was raised to life - is at the right hand of God and is also interceding for us"* (Romans 8 v 34).

Out of his deep love for us, he is constantly seeking to connect our heart to the Father's heart. He speaks in heaven on our behalf because we continue to sin and fail here on earth, so his intercession brings into reality what his atonement has accomplished.

What a comfort to know that Jesus is praying for you and me right now!

What is our response to knowing that Jesus' heart towards us is one of settled compassion and mercy, despite our current failures, weakness or sin? Or, that he is constantly interceding on our behalf? It should surely propel us to do what we have been encouraged to do - confidently enter his presence to receive mercy and find grace to help us in the time of our need.

Abundantly Pardon

Our own thoughts of God are so small in relation to his compassion and readiness to forgive and restore us to himself. Because we have difficulty ourselves in forgiving others and restoring our broken relationships, we tend to think God is like us. But God's disposition is far different to our own. Consequently, this mismatch can be another reason we do not always enter and embrace the provision our Heavenly Father has provided for us in Jesus. The prophet Isaiah gives expression to this when he says:

> "For my thoughts are not your thoughts,
> neither are your ways my ways,"
> declares the Lord.
>
> "As the heavens are higher than the earth,
> so are my ways higher than your ways
> and my thoughts than your thoughts."
>
> (Isaiah 55 v 8 - 9)

(The word translated as *"thoughts"* means not simply mental reflection but plans, devices, intentions and purpose.)

For some people, this verse appears to relate to the mysterious way God operates in his world, which can leave us at times surprised or perplexed. But I suggest that if we look at the context, we can see that the passage teaches us more about God's heart of compassion and his desire to forgive sinners. And more than this, not only to abundantly pardon them, but give them a glorious future:

> "Seek the Lord while he may be found;
> call on him while he is near.
> Let the wicked forsake their ways
> and the unrighteous their thoughts.
> Let them turn to the Lord, and he will have mercy on them,
> and to our God, for he will freely pardon..."
>
> "You will go out in joy
> and be led forth in peace;
> the mountains and hills
> will burst into song before you,
> and all the trees of the field
> will clap their hands.
>
> "Instead of the thornbush will grow the juniper,
> and instead of briers the myrtle will grow.
> This will be for the Lord's renown,

> for an everlasting sign,
> that will endure forever."

(Isaiah 55 v 6-7, 12-13)

We must learn not to measure God by our own standards. His love and compassion towards us in our sin, is far beyond what we can easily conceive of or comprehend. Look at John Calvin's comment on this passage:

> *Men are wont to judge and measure God from themselves: for their hearts are moved by angry passions, and are very difficult to be appeased: and therefore, they think that they cannot be reconciled to God, when they have once offended him. But the Lord shows that he is far from resembling men.*[3]

If we continue to seek the Lord, call upon him with a contrite heart, and lay out before him our sins, misdeeds and shortcomings, then he will abundantly pardon us. He will renew his love to us and sweep us up into the glorious future he has planned, as we receive the grace and mercy to help us now in our time of need.

Consider the richness of Martin Luther's commentary on Galatians:

> *The freeness of God's grace and love is not only the gateway but also the pathway of the Christian life.*[4]

Notes

1. The Heart of Christ by Thomas Goodwin, Puritan Paperbacks, Published by The Banner of Truth Trust, 2011, Page 63
2. Gentle and Lowly, The Heart of Christ for Sinners and Sufferers, Dane Ortlund, Copyright © 2020, Page 71. Used by permission of Crossway, a publishing ministry of Good News Publishers, Wheaton, IL 60187, www.crossway.org
3. Calvin's Commentary on Isaiah 55 v 8, www.biblehub.com/commentaries/calvin/isaiah/55.htm
4. Crossway Commentaries, Galatians by Martin Luther, ed. A Mc Grath and J. I. Packer, Published 1998. Used by permission of Crossway, a publishing ministry of Good News Publishers, Wheaton, IL 60187, www.crossway.org

CHAPTER SIX

True Freedom

In his book, "The Second Mountain - The Quest for a Moral Life," American author David Brooks states that in the last 50 years, the dominant ethos of society in the West has been individualism. The extent of this attitude led Brooks to use a new term, "hyper-individualism," to describe the way Western culture has evolved. His conviction is that the overarching narrative of today is, "I'm free to be myself," which translates in most people's minds to:

> *Each individual has the right to live in any way he or she pleases as long as they don't interfere with other people's rights to live as they please.*

Making one's own choice about how to live, and doing one's own thing, is increasingly considered in society to be "the best social arrangement and that which guarantees the widest possible freedom". There is also a growing belief that "spiritual formation happens best in total freedom, not within obligation".

To illustrate this modern idea of self-determined meaning and purpose, Brooks cites a comment made by Justice Anthony Kennedy during a famous US Supreme Court decision:

> *"At the heart of liberty is the right to define one's own concept of existence, of meaning, of the universe, and of the mystery of human life."*[1]

And so, it leads us to ask whether true freedom is really found in defining, and then living, one's own truth?

Biblical Freedom

For followers of Jesus, the Bible reminds us we are not at liberty to choose our own way of living, nor are we left to decide for ourselves the purpose and meaning of life. Instead, we see a radically different view of the meaning of freedom, as described here by the American Pastor Kevin De Young:

> *The Bible gives us a different way of talking about freedom. Real freedom is not the ability to be whoever you want to be. Real freedom is the ability to be who you ought to be. There is a right way to live. This means that there is a purpose to our freedom.*[2]

This purpose is that we may live godly and upright lives, so we can bring honour and praise to God. Hence, we see both Paul and Peter encourage early followers of Jesus not to use their freedom *"to indulge the flesh,"* (Galatians 5 v 13) or *"as a cover-up for evil"* (1 Peter 2 v 16).

The Bible reveals there is a real danger of sabotaging the freedom we have attained through Christ. We can mistakenly return to a way of living where we seek to obtain God's favour through our behaviour, using our performance as a kind of barometer of his approval and acceptance. Instead of living by grace and faith in the power of the Holy Spirit, we start associating our day-to-day emotional well-being with how well we perceive ourselves to be keeping the 'rules.' And we often find many of these 'rules' are of our own making! Although we know we have been saved by grace alone, we let our performance regulate our relationship with God, along with our perception of his acceptance and favour. It's a recipe for misplaced confidence, unhealthy thinking and unstable feelings of self-worth.

I am sure many of us have fallen into the trap of evaluating our lives based on how well we feel we are doing or living. Our assessment can cover a host of areas, like whether we have had an early morning devotional time, read our Bibles or prayed before leaving home. Or whether or not we have been able to tell someone about Jesus or performed a kind deed. It could be whether we have managed to keep our thought life 'really pure' for three days in a row! And let's not forget about whether we are showing the signs of being an exemplary student or employee, serving sacrificially in church life, or being able to finally make a half decent job of being a parent or spouse!

These are all common thoughts. But, of course, the list could go on.

We attempt to convince ourselves if our external behaviour comes up to scratch, then it will draw down God's favour and blessing on our lives. Yet internally we remain insecure. We continue unsure whether we are, in fact, living up to God's standards, or even our own. There's a fear of our status changing. Yet this battle should come as no surprise, for we've been surrounded by and saved from a world where perception, reputation and performance is king!

In light of this, there is a very real risk in how we relate to God and those around us. When we judge we are doing well, we can come across as either superior, or super sensitive to any criticism of our own lifestyle and behaviour. And should our prayers continue to go unanswered, we can end up feeling God owes us an answer because of all our 'right' living!

Loved And Accepted

What we all need to know in the depth of our being is that God's grace means we are fully loved and accepted, whatever our performance. Our relationship with him can never be based on how well we are doing (or rather not doing). I remember reading Philip Yancey's book, "What's So Amazing About Grace." I was struck by the truth that there is nothing you can do to make him love you more, and there is nothing you can do to make him love you any less. In a similar statement, Tim Keller has said, "If you didn't earn your salvation how are you going to un-earn it?"[3]

These statements combine incredible richness with beautiful simplicity. God's acceptance and love for us is based upon the finished work of Jesus and his life, death and resurrection. His perfect life has been credited to our account.

J. I. Packer expresses the wonderful security of our position in Christ:

> *To justify in the Bible means to "declare righteous": to declare, that is, of a man on trial, that he is not liable to any penalty but entitled to all the privileges due to those who have kept the law.*
>
> *We are children of God loved eternally by a perfect Father. It is only out of this place of knowing that you are loved because of Jesus, that you can really live for him and experience the emotional stability and security that allows us as an individual, and we as a church, to live as God's radically different community.*[4]

When Freedom Is Threatened

To help us understand more clearly how to avoid the dangers of falling back into a performance or 'works' way of living, we can look closely at Paul's letter to the Galatians (see Chapter 5 v 1 - 15).

The background is that Paul is writing to the churches he had founded in Galatia. They were being shaken by false teachers, as not only had they mounted a fierce attack on Paul's authority, but also on the gospel he preached to them.

These false teachers were Jewish Christians who believed that some ceremonial practices of the Old Testament were still binding on the New Testament church. They taught that Gentile converts needed to abide by certain rites, especially circumcision. Beyond just having faith in Christ, they declared the importance of these traditions in securing their identification as children of Abraham and receiving the blessings promised to him. The gospel of grace was being distorted.

We also see this idea confronted in the book of Acts:

> Certain people came down from Judea to Antioch and were teaching the believers: "Unless you are circumcised, according to the custom taught by Moses, you cannot be saved."
> (Acts 15 v 1)

For the false teachers, circumcision was a theological symbol rather than just a physical operation or ceremonial rite. They considered it a sign of belonging to God's covenant people, such that on the day of the Lord, they would be found righteous. For them, it stood for a particular kind of religion - salvation by faith in Christ, *plus* obedience to the law. It was a kind of legalism that centred on human effort and achievement, so was at odds with the message of freedom and grace to which the Gentiles had first responded. It had the potential to destabilise the foundations of their faith.

It's no surprise, therefore, to find Paul immediately affirming the truth of the new life and identity inherited by the Galatians:

> It is for freedom that Christ has set us free.
> (Galatians 5 v 1)

Paul talks about having been set free. It's important to note it as a past action that has been completed. It is an action that is done and doesn't need revisiting.

Paul is not speaking about freedom from sin here, although this is taught in other parts of Scripture. When speaking to the Jews who had believed in him, Jesus said, *"So if the Son sets you free, you will be free indeed"* (John 8 v 36). He was referring to freedom from both the guilt, and the life-controlling power of sin. Similarly, Paul addresses sin when writing to the Romans:

> For we know that our old self was crucified with him so that the body ruled by sin might be done away with, that we should no longer be slaves to sin - because anyone who has died has been set free from sin.
> (Romans 6 v 6 - 7)

In the letter to the Galatians, Paul is talking about freedom from the tyranny of the law. From its control. He is not, so much, talking about setting our will and desires free from slavery to sin, or our conscience being free from the guilt of it.

So, what did freedom from the law mean for the Galatians? It meant freedom from the dreadful struggle to keep it, even a watered-down version made to make it more manageable! It meant they were free to stop trying to win the favour of God, by adding human effort and achievement to the faith by which they had begun to follow Jesus. It meant they were free to live lives of obedience with the new heart given to them, through daily faith in Jesus Christ, and by learning to rely on the Holy Spirit. The false teaching threatened this by adding burdens and a *"yoke"* they could not hope to bear (see Acts 15 v 10).

Stand Firm

Paul was uncompromising. This threat was such a serious issue that he gives them the command to *"stand firm"* – a military term signifying vigilance and responsibility:

> Stand firm, then, and do not let yourselves be burdened again by a yoke of slavery.
> (Galatians 5 v 1)

Paul wants them to enjoy the freedom brought to them by Christ, through the forgiveness of their sin. He does not want them to be continually trying to win God's favour by their own self-effort, legalistic strivings, and trying to keep the 'rules.' To help them grasp what he is saying, he introduces the picture of an ox bowed down by a heavy yoke – that yoke being the study and practice of the law.

Paul understood that seeking to obey the law, particularly circumcision, would return them to a position of slavery they had experienced in their past lives. They would become burdened by demands they could not meet and fearful of condemnation for their disobedience. Yet Christ, through his life, death and resurrection had lifted off the yoke of the law by fully meeting the demands of it. He had died for their disobedience and bore their condemnation by standing in their place:

> Christ redeemed us from the curse of the law by becoming a curse for us.
> (Galatians 3 v 13)

So, as Christ had removed the yoke from them, Paul wanted them to *"stand firm"* again and not lose out on the freedom gained for them at such a cost. He implored them to not let themselves be loaded down again with the crushing yoke of slavery. It was imperative they didn't return to rule keeping as their way of finding acceptance with God or gaining his favour.

For freedom has always been God's heart for his people. After God delivered Israel from literal slavery in Egypt, he spoke these words to his people:

> I am the Lord your God, who brought you out of Egypt so that you would no longer be slaves to the Egyptians; I broke the bars of your yoke and enabled you to walk with heads held high.
> (Leviticus 26 v 13)

What God wanted for his children of old, and what Paul wanted for the Galatian believers, was for them to walk with their heads held high!

Paul is so concerned for their spiritual welfare, he proceeds to give them a solemn warning. He tells them that if they are circumcised and return to their rule keeping ways as the basis of their acceptance and relationship with God, then Christ would be of no value or benefit to them. Rather, they will end up separated, severed, and alienated from Christ (see Galatians 5 v 2 - 4). It would be like crossing a border back into an occupied territory where law rules!

By seeking favour with God through their own human efforts and energy, they would not only have fallen away from grace and turned their back on God, but in choosing to keep the law again they would lose Christ. For it was impossible for them to receive Christ and acknowledge they could not save themselves, while at the same time continuing to insist on following the law as the basis for their salvation.

Paul is unambiguous. You cannot add anything to Christ for salvation, not circumcision, law keeping, rule keeping, good works, or anything! Christ alone is sufficient for salvation, or, as the Reformers agreed, salvation is *in Christ alone, by grace alone, through faith alone.*

If you add anything to Christ, then you lose him and become obligated to obey the whole law:

> For whoever keeps the whole law and yet stumbles at just one point is guilty of breaking all of it.
> (James 2 v 10)

And this is why Paul is eager to remind them of the glorious hope they have in Christ:

> For through the Spirit, we eagerly await by faith the righteousness for which we hope.
> (Galatians 5 v 5)

Faith To Wait

Hope in the fullness of Christ's salvation is critical. They are being reminded to wait for their future salvation and their final glorification, when they will spend eternity with Jesus in a new heaven and earth. But notice in verse five, Paul says they should be *waiting* for it. He doesn't say working for it or trying to earn it by good works. Neither does he remind them to strive anxiously to obtain it – for their hope comes from *knowing* this free gift from God is on its way. They are to wait with eager anticipation.

And they must wait for it by *"faith"*, trusting in Christ crucified and his work on their behalf. Trusting that Jesus has accomplished all that is necessary for them to be accepted with God and to be found in Christ. Trusting in the certainty of both their present and future acceptance by God. And, while they wait, they must remember, *"the only thing that counts is faith expressing itself through love"* (Galatians 5 v 6).

It's also important to look at Paul's encouragement for them to eagerly await righteousness, *"through the Spirit...by faith"*. They have not only been called to a life of faith, but also to a life in the Spirit. The indwelling Spirit produces the good works of love, not human effort or moral exertion. As such, good works shouldn't be added to faith as some kind of subsidiary ground for acceptance with God, rather deeds are born out of faith and the power of God's Spirit. For the Spirit's presence marks them out as recipients of God's new covenant blessing, helping them while they await their full hope of righteousness. And the faith that saves, is also a faith that works to energise and motivate them to love.

Douglas J Moo explains the role of faith and the Spirit when he says:

> *Faith is the means not only of entering into a relationship with God, but also maintaining that relationship and of confirming that relationship on the day of judgement.*
>
> *It is by appropriating and living out of the power of the Spirit that believers confidently wait for the ultimate confirmation of their righteous status before God.*
>
> *Those who are "in Christ" by faith need to live by faith, a faith that produces works of love pleasing to God through the Spirit; and it is by living in this way that people can have a sure hope of righteousness.*[5]

You can sense Paul's disappointment and frustration at the change of thinking and behaviour in Galatia when he exclaims, *"You were running a good race. Who cut in on you to keep you from obeying the truth?"* (Galatians 5 v 7).

Paul often likens the Christian life to a race. When he says they were running well, perhaps he means they had been doers of God's word and not simply hearers. Maybe, their belief had matched their behaviour, such that their way of living had been governed by the fact they were Spirit-filled and full of faith. But now an obstacle had been thrown on the track to steer them away from this path and hinder their spiritual progress.

These false teachers were contradicting the gospel by introducing a doctrine of merit rather than of grace, which resulted in believers in Galatia no longer obeying the truth of Paul's gospel. They had forsaken Christ and fallen from grace. More than that, their teaching was beginning to spread among the Christian community, contaminating the whole church. Paul is adamant this teaching is not of God; the God who called them, called them in grace and powerfully brought them into relationship with himself:

> I am astonished that you are so quickly deserting the one who called you to live in the grace of Christ and are turning to a different gospel - which is really no gospel at all.
> (Galatians 1 v 6 - 7)

Has Paul lost hope in them? By no means! Paul is confident in the Lord that they will return to his own view of the gospel, but he is nevertheless angry that the false teachers are unsettling them and throwing them into confusion. So much so, he wishes these false teachers would mutilate (castrate) and make eunuchs of themselves (see Galatians 5 v 12). He uses this very strong language because he considers this teaching not only to be in error, but a grave evil!

Paul alludes to the possible motivation behind the false teaching. Preaching to people about keeping the law and saying that full salvation depends on man's achievements, may result in making a person popular or helping them to avoid persecution. But Paul reminds them he is still facing persecution at the time of his writing, because he preaches Christ crucified. To tell people that only faith in Christ can save them will always result in persecution, for it is offensive to human pride. Salvation for Paul is, from start to finish, a divine accomplishment. There is no compromise on this truth.

From Galatia To Today

This passage demonstrates how important it is for us to grasp this vital truth. We must not let ourselves or our church communities become burdened again by living under the yoke of slavery, either that of Old Testament law or human effort. But Paul is not finished. He has more to say to the Galatians, and us, about how we are to use our freedom in Christ. For salvation by grace alone does not mean we can live as we like.

The true nature of Christian freedom sees the Spirit enable us to overcome the continuing power of the flesh (sinful nature) by stimulating love for others, and providing for the true fulfilment of the law. The Spirit-filled life is not only fully adequate to maintain and confirm one's status of righteousness before God, but the Spirit can also produce the daily life of righteousness God expects of his people. The Spirit is entirely sufficient to subdue the impulses of the flesh and meet all the demands of righteous-living.

Therefore, Paul explains that true Christian freedom is not licence to indulge the flesh.

> You, my brothers and sisters, were called to be free. But do not use your freedom to indulge the flesh; rather, serve one another humbly in love.
> (Galatians 5 v 13)

The sinful nature, or 'flesh' as it is sometimes translated, is not what clothes our bodily skeleton. Rather, it refers to our fallen human nature inherited from our parents, which they inherited from theirs – one that is self-centred and prone to sin. So, Paul says we must not *"indulge"* it or give it an opportunity. The original word Paul uses means 'a starting point'. The imagery here denotes a base of operations in a war, or a place from which another action or offensive is launched.

Paul says, don't let your freedom in Christ become a pretext for other action or for self-indulgence. In Christ we have been given freedom *from* sin, not freedom *to* sin. We have freedom to approach God as our Father and become more like him, not freedom to give in and satisfy our own selfishness and pride. We have been saved for so much more.

The New English Bible is helpful in its translation of Galatians 5 verse 13 when it says, *"Do not turn your freedom into licence for your lower nature."* Look again at the term *"lower nature"* used here. Indulging in this is not freedom; it's choosing to return to slavery. Jesus said, *"Very truly I tell you, everyone who sins is a slave to sin"*. It is true that at one time we were *"foolish, disobedient, deceived and enslaved by all kinds of passions and pleasures. We lived in malice and envy, being hated and hating one another"*. But that is no longer true. Paul reminds us, *"Those who belong to Christ Jesus have crucified the flesh with its passions and desires."*

In other words, they have said, "No!" to the claim of their lower nature to rule over them (John 8 v 34; Titus 3 v 3; Galatians 5 v 24).

Walking By The Spirit

People today will speak of being free. But, in reality they remain slaves to appetites and passions they cannot control - it's the human condition. However, as followers of Jesus we now seek to walk in the Spirit, relying on the promise of power to walk in true freedom. Paul reminded the Galatians of this hope:

> So I say, walk by the Spirit, and you will not gratify the desires of the flesh.
> (Galatians 5 v 16)

It follows, therefore, that walking by the Spirit shapes how we relate to others. Paul makes it clear our salvation is not freedom to exploit our neighbour, but rather to *"serve one another humbly in love"* (Galatians 5 v 13). We are not free to do as we please, without thought for the impact on those around us. We are not free to ignore, exploit or neglect our fellow man, but rather we are called to love him. The Spirit indelibly changes our thinking, meaning we don't see other people as being here to serve us - we are to give ourselves to serve them. There should be a willingness to give up our own status and position for the benefit of others, or as one person has put it, "to be one poor slave with a lot of masters!"

Such humility shapes the culture in churches and communities; love demands reciprocal concern for others in the community and self-sacrifice for the good of others. We are called to service and not selfishness, the outworking of which means we will not bite, devour or destroy one another with malicious talk or actions (see Galatians 5 v 15). Instead, we will serve one another in love.

Paul helps us understand how this life is made possible by the Holy Spirit's tangible work. As the fruit of the Spirit grows in our very being, we are changed so that love, joy, peace, patience, kindness, goodness, faithfulness, gentleness and self-control abound (see Galatians 5 v 22 - 23).

Remember, *"God is love"* (1 John 4 v 16), so as we let him reign in our life, we too become characterised by love. Love is constructive not destructive. It thinks kind thoughts, it performs good actions, it is faithful, dependable, reliable, trustworthy, and it bears another's burdens. True love is expansive and never possessive, for to love somebody is not to possess them for oneself, but to serve them solely for their benefit and gain.

Look at the words of two recent presidents, both recipients of the Nobel Peace Prize, heralding the importance of using freedom to bless others.

Nelson Mandela, President of South Africa:

> *For to be free is not merely to cast off one's chains, but to live in a way that respects and enhances the freedom of others.*[6]

Oscar Arias Sanchez, President of Costa Rica:

> *The more freedom we enjoy, the greater the responsibility we bear, towards others as well as ourselves.*[7]

You can see our world, with all its brokenness, yearns for this kind of love. Sometimes people catch hold of it and speak about it, but it is Christ who brings about this true freedom.

Paul knew this and would not let the truth of it be stolen from the Galatians. He reminds them, *For the entire law is fulfilled in keeping this one command: "Love your neighbour as yourself"* (Galatians 5 v 14). The whole law aims at doing good to others; if one loves truly and consistently, then everything the old law was aiming at is also accomplished.

This way of life starts and ends with freedom in Christ! We do not exchange the mercy we've received for personal morality. Rather, having received mercy without merit, through faith in him, we keep the law out of love for the one who redeemed us at such cost. We obey, not because we must, but because we love to and are enabled to do so by the indwelling power of the Holy Spirit.

Notes

1 From The Second Mountain by David Brooks, published by Penguin, Copyright © David Brooks, 2019. Reprinted by permission of Penguin Books Limited

2 The Cross in Four Words by Kevin de Young, Richard Coekin and Yannick Christos-Wahab, Page 26, published by The Good Book Company, 2020. Used by kind permission, www.thegoodbook.com

3 @timkellernyc (Timothy Keller (1950-2023)) Twitter/X, 7 September 2021, x.com/timkellernyc/status/1435174508013531137. Accessed: 23 November 2024.

4 God's Words by J I. Packer. Copyright J I. Packer © 1981. Published by Inter-Varsity Press 1981. Pages 139 & 140. Retitled and printed by Christian Focus Publications Ltd 2007 under the title "18 Words – The most important words you will ever know"

5 Galatians – Baker Exegetical Commentary On The New Testament by Douglas J. Moo. Copyright © 2013 Douglas J. Moo. Published by Baker Academic. Pages 329 & 331

6 www.britannica.com/list/nelson-mandela-quotes

7 www.humanrights.com/voices-for-human-rights/oscar-arias.html

CHAPTER SEVEN

Paradox

You are fully loved and accepted in Christ.

What a truth this is! In the last chapter we talked about the importance of not giving up this freedom by returning to the yoke of slavery of the law. We must not look back at the law and our morality as a way of finding acceptance with God, or to win his favour by our own human achievement.

But this challenge leaves us with the question of how to navigate our relationship with the law so we honour God in the present? We only need to look at Jesus' words in the "Sermon on the Mount," to know God hasn't compromised his standards:

> "Do not think that I have come to abolish the Law or the Prophets; I have not come to abolish them but to fulfill them. For truly I tell you, until heaven and earth disappear, not the smallest letter, not the least stroke of a pen, will by any means disappear from the Law until everything is accomplished. Therefore anyone who sets aside one of the least of these commands and teaches others accordingly will be called least in the kingdom of heaven, but whoever practices and teaches these commands will be called great in the kingdom of heaven. For I tell you that unless your righteousness surpasses that of the Pharisees and the teachers of the law, you will certainly not enter the kingdom of heaven."
> (Matthew 5 v 17 - 20)

This passage not only speaks of the longevity of the law, but also of the blessing of those who practise and teach the commands within it. Similarly, in other parts of the New Testament, we find teaching that talks about upholding or obeying the law:

> Do we, then, nullify the law by this faith? Not at all! Rather, we uphold the law.
> (Romans 3 v 31)

> I am not free from God's law but am under Christ's law.
> (1 Corinthians 9 v 21)

> This is love for God: to keep his commands. And his commands are not burdensome.
> (1 John 5 v 3)

However, other statements in the New Testament clearly affirm that our lives are no longer subject to the authority of the law. We have been released or discharged from its hold; it has no further claim on us:

> For sin shall no longer be your master, because you are not under the law, but under grace.
> (Romans 6 v 14)

> You also died to the law through the body of Christ.
> (Romans 7 v 4)

So, which is it? Are followers of Jesus no longer under the law, or do they need to be obedient to it and uphold it? Is there a way of reconciling both these statements? Can both be true at the same time?

It appears like these passages equate to a **paradox,** where the seemingly self-contradictory ideas can both be true. Think about these sentences for a moment:

- Nobody goes to that restaurant; it's too crowded
- Don't go near the water until you have learnt how to swim
- The man writing such stupid sentences cannot write at all

We know exactly what they mean, yet they make no sense if taken at face value, away from context and prior understanding.

For us, this means there is much to grapple with and consider, so we can understand what the truth of our freedom means for how we live our lives today.

As such, let's look at these questions about the law and our lives by presenting a paradox:

> *Christians* ***no longer have to*** *keep the law of God, but they* ***must do so*** *if they want to become God's treasure and a radically different community.*

As we work towards practical understanding, we need to start in the Old Testament with the giving of the law to God's people, the Israelites. The law was not only The Decalogue, the Ten Commandments given to Moses on Mount Sinai (see Exodus 20), but also included the Torah. Torah was the name given to the first five books of the Bible, from Genesis to Deuteronomy. The books include much narrative, meaning there is rich teaching and guidance here, as well as law in the sense of statutes and legislation.

Grace Before Law

The key point to note is that it was God's prior action, in 'redemptive grace,' that called for Israel's obedience to God's law. In other words, the law was given after God's act of rescue and deliverance, not before. The Exodus was God's initiative, born of his love, mercy and compassion for his people. God had seen their suffering and came down to rescue them:

> "I have indeed seen the misery of my people in Egypt. I have heard them crying out because of their slave drivers, and I am concerned about their suffering. So, I have come down to rescue them from the hand of the Egyptians and to bring them up out of that land into a good and spacious land, a land flowing with milk and honey..."
> (Exodus 3 v 7 - 8)

After their deliverance, God gave this message to Moses for his people:

> "You yourselves have seen what I did to Egypt, and how I carried you on eagles' wings and brought you to myself. Now if you obey me fully and keep my covenant, then out of all nations you will be my treasured possession. Although the whole earth is mine, you will be for me a kingdom of priests and a holy nation."
> (Exodus 19 v 4 - 6)

Let's consider God's order of things. God did not give Moses the law at the burning bush. Nor did he ever state the deliverance of the Israelites would depend on them keeping it. There was no instruction to Moses saying, 'This is my law, and if you obey it fully, I will come down and rescue you.' God gave the law following their deliverance, after he had redeemed them from their cruel bondage. God was looking for them to respond to his amazing grace with their love and obedience, as a genuine expression of their gratitude for his mercy. Obedience and holy living were to be the fruit of their liberation. Grace before law.

In fact, throughout her history, Israel was to see obedience to the law as a signpost to the Exodus and God's prior covenant of grace with them.

You can imagine their children and their children's children asking, 'What do God's laws and commandments mean?'

When this question came, the answer wouldn't be, 'We obey them to please him and be accepted by him, and if we do, we can earn his love and blessing.' Rather they would tell their children the story of the Exodus and God's powerful initiative in redeeming and delivering his people. They would speak of love, faithfulness and grace:

> "We were slaves of Pharaoh in Egypt, but the Lord brought us out of Egypt with a mighty hand. Before our eyes the Lord sent signs and wonders—great and terrible—on Egypt and Pharaoh and his whole household. But he brought us out from there to bring us in and give us the land he

promised on oath to our ancestors. The Lord commanded us to obey all these decrees and to fear the Lord our God, so that we might always prosper and be kept alive, as is the case today. And if we are careful to obey all this law before the Lord our God, as he has commanded us, that will be our righteousness."
(Deuteronomy 6 v 21 - 25)

Treasure, Delight And Celebration

God's laws reveal the kind of God he really is, for they are not arbitrary, but intimately related to his character and ways. He wanted Israel to obey his commands and keep his covenant, so they might become his *"treasured possession"* (see Exodus 19 v 5). His laws demonstrate what he delights in, including honesty, integrity, justice and mercy. Throughout, we see how he is on the side of the poor and oppressed, and how he highly values compassion and generosity. The fullness of his covenant shows how he delights to express his love and care for *all* parts of his creation.

God wanted his people to delight in these same things and find their joy in being and doing what pleases him. He envisaged a mutual delight, leading to a rich intimate relationship between them. Through grace, he longed for Israel to find its joy and happiness in him, with him also delighting in them as his treasured possession. As John Piper reminds us:

God is most glorified in us when we are most satisfied in him.[1]

We can tend to become very negative in our thinking about the law. In the last chapter, we explored Paul's direct rebuttal of Jewish false teachers in the book of Galatians. They had turned obedience to the laws of the Torah into something it was never meant to be, and this was unequivocally wrong. But as Christopher Wright points out, the law was a gift of God to his people and something to be celebrated:

> *The law is not a burden imposed by God as a condition of righteousness and salvation. The law is the gift of God to people already redeemed, in order to enable them to go on living within the sphere of his blessing. It is given on the foundation of God's grace that has been demonstrated in the redemption already accomplished, and it is given in order to help them respond appropriately and live in the way God wants. Devout and godly Israelites celebrate the law as something good and positive, something sweet and precious, something to delight in and be nourished by.*[2]

It is no surprise, therefore, that a healthy understanding of the relationship between the law and grace needs time (and careful teaching) to develop.

In Psalm 19, we read King David's celebration of the law and how the Israelites valued and delighted in it:

> The law of the Lord is perfect, refreshing the soul. The statutes of the Lord are trustworthy, making wise the simple. The precepts of the Lord are right giving joy to the heart. The commands of the Lord are radiant, giving light to the eyes. The fear of the Lord is pure, enduring forever. The decrees of the Lord are firm, and all of them are righteous. They are more precious than gold, than much pure gold; they are sweeter than honey, than honey from the honeycomb. By them your servant is warned; in keeping them there is great reward.
> (Psalm 19 v 7 - 11)

And in Psalm 119, we find the psalmist rejoicing in God's law:

> With my lips I recount all the laws that come from your mouth. I rejoice in following your statutes as one rejoices in great riches. I meditate on your precepts and consider your ways. I delight in your decrees; I will not neglect your word.
> (Psalm 119 v 13 - 16)

In a similar fashion, Psalm 1 states that the man who is blessed, fruitful and prosperous, is the man whose *"delight is in the law of the Lord, and who meditates on his law, day and night"* (verse 2). Those who live their lives in joyful obedience to God's law discover all kinds of benefits and blessings! I love Christopher Wright's summary of the life we can enjoy:

> *This is not a code of religious slavery but a recipe for responsible freedom and joy in living life in the presence of the living God.*[3]

Holy Nation

If we look again at the Exodus story, we see that one of the purposes God had for his chosen people in their deliverance from Egypt, was for them to become a holy nation:

> '...Although the whole earth is mine, you will be for me a kingdom of priests and a holy nation.'
> (Exodus 19 v 5 - 6)

It was in the creation of this holy nation that the law had another important part to play. It was given to mould them together into a radically new community; one based upon completely different principles and values to the nations around them. If Israel would fully keep God's law, then love, righteousness and justice would reign in their nation, and they would become a people living the way God had always intended mankind should live. Their corporate life together was to reflect the nature and character of God and mirror his divine activity.

They were to be a nation where relationships were based on unconditional love. Where sex was used in its right context to build up and bring marriage partners together. Where power and money were used for the good of the community to nourish, protect and provide. Where the created world was not worshipped or exploited but enjoyed and stewarded as a gift from God. And where the widow, foreigner, stranger and the marginalised in society felt valued, like they had found a real home where they belonged.

God imagined a nation where his shalom (peace) was being restored within a broken world. And as such, he gave them his law to shape them, so they could be a model to the nations.

Kingdom Of Priests

If Israel fully obeyed the law and lived as a holy nation, then they would become a kingdom of priests. A priest's role is to bring people to God, to act as a mediator between God and man, and to help people see and know who God really is. God's desire for Israel was that the quality of their collective lives should reflect his character to the world, and so draw other nations to him.

Christopher Wright summarises it this way:

> *God envisages a people who, by living as a society governed by God's values and standards, will become a visible model to the nations, bearing witness to the presence of the God they worship by the admirable quality of their whole social system.*[4]

What Israel modelled was intended to have relevance and application beyond the geographical, historical and cultural borders of Israel. It was to spark admiration and raise questions among the rest of the nations. Moses spoke of this when addressing God's people before their entry to the promised land:

> See, I have taught you decrees and laws as the Lord my God commanded me, so that you may follow them in the land you are entering to take possession of it. Observe them carefully, for this will show your wisdom and understanding to the nations, who will hear about all these decrees and say, "Surely this great nation is a wise and understanding people." What other nation is so great as to have their gods near them the way the Lord our God is near us whenever we pray to him? And what other nation is so great as to have such righteous decrees and laws as this body of laws I am setting before you today?
> (Deuteronomy 4 v 5 - 8)

Israel had been saved *from* something when rescued from slavery in Egypt, but more than this, she had been saved *for* something. Israel was to become the people of God, with the mission to be a light to the nations:

> "It is too small a thing for you to be my servant
> to restore the tribes of Jacob
> and bring back those of Israel I have kept.
> I will also make you a light for the Gentiles,
> that my salvation may reach to the ends of the earth."
> (Isaiah 49 v 6)

The sad fact of history is that although Israel had her bright moments, she failed to live up to her calling. She failed to fully obey God's law and become the light to the nations they so desperately needed. Her history was littered with times when she was not a loving, generous, forgiving, merciful and just nation.

Did this mean that God's law was in some way deficient? Not at all. For as Paul reminds us in the book of Romans:

> The law is holy, and the commandment is holy, righteous and good.
> (Romans 7 v 12)

There was, and is, nothing wrong with the law. The trouble was on Israel's side. Both Israel, and we ourselves today, find that in our natural state we cannot keep the law. Our fallen, sinful nature has a disposition towards wrongdoing. In fact, the law shows up the true nature of our hearts and arouses our sinful passions. We not only find we are unable to keep God's law, but also that we don't want to keep it. Under God's searchlight of the law, we find ourselves exposed and our unbelieving, rebellious, self-centred hearts are shown for their true nature. And, as James reminds us, if we break any part of God's law, we are found guilty as if we had broken all of it (see James 2 v 10).

What Israel needed, and what we need, is a new heart and a new nature. This is exactly what God had promised to Israel and what he promises to us today!

New Covenant

Did you know, as followers of Christ, we're now living in the promises given to Israel all those years ago?

> "This is the covenant I will make with the people of Israel
> after that time," declares the Lord.
> "I will put my law in their minds
> and write it on their hearts.
> I will be their God,
> and they will be my people."
> (Jeremiah 31 v 33)

> 'I will sprinkle clean water on you, and you will be clean; I will cleanse you from all your impurities and from all your idols. I will give you a new heart and put a new spirit in you; I will remove from you your heart of stone and give you a heart of flesh. And I will put my Spirit in you and move you to follow my decrees and be careful to keep my laws.'
> (Ezekiel 36 v 25 - 27)

This new heart and nature are given to us by a sovereign work of God. He makes us spiritually alive by imparting new life to us by his Holy Spirit. God brings about our new birth through his word of truth as we hear the gospel, the good news of our Lord Jesus Christ, and as the Holy Spirit unites us to him.

Through the indwelling presence of the Holy Spirit, he starts to work in us and give shape and character to our new nature. We begin to keep God's law as the Spirit moves us to follow God's decrees, not from dutiful observance but by an obedience of the heart that comes by faith:

> Therefore, my dear friends, as you have always obeyed—not only in my presence, but now much more in my absence—continue to work out your salvation with fear and trembling, for it is God who works in you to will and to act in order to fulfil his good purpose.
> (Philippians 2 v 12 - 13)

New birth is only possible because the Father took the initiative of sending his only Son into the world to save us. Jesus did what Israel failed to do. Not only did he fully reveal the character and nature of his Father, but he also fully obeyed and fulfilled all the law and the prophets. Only Jesus could make the claim, *"I always do what pleases him"* (John 8 v 29), and could challenge the Jews of his day with the statement, *"Can any of you prove me guilty of sin?"* (John 8 v 46).

Peter, writing in his first letter, says of Jesus, *"He committed no sin, and no deceit was found in his mouth"* (1 Peter 2 v 22). And this was visible to all, including those whose way of life he directly challenged! Such was his perfect life, even at his death, the criminal crucified with him could say, *"But this man has done nothing wrong,"* and the Roman Centurion exclaimed, *"Surely this was a righteous man"* (see Luke 23 v 41, 47).

It was at the cross that Jesus took the curse of the law upon himself:

> Christ redeemed us from the curse of the law by becoming a curse for us, for it is written: "Cursed is everyone who is hung on a pole."
> (Galatians 3 v 13)

The penalty for our lawbreaking was fully met by Jesus on the cross. The innocent stood in the place of the guilty and made atonement for our sin and wrongdoing. So, as we place our faith in Jesus, God can declare us righteous in his sight. The law is met and fulfilled by Jesus, as Paul declares:

> Christ is the culmination of the law so that there may be righteousness for everyone who believes.
> (Romans 10 v 4)

Do Christians have to keep the law?

Certainly not - if we're equating keeping the law with how we may be saved! Jesus kept the law *for* us, so that we might be saved through his perfect life, death and resurrection. There is no way we can earn our salvation by keeping the law. Our own good works or trying hard to make ourselves acceptable to God through efforts and achievements, do not earn us more favour. We are saved by believing that, in Jesus, the law has been completely fulfilled and God has accepted the sacrifice of his perfect life on the cross. In his death, the penalty for sin that was rightly ours fell on him, and by his bodily resurrection he has secured for us eternal blessings. Through him, we have been reconciled back into an intimate and eternal relationship with God, our Heavenly Father.

So having started by faith, we continue to walk by faith, growing daily in our relationship of unconditional love and acceptance with Jesus and the Father. Day by day we can trust more in the mercy, love and grace of God, relying on the power of the Holy Spirit to enable us to walk as Jesus walked.

But do we have to keep the law to become a radically different community?

Yes, we do - just like God had planned for Israel. As God's grace and mercy has redeemed us from being slaves to sin, our own obedience is meant to be the fruit of this freedom. We are to live in such a way that we reflect and make known God's glory to the world, with the church standing out as a radically different community, showing his character and heart for people. And we do this, not because we must, but as a genuine response and expression of gratitude to him for saving us.

Look at how Peter describes those who have been saved and redeemed:

> But you are a chosen people, a royal priesthood, a holy nation, God's special possession, that you may declare the praises of him who called you out of darkness into his wonderful light. Once you were not a people, but now you are the people of God; once you had not received mercy, but now you have received mercy.
> (1 Peter 2 v 9 - 10)

As we read this, we must know the same is true of us today. God is still actively forming a people who are his treasured possession, a holy nation and a kingdom of priests.

Walk By The Spirit

As God's chosen people, we are called to live a life in keeping with our new identity and new hearts. It is here, in our hearts, where God has written his laws, and we receive power to respond to them by the indwelling Spirit of God. In his book, "God's Empowering Presence," Gordon Fee helpfully reminds us of the Spirit's sufficiency in our lives. The Holy Spirit can achieve a righteousness in us that the Torah was not able to, so that those who walk by the Spirit can fulfil the law's righteous commandments.[5]

In other words, the old covenant called for righteousness but couldn't produce it. Though the Spirit, our sure promise of the new covenant in Christ, can produce this right kind of living and behaviour. The Spirit enables us to live in the way the law originally intended the Israelites to live.

Praise God for the fruit we will see grow in our lives:

> But the fruit of the Spirit is love, joy, peace, forbearance, kindness, goodness, faithfulness, gentleness, and self-control. Against such things there is no law.
> (Galatians 5 v 22 - 23)

Be encouraged. People filled with the Spirit of God not only want to please God, but they are also empowered to do so.

For God is not just saving individuals and preparing them for an eternity with him. He is creating a united and diverse people, among whom he can dwell and who reflect his character by how they live. He is gathering an eschatological people, who bring the truth of God's future into the present. God's people will be radically different in each aspect of their lives because their hope is built on different values to those around them. As such, they'll be a community that exhibits a different quality of life, living out what they have become through God's amazing grace, in the person of Jesus, his Son. And they'll live in freedom, no longer seeking through personal strength or ability to obey an external code of laws, but obeying the law from their new hearts, in the power of the Spirit.

Our Relationship With The Law

Although the law no longer binds us today, it still provides a rich source of wisdom to inform our Christian conduct:

> For all Scripture is God-breathed and is useful for teaching, rebuking, correcting and training in righteousness, so that the servant of God may be thoroughly equipped for every good work.
> (2 Timothy 3 v 16 - 17)

John Calvin (1509 – 1564) confirms the need to heed Christ's affirmation of the continuing importance of the law and the prophets. It readies us for the good works God has prepared in advance for us to do (see Ephesians 2 v 10) and remains a primary guide for how God wants his people to live. Speaking of believers, in whose hearts the Spirit of God already lives and reigns, he says of the law:

> *Here is the best instrument for believers to learn more thoroughly each day the nature of the Lord's will to which they aspire, and to confirm them in the understanding of it... And because we need not only teaching but also exhortation, the servant of God will also avail himself of this benefit of the law: by frequent meditation upon it to be aroused to obedience, be strengthened in it and be drawn back from the slippery path of transgression.*[6]

Now let's look at the way some Messianic Jews approach Old Testament law, something which is often overlooked but is interesting to observe. Chris Wright notes they may choose to keep these laws and customs, and do so enthusiastically. However, they are not obliged to, nor are they in any way linked to their salvation. Salvation is exclusively grounded in the Messiah's sacrifice on the cross:

> *Messianic Judaism argues further that in the light of the New Testament the very idea of Torah must be refined. It cannot be confined to (though it still includes) the Old Testament Torah, but now encompasses for the Christian the "Torah of the Messiah". This includes not only the specific commands of Jesus, but also the total way of obedience and practical holiness to which Christians are called in the New Testament. But then, the full understanding of New Testament moral teaching actually requires knowledge of Old Testament law, which forms the basis for so much of it.*

> *Old Testament law retains its moral authority for believers, but that it must be set within its total Christian canonical context as part of the new Messianic Torah of the New Covenant.*[7]

And remember Jesus' teaching to his disciples relating to his commands and their lifestyle:

> "If you keep my commands, you will remain in my love, just as I have kept my Father's commands and remain in his love. I have told you this so that my joy may be in you and that your joy may be complete."
> (John 15 v 10 - 11)

> "Whoever has my commands and keeps them is the one who loves me. The one who loves me will be loved by my Father, and I too will love them and show myself to them."
> (John 14 v 21)

It is worth repeating. The law is not a burden imposed by God as a condition of righteousness and salvation. The law is the gift of God to his people already redeemed, which enables them to go on living within and enjoying his blessing.

Our obedience in faith, through the power of the Holy Spirit, enables us to remain in the love of the Father and the Son, bringing his joy into our lives no matter what our circumstances. Our identity and status don't change, but our ability to truly reflect them does. From here, we are empowered to give witness to the world that we are truly a people whose *"work is produced by faith, our labour prompted by love, and our endurance inspired by hope in our Lord Jesus Christ"* (1 Thessalonians 1 v 3).

Greatest Commandment

Jesus was once asked by an expert in the law about the most important commandment. Take note of Jesus' reply:

> Jesus replied: "'Love the Lord your God with all your heart and with all your soul and with all your mind.' This is the first

> and greatest commandment. And the second is like it: 'Love your neighbour as yourself.' All the Law and the Prophets hang on these two commandments."
> (Matthew 22 v 37 - 40; see also Mark 12 v 29 - 31)

Similarly, the Apostle Paul stresses the importance of loving one's neighbour because, in doing so, it fulfils the law:

> For the entire law is fulfilled in keeping this one command: "Love your neighbour as yourself."
> (Galatians 5 v 14)

> Let no debt remain outstanding, except the continuing debt to love one another, for whoever loves others has fulfilled the law. The commandments, "You shall not commit adultery," "You shall not murder," "You shall not steal," "You shall not covet," and whatever other command there may be, are summed up in this one command: "Love your neighbour as yourself." Love does no harm to a neighbour. Therefore, love is the fulfilment of the law.
> (Romans 13 v 8 - 10)

And so, we are moved to love. In fact, we find ourselves eagerly desiring to do so.

But what is the true nature of this love that we are to show? We will explore the answer in the next chapter.

Notes

1 www.desiringgod.org/messages/our-grand-obligation

2 The Old Testament in Seven Sentences by Christopher Wright. Copyright © Christopher Wright 2019. Published by Inter Varsity Press. Page 63

3 The Old Testament in Seven Sentences by Christopher Wright. Copyright © Christopher Wright 2019. Published by Inter Varsity Press. Page 153

4 The Old Testament in Seven Sentences by Christopher Wright. Copyright © Christopher Wright 2019. Published by Inter Varsity Press. Page 65

5 God's Empowering Presence - The Holy Spirit In The Letters Of Paul by Gordon D. Fee. Published by Hendrickson Publishers Inc, April 2001. ISBN-10: 094357594X

6 Calvin, Institutes 2.7.12. Quoted in OT Ethics for the People of God by Christopher J.H. Wright. Copyright © Christopher J. H. Wright 2004. Published by Inter-Varsity Press, Page 393

7 OT Ethics for the People of God by Christopher J.H. Wright. Copyright © Christopher J. H. Wright 2004. Published by Inter-Varsity Press, Page 412. Reproduced with permission of the Licensor through PLSclear.

CHAPTER EIGHT

Love Your Neighbour

One of the abiding memories of my teenage years was the song, "All you need is love," written by the Beatles. The song was released in May 1967 against the backdrop of the Vietnam War and was Britain's contribution to, "Our World," the first live global television link. The programme was broadcast via satellite and seen by an audience of over 400 million, across 25 countries.

John Lennon's lyrics were deliberately simplistic. The purpose was to allow the show's international audience to capture the utopian ideals associated with the "Summer of Love," (which also encompassed the hippie music, hallucinogenic drug, anti-war and free-love scene of the West Coast of America).

The song also became an anthem for the counterculture's embrace of the "Flower Power" philosophy, and a symbol of passive resistance and nonviolence. Yet later, Lennon's lyrics were criticised by music journalists for this same simplicity, being described by some as naïve. In their opinion, the world needed much more than love if world peace was to be achieved and the nations saved.[1]

Some five decades on, people still espouse the view of love being all we need for the majority of the world's problems to be solved. However, the detailed character of such love is rarely defined. Most dictionaries settle for defining love as, "a strong feeling of affection and concern toward another person, as that arising from kinship or close friendship," or "a strong feeling of affection and concern for another person accompanied by sexual attraction."[2]

Love is needed without doubt, but the nature, extent and practical outworking of the love required is clearly important.

In English we have only one word for love, whereas the ancient Greeks broke down love into three categories: *Philia,* meaning tender affection or brotherly love that exists between friends; *Storge,* referring to family love that exists between family members, and sometimes between very close friends; and *Eros,* which is romantic love between partners, physical or 'sexual' desire, and the root of the word 'erotic'.

However, the New Testament uses the Greek word, *agape.* 'Agape' speaks of the active love of God for his Son and his people, along with the active love his people are to have for God, each other and even their enemies. The best description of this love is found in 1 Corinthians Chapter 13 – Paul's teaching here is one of the most famous chapters in the Bible. It's a passage often read at weddings, and sometimes at funerals. For example, the words were read at the funeral of Princess Diana in 1997 by Tony Blair, the Prime Minister at the time.

Before we look at the detail of this passage, we need to remind ourselves of the context of Paul's description of love. In the preceding chapter, Paul had been speaking about spiritual gifts and how they had been given for the common good of the church. He reminded them, though the people of Corinth were many, they had been baptised by one Spirit, into one body. Then, in the following chapter, he instructs them on the right use of spiritual gifts and how to conduct themselves in their times of corporate worship.

In Chapter 13, sandwiched between these two important teachings, we find the wonderful description of love. Here, Paul instructs them that the use of charismatic gifts, service to the poor, and even martyrdom, must be rooted in the authentic love of God. Without love, their spiritual activities would amount to nothing and would gain them nothing. For Paul, there was a more excellent way to live – the way of love. What mattered for him, was living an authentic lifestyle that reflected God, who himself is love (see 1 John 4 v 16).

So, from here, let's look closely at Paul's description:

> Love is patient and kind; love does not envy or boast; it is not arrogant or rude. It does not insist on its own way; it is

> not irritable or resentful; it does not rejoice at wrongdoing, but rejoices with the truth. Love bears all things, believes all things, hopes all things, endures all things.
>
> Love never ends. As for prophecies, they will pass away; as for tongues, they will cease; as for knowledge, it will pass away.
>
> (1 Corinthians 13 v 4 - 8 ESV)

In these verses, Paul describes the character of love by sharing what it is, as well as what it isn't. The phrases are full of richness, so we'll look at each in turn to see how we can apply them, both in terms of God's love for us, and us loving our neighbours as ourselves.

Love Is Patient (Long-Tempered Or Long-Suffering)

Love gives others time to change. It enables us to give our neighbours room to grow up and develop as human beings created in the image of God. It is not easily irritated by immature behaviour, nor by the faults and failings of others. It recognises that all people grow and develop at a different pace and in different ways.

Love does not despise people or write them off. Instead, it understands that people don't all start life from the same position: we don't have the same privileges; we come from different family, ethnic and social backgrounds; we have not had equal opportunities for progress in life.

Have you noticed this in yourself? Our impatience can be most active when we see faults and failings in others that we have overcome and conquered in our own lives. Or similarly, we can be less patient when we have obtained some form of stability and contentment in life and feel we're on an upward trajectory!

There is always a very real danger of becoming like the Pharisee in Jesus' parable, parading our own goodness while looking down on the failings of others (see Luke 18 v 9 - 14). Instead of seeing the potential or progress in others, we instead magnify their failings and run them down in our minds, even if not to their face!

We would all do well to listen to Paul's instruction to the church at Thessalonica:

> And we urge you, brothers and sisters, warn those who are idle and disruptive, encourage the disheartened, help the weak, be patient with everyone.
> (1 Thessalonians 5 v 14)

Love calls us to be active in helping people to advance from where they are presently, to grow in maturity, and to reach their God-given potential in life. However, being patient with people and cutting them some slack, needs to be accompanied by genuine encouragement, guidance and admonition where needed.

As we shall see when we look at the other phrases in this passage, Jesus is our supreme example of radical love. When Philip says to Jesus, *"Show us the Father and that will be enough for us,"* we don't see Jesus rebuking him for his slowness to comprehend his oneness with God. Rather, we find him receiving another patient explanation from Jesus to help him to grasp the reality of this truth (see John 14 v 8 - 11).

At the Last Supper, we see a dispute arising among the disciples, as to which of them was considered the greatest. By this time, one would have thought they would have grasped the truths of humility and servanthood being taught and embodied by Jesus among them... but evidently not! Yet, Jesus patiently teaches them once again this vital truth (see Luke 22 v 24 - 30).

Love Is Kind
(Actively Generous; Helpful; Good And Gracious)

Love is constructive and actively seeks to do good to others. It looks for and searches out ways to be helpful, encouraging, affirming and appreciative. Most importantly, it does not wait to be asked!

Most people in the United Kingdom today seem willing to help others out when asked, whether that is in the church, the workplace or the wider community. For example, an increasing number of people here in the United Kingdom are ready to respond to large charity events like Red Nose Day and Children in Need, often expending enormous amounts of energy and ingenuity to raise funds for such worthy causes. It's attractive and meaningful to play a part when called upon; indeed, it points towards the desire of our hearts to know something of this true love.

However, the love described by Paul goes beyond this; it does not wait to be asked, nor does it expect to get anything back in return! Moreover, there's precedent for it throughout the Bible. Jesus taught his disciples that they should not only love those who love them, but to do good even to their enemies without expecting anything back in return. He spoke of going the extra mile and repaying good for evil so, as they modelled love, his disciples would reflect their Father (the Most High) who is *"kind to the ungrateful and wicked"*. Love is central to God's agenda and the prophet Jeremiah reminds us that God declared, *"I am the Lord, who exercises kindness, justice, and righteousness on earth, for in these I delight"* (see Luke 6 v 35 - 36; Matthew 5 v 41 - 48; Jeremiah 9 v 24).

Such loving behaviour is as counter-cultural today as it was in the past. It is the opposite of the world's ways, which tends to ask, 'What's in it for me?' rather than, 'What's in it for them?' Followers of Jesus are called to look out for their neighbours first and think about how they can express kindness to them.

The greatest act of kindness to us was Christ's death on our behalf, which he did freely, *"while we were still sinners"* (Romans 5 v 8). Paul expresses this kindness when he writes to Titus:

> At one time we too were foolish, disobedient, deceived and enslaved by all kinds of passions and pleasures. We lived in malice and envy, being hated and hating one another. **But when the kindness and love of God our Saviour appeared,** he saved us, not because of righteous things we had done, but because of his mercy. He saved us through the washing of rebirth and renewal by the Holy Spirit, whom he poured out on us generously through Jesus Christ our Saviour, so that, having been justified by his grace, we might become heirs having the hope of eternal life.
> (Titus 3 v 3 - 7; emphasis added)

The amazing thing about God's love is that it progressively transforms and redirects our personality and actions towards the good of others. It deals with our self-centred, old nature and enables us to demonstrate Christlikeness in our everyday lives. Kindness and care for others comes increasingly to centre stage.

The next few phrases show what love is not and does not do, helping us to see the kind of transformation possible for us.

Love Does Not Envy

Envy means, "to desire, (and) to deprive another of what he (or she) has."[3] Sadly, the world today is full of the envy of others. From a young age, we're pitted in competition against each other, such that comparison becomes the yardstick by which we measure success (we've explored the negative impact this has on our identity previously). As such, people are envious of the appearance, talents, status, success and material possessions others have. So much so, they desire what isn't theirs and scheme to obtain them.

This attitude sometimes shows itself in a subtle wish to see another person discredited or their fortunes change for the worse. It can even be taking pleasure in seeing another person fall on hard times. Even if we hide it externally, in our most reflective moments we might be aware of this battle internally... but the call to love is not like that.

Love desires the very best for the other person. It's glad when that person is preferred before them or becomes more successful. It rejoices when someone else is promoted or honoured, when their sphere of influence or effectiveness is enlarged:

> But if you harbour bitter envy and selfish ambition in your hearts, do not boast about it or deny the truth...
>
> For where you have envy and selfish ambition, there you find disorder and every evil practice.
>
> (James 3 v 14, 16)

Love Does Not Boast

Love is not out to impress or feign moral superiority, parading its abilities and achievements before others. Instead, it recognises that all they possess or have achieved, has been the result of God's goodness. Love lets a person readily admit that any talents and abilities they enjoy are a direct result of a gift from God:

> For who makes you different from anyone else? What do you have that you did not receive? And if you did receive it, why do you boast as though you did not?
> (1 Corinthians 4 v 7)

Love Is Not Proud

Love is not arrogant or puffed up with a sense of its own self-importance. It does not think it has 'arrived' with nothing more to learn, or flaunt its knowledge and experience of life before others. Agape love produces a man or woman who is humble and able to make a true estimate of themselves, forming a sober judgement of their capabilities and achievements. Love allows them to be teachable and open to reason, using their knowledge to help and strengthen others. It will not try to dominate conversations with tales from an inflated ego, but rather demonstrates a genuine interest in the welfare of others:

> For by the grace given me I say to every one of you: Do not think of yourself more highly than you ought, but rather think of yourself with sober judgement, in accordance with the faith God has distributed to each of you.
> (Romans 12 v 3)

> All of you, clothe yourselves with humility toward one another, because God opposes the proud but shows favour to the humble.
> (1 Peter 5 v 5)

Love Is Not Rude

Love doesn't behave badly, causing others embarrassment by what it says or does. Nor does it sail close to the wind by using innuendo, double meaning or coarse joking. It does not deliberately set out to offend or belittle others but considers the effect its speech and behaviour will have on them. It shows respect for other people's views and feelings:

> Do not let any unwholesome talk come out of your mouths, but only what is helpful for building others up according to their needs, that it may benefit those who listen. (Ephesians 4 v 29)

Love Is Not Self-Seeking

Love is not looking for selfish advantage or to get its own way. Love is open to the perspectives of others, taking into account and elevating their needs and welfare. In the workplace, it is not only concerned about its own career prospects, but also the advancement of other colleagues and the prosperity and success of their company or employer.

While it wants the best education possible for its own children, it also fights for the best education for all the children in their community. When elections come around, it not only considers voting for a candidate who will work to meet its own aspirations, but considers thoughtfully what will be the best option to enhance the quality of life for all. Then, in church life, it will try to support and engage in all aspects of the local church family, not simply those parts meeting its own needs. Love remains committed to the wellbeing of all church members, whatever their ethnicity or social background, seeking to live together with others as a true expression of the one new humanity in Christ:

> Do nothing out of selfish ambition or vain conceit, but in humility consider others better (more important) than yourselves. Each of you should look not only to your own interests, but also to the interests of others.
> (Philippians 2 v 3 - 4; parentheses added)

Love Is Not Easily Angered

Love can help us in the face of being sinned against, enabling us to react in a godly manner when we have been hurt, offended or abused. But, more than that, it helps us not be easily provoked or stirred up. It is not irritable or touchy or quick to be offended.

It is not uncommon to find people around us who appear easily offended or have a short fuse! Think about comments like: 'You will need to catch her at the right moment,' 'You will have to choose your words carefully when you are talking with him,' or, 'He doesn't like it when you disagree with his opinion.' They are relatively common to hear. Maybe they have been, or could be said, of you or me at times? Yet love means these kinds of comments can be avoided, so they are never voiced about the follower of Jesus:

> In your anger do not sin: Do not let the sun go down while you are still angry, and do not give the devil a foothold.
> (Ephesians 4 v 26 - 27)

> My dear brothers and sisters, take note of this: Everyone should be quick to listen, slow to speak and slow to become angry, because human anger does not produce the righteousness that God desires.
> (James 1 v 19 - 20)

Love Keeps No Record Of Wrongs

Love doesn't hold grudges, nor is it resentful and bitter. Love doesn't provide a harbour into which ships of offence can sail in and moor up!

The word Paul uses here is an accounting term, meaning 'to reckon or to add up.' Love does not keep a register of wrongs or calculate how many times it has been sinned against. It does not compile statistics of different types of wrong done to it or keep a record of past hurts and wounds.

Love wipes the slate clean, or in our modern terminology, clears the computer screen and 'erases the memory!' How many friendships with neighbours have been destroyed because past hurts or grievances have not been laid to rest and given a proper funeral?

> If you, Lord, kept a record of sins,
> Lord, who could stand?
> But with you there is forgiveness,
> so that we can, with reverence, serve you.
> (Psalm 130 v 3 - 4)

> Make every effort to live in peace with everyone and to be holy; without holiness no one will see the Lord. See to it that no one falls short of the grace of God and that no bitter root grows up to cause trouble and defile many.
> (Hebrews 12 v 14 - 15)

Love Does Not Delight In Evil

Love is not pleased when wrong or evil prevails, and it is disturbed when good is spoken of as evil. It is not indifferent or apathetic towards evil, for it cannot see injustice or oppression and pass by on the other side of the road. Rather, it longs to rectify situations and put them right, acting to bring about change so that what is good and true, prevails.

Love does not sit on the sidelines grumbling, complaining and tut-tutting, but rolls up its sleeves and gets its hands dirty to alleviate pain and suffering. It cares enough about its neighbourhood, community, country and the nations to become actively involved in playing its part in seeing transformation:

> To fear the Lord is to hate evil;
> I hate pride and arrogance,
> evil behaviour and perverse speech.
> (Proverbs 8 v 13)

> Love must be sincere. Hate what is evil; cling to what is good.
> (Romans 12 v 9)

Paul then continues by extolling, again, what love is and does.

Love Rejoices With The Truth

Love is never happier than when truth is winning the day. Not simply when truth, sincerity and integrity spread through society, but when God's truth is proclaimed and acted upon. It rejoices when neighbours are impacted and influenced by God's word and begin to seek the kingdom of God. The apostle John expressed having this kind of joy in the truth in his third letter:

> It gave me great joy when some believers came and testified about your faithfulness to the truth, telling how you continue to walk in it. I have no greater joy than to hear that my children are walking in the truth.
> (3 John v 3 - 4)

Scripture reminds us of Jesus' great example of these last two characteristics of love. The writer to the Hebrews quotes the Old Testament when declaring the glory of the Son, which is shown by his rejection of evil and his love of what is true:

> Your throne, O God, will last for ever and ever;
> a sceptre of justice will be the sceptre of your kingdom.
>
> You have loved righteousness and hated wickedness;
> therefore God, your God, has set you above your companions
> by anointing you with the oil of joy.
>
> (Psalm 45 v 6 - 7; see Hebrews 1 v 8 - 9)

As we look at the next few phrases, we'll see Paul show something of the enduring and abiding quality of love.

Love Always Protects

Love always seeks to defend others from danger and harm, enduring hardship or pain, even forgoing its own legitimate rights to protect others.

We have a wonderful picture of this when Judas and the temple guard come to arrest Jesus in Gethsemane. Having identified himself as the one they wanted, Jesus intercedes on behalf of his disciples:

> Jesus answered, "I told you that I am he. If you are looking for me, then let these men go." This happened so that the words he had spoken would be fulfilled: "I have not lost one of those you gave me."
> (John 18 v 8 - 9)

Love Always Trusts

Love credits others with good intentions and believes the best about them, continuing like this until proven wrong by the clear presentation of contrary evidence. Even then, it remains loyal, faithful and committed to friendship and the good of the other person. It goes on trusting, despite being let down or hurt.

We are not talking here about gullibility, nor meaning that love is naïve, undiscerning or credulous. However, it does mean not being suspicious or doubting another's character and motives without good reason. A person may have a chequered history, or be obviously undeserving of trust, yet love is able to find a way to put the past behind and express fresh confidence in them.

In one of his resurrection appearances, Jesus made breakfast for his disciples on the shore of the Sea of Tiberias. When they had finished eating, he took Simon Peter aside and asked him three times whether he loved him? These three questions mirrored Peter's denial of Jesus three times in the high priest's courtyard. Each time Peter answers in the affirmative, and each time Jesus asks Peter to take responsibility for the care of his sheep. There is a beautiful redemptive symmetry, full of healing, full of trust, and full of love. Despite his past failures, Jesus' love for him led him to entrust into Peter's hands, the future shepherding of his flock (see John 21 v 15 - 19).

Love Always Hopes

Hope is a confident expectation of a good outcome, so love is always expecting better things for people and circumstances. It is thoroughly optimistic and sees better prospects ahead. Love believes the seemingly unchangeable can be changed, and that broken lives can be mended and transformed. Therefore, it refuses to label its neighbour too far gone, as 'never amounting to much,' or as a hopeless case. What a hope this is for those around us! What a hope this is for you and me!

Paul's teaching is shaped by his own experience and conviction that love always hopes. When reminding the church in Corinth of the kinds of people who will not inherit the kingdom of God, he is able to confidently say of the believers:

> And, that is what some of you were. But you were washed, you were sanctified, you were justified in the name of the Lord Jesus Christ and by the Spirit of God.
> (1 Corinthians 6 v 11)

Love knows there is hope for others because the gospel is the power of God for the salvation of everyone who believes.

Love Always Perseveres

Love courageously endures to the end, giving itself tirelessly for others. It never gives up on people. Like a solid sea defence, it holds against the constant beating of every destructive wave that crashes upon it. Whether we face waves of discouragement, misunderstanding, rejection, lack of recognition or lack of reward, love stands up to them and stands strong.

John was able to speak of how Jesus loved his disciples to the very end, even to the point of his death on the cross:

> It was just before the Passover Festival. Jesus knew that the hour had come for him to leave this world and go to the Father. Having loved his own who were in the world, he loved them to the end.
> (John 13 v 1 ESV)

Love Never Fails

Love always has the resource, tools, wisdom or touch needed for the task. It is never reduced to inactivity or stumped as to know what to do. This love will never collapse or fall like the house built without strong foundations in Jesus' story of the wise and foolish builders (see Luke 6 v 49).

There is no ruin or destruction in the place (or heart) where love reigns supreme.

God Is Love

When we think of the kind of love Paul describes, we are immediately aware of the fact he is not speaking of a love that comes naturally to us. Indeed, if we substitute our own name for 'love' in the phrases Paul uses, we become quickly acquainted with our own shortcomings and failure to love as we should. We may even feel that this kind of love is impossible to live out – a wonderful ideal, but far too radical! We know that the world would be a better place if everyone loved like this, but we can't see ourselves hitting the bullseye on this one! Loving our neighbour with this kind of love is way beyond our reach.

However, we are not left stranded back at the beginning of Chapter 8, with just a wishful song. Rather, we are reminded clearly that, *"God is love"* (see 1 John 4 v 16). Love is who he is! So, if we substitute the name 'Jesus' for 'love,' a different story emerges. For in his incarnate life and ministry, Jesus personified agape love and perfectly lived a life of love. Now that we have been born again by the Spirit of God, we have been joined to him, and it is in our union with God through Jesus that we are enabled to live this supernatural life of love.

It follows that we can confidently expect to see this love growing in us, as Paul encourages when speaking of the indwelling work of the Holy Spirit. Over time, our lives will beautifully reflect the fullness of God's love as the fruit of the Spirit emerges within us:

> But the fruit of the Spirit is love, joy, peace, forbearance, kindness, goodness, faithfulness, gentleness and self-control.
> (Galatians 5 v 22 - 23)

Now we are in Christ, who is love, it is gloriously possible for us to live this life and increasingly love our neighbour with the same unconditional and sacrificial love of Jesus.

Notes

1 Wikipedia, All You Need Is Love. Available at: en.wikipedia.org/wiki/All_You_Need_Is_Love (Accessed 31 January 2025)

2 Expository Dictionary of New Testament Words by W.E. Vine. Published by Oliphants 1975. ISBN 0 551 00282 4

3 Expository Dictionary of New Testament Words by W.E. Vine. Published by Oliphants 1975. ISBN 0 551 00282 4

CHAPTER NINE

Do Not Judge

It might seem strange to follow a chapter on loving one's neighbour with a chapter about not judging others. But if we're honest, we all know we have a tendency or inclination to criticise and judge other people from time to time. Whether coming from insecurity and a need to compare, or from a place of frustration and hurt, judging others can be the unhealthy thinking that results. Jesus underlined the importance of the subject in the "Sermon on the Mount," in Matthew's gospel (see Matthew 7 v 1 - 6). His teaching was not only challenging to those listening, but remains critically important today. Many of us live in a cultural context where public and private criticism of others is increasingly seen as both normal and acceptable.

This trend is not only seen in the world of social media, but also nearer to home whenever we gather to socialise. In today's world, it seems everybody is entitled to a view on everything! And many people will share that view at the drop of a hat, even without being asked.

You may have noticed the trend that people seem compelled to present themselves as 'experts' in areas they have very little knowledge of, have never trained in, nor have significant experience of! Yet, they still tell others how they ought to run, manage, execute or improve things in any given area of life. It's all around us! Consider the advice you might hear as people freely share their opinions on: how to run the country, educate children, cure unemployment, end teenage pregnancy, parent, reduce crime, promote community well-being, manage their favourite football team, or how to effectively order their personal lives!

Yet on the other hand, we live in a generation where the mantra of the day is 'tolerance.' Everyone is entitled to express his or her own view, however outrageous and offensive it may appear to others. It's a world where there are few moral absolutes, so everything becomes relative. Any distinctions between what is right or wrong, good or bad, and beneficial or detrimental, has become blurred and irrelevant. All modes of behaviour, however bizarre, must be accepted and tolerated no matter what their effect on the wider community. To utter criticism or suggest one way is better than another, let alone 'the right way,' is to find yourself branded narrow minded, arrogant, opinionated, bigoted or fanatical. And, in the field of identity politics and its application to sexual issues, any disagreement is generally seen as an attack on the person, rather than an objection to a viewpoint. There seems to be tolerance for all, except for anyone who might ask if some boundaries or truths are in fact a good thing. We're dealing with an area needing careful navigation.

The Tendency Towards Self-Righteousness

Before we look more closely at Jesus' teaching, let's remind ourselves of a couple of the ways judging others reveals itself in our own lives. The first is having a self-righteous attitude and feeling superior to those around us. This feeling happens when we draw our own moral lines which are attainable by us, but not by others. While we can exhibit this assumed 'correct' behaviour, other people's behaviour falls far short of these 'right' standards. There's truth in what the nineteenth-century American Poet, Henry Wadsworth, pointed out – we'd do well to consider it:

> *We judge ourselves by what we feel capable of doing, while others judge us by what Good we have done.*[1]

The Pharisee in Jesus' parable of the Pharisee and the tax collector (see Luke 18 v 9 - 14) demonstrates the kind of attitude we are talking about when he compares himself to those around him:

> 'God, I thank you that I am not like other people—robbers, evildoers, adulterers—or even like this tax collector. I fast twice a week and give a tenth of all I get.'
> (Luke 18 v 11 - 12)

We rightly condemn such an attitude. Though I wonder whether we would be so aware of its modern equivalent, often expressed in church life... even if the words themselves are not spoken out loud!

- Their vision is not as large as mine
- Their faith is not as stable
- Their grasp of deep truths is not as masterful
- Their serving record is not so impressive
- Their efforts are not so substantial

You could extend these judgements to thoughts we may have on how others use their money, the behaviour and noisiness of other people's children, or even how close to the start of a service (or how far into the first song) someone arrives on a Sunday!

The trouble with a self-righteous attitude is that other people become diminished in our eyes. Without even knowing it, we can begin assessing their value or success as people as being inferior to our own. This serves no-one, especially not our own hearts and the way we are able to truly love and care for others.

Remember criticism is the disapproval of people, not for having faults, but for having faults different from our own!

The Temptation To Find Fault

Next, there is the hypercritical attitude or arch critic, who is always finding fault and actively seeking out people's failures. It seems they live with an expectation of finding error; they appear to receive pleasure and enjoyment in doing so. Others obtain a kind of malicious satisfaction in discovering other peoples' shortcomings and blemishes. How often have we felt pleased when we have heard about the mistakes of another person, especially if we've been jealous or envious of them? And, even if we've not felt overtly happy, we've maybe felt a little better about ourselves in comparison. This response is rooted in judgement.

The arch critic tends to major on the minors, or the unimportant rather than the important, and this approach misses the mark. Paul, speaking in Romans 14 about *"disputable matters,"* reminds the believers that *"the kingdom of God is not a matter of eating and drinking, but of righteousness, peace and joy in the Holy Spirit"* (Romans 14 v 1, 17 - 18). The Spirit does not bring about peace and joy through freedom-sapping criticism!

The arch critic attempts to build themselves up by knocking others down. They're ready to give judgement on matters of no concern to them, or on people with whom they have no direct dealing. We can't deny this is a temptation for all, though hopefully our attitudes are somewhat different.

Teaching Of Jesus

Let's take a closer look at what Jesus taught about judging others:

> "Do not judge, or you too will be judged. For in the same way you judge others, you will be judged, and with the measure you use, it will be measured to you.
>
> "Why do you look at the speck of sawdust in your brother's eye and pay no attention to the plank in your own eye? How can you say to your brother, 'Let me take the speck out of your eye,' when all the time there is a plank in your own eye? You hypocrite, first take the plank out of your own eye, and then you will see clearly to remove the speck from your brother's eye.
>
> "Do not give dogs what is sacred; do not throw your pearls to pigs. If you do, they may trample them under their feet, and turn and tear you to pieces."
>
> (Matthew 7 v 1 - 6)

The larger context here is that Jesus is teaching what it means to be the true people of God and how, as God's people, we are called to show the presence of the kingdom of God in the small details of our shared life together.

At this time, the Pharisees prided themselves on keeping the law (Torah). They saw observance of the law as the way God would vindicate them and elevate them as being his true people. But they also looked down on those who did not keep the law, as they perceived it. For them, fellow Jews who fell short of their standards were seen as 'sinners,' just like the Gentile pagans; they were viewed as being outside of God's future blessings. The expectation was that they would, one day, receive their just deserts. As such, they wrote them off.

Judgement indeed.

In his paraphrase of Luke 18, Eugene Peterson describes the Pharisees as those *"...who were complacently pleased with themselves over their moral performance and looked down their noses at the common people"* (Luke 18 v 9 - 12 MSG).

It was against this backdrop that Jesus said, *"Do not judge."* Challenging back then and also today, it's teaching that immediately raises important questions for us in the way we live our lives.

To Judge Or Not To Judge?

Does this statement mean we must never express an opinion about anything or anyone? Is Jesus calling us to suspend all our critical faculties? Can we never make value judgements or choose between different policies and plans of action? For three reasons, I would suggest the answer to all these questions is no.

The first reason is common sense. It would be unnatural for us to overlook, fail to criticise or offer any opinion on the serious wrongs or problems that beset our world and society. For example, issues such as genocide, economic exploitation, trafficking of young women for prostitution, the destruction of our environment, and many more, demand a Christian response. In a similar way, it's often pointed out that the considered criticism of literature, art and music involves a high exercise of the human mind, and our mind is a God-given faculty.

The second reason centres on the teaching of Jesus in this passage. In verse 6, it states very clearly that Jesus expects us to exercise discernment, to avoid giving dogs what is sacred or throwing our pearls to pigs! Later in the same chapter, he also expects us to be able to distinguish between true and false prophets by assessing their teaching and evaluating their lives. And, during one of his confrontations with the Jews recorded in John's gospel, he tells them to, *"Stop judging by mere appearances, but instead judge correctly"* (Matthew 7 v 15 - 20; John 7 v 24).

The third reason is that throughout the New Testament, we find an expectation that judgements will take place in relation to different aspects of human life. For example, governing authorities instituted by God and acting as God's servants, are expected to make judgements about how society should be run.

Similarly, within the church, leaders are called to exercise discipline in the form of judgement. For example, in the church at Corinth, Paul not only exalts leaders to act over a case of gross sexual immorality, but also speaks of himself having already passed judgement on the offending brother. He also addresses that some believers in the church are taking each other to court to have disputes settled by secular authorities. Paul is adamant such disputes between believers should be judged and settled in the church, rather than going to court (see Romans 13 v 1 - 5; 1 Corinthians 5 v 1 - 5; 6 v 1 - 6).

We also find both Paul and John were not afraid to distinguish and judge between truth and heresy – they encouraged the believers to do the same. How else would we grow in maturity and understanding, so not to be thrown off course by unhelpful teaching? And finally, Paul had some hard things to say about those promoting wrong teaching and how the church should act towards them (see Galatians 1 v 8 - 9; 2 v 11; 5 v 12; 1 John 4 v 1 - 3)!

So, if this critical approach and these judgements are legitimate, what exactly did Jesus mean when he said, *"Do not judge,"* in his teaching?

Pronouncing Judgement

The word *"judge"* used by Jesus, means to discern or distinguish, to decide mentally or judicially, or to give one's verdict or pass sentence. Hence, it means to assume the office of a judge who tries, condemns, damns and punishes. Specifically, it refers to pronouncing judgement in a final sense.

There is all the difference in the world between expressing an enlightened, intelligent criticism of a man's views and theories, his doctrine, his teaching or his mode or manner of life, compared to passing judgement on the *person* themselves. It was passing judgement on the person that was happening in Jesus' time. Some Jews had acted, and were acting, in ways that belonged only to God. Gentiles and Jewish 'sinners' had already been judged to be beyond the mercy of God - written off, condemned, and consigned to the rubbish heap!

But this kind of condemnation was never to be the activity of the true people of God, including us today. When God chose Israel in the first place, it was so they might be a light for the Gentiles and bring God's salvation to the ends of the earth. God's purpose for mankind was, and always has been, salvation not condemnation (see Isaiah 49 v 6).

God The Judge

We should not judge because judgement belongs to God alone, or as John expresses it in his gospel, it belongs to Jesus Christ:

> "The Father judges no one, but has entrusted all judgement to the Son..."
>
> "And he has given him authority to judge because he is the Son of Man."
>
> (John 5 v 22, 27)

Writing to the church in Rome, Paul makes it clear they are not to sit in judgement on one another in this way:

> Who are you to judge someone else's servant? To their own master, servants stand or fall. And they will stand, for the Lord is able to make them stand.
> (Romans 14 v 4)

When he writes to the church in Corinth, he underlines that the Lord himself is our judge. Even if his own conscience was clear, this did not make him innocent. He must wait for the day of judgement, where God's overall authority will be clear:

> My conscience is clear, but that does not make me innocent. It is the Lord who judges me. Therefore, judge nothing before the appointed time; wait until the Lord comes. He will bring to light what is hidden in darkness and will expose the motives of the heart. At that time each will receive his praise from God.
> (1 Corinthians 4 v 4 - 5)

Judgement belongs to God alone, the creator and master of us all. He alone knows our actions, and also the motivations and secrets of our hearts. One day we will all stand before the judgement seat of Christ:

> We must all appear before the judgement seat of Christ, that each of us may receive what is due us for the things done while in the body, whether good or bad.
> (2 Corinthians 5 v 10)

Judgement Now

In addition to this final judgement, the Bible says we may also be on the receiving end of God's judgement in this life. This is not simply the natural law of reaping what we sow – if we are critical of others, we should not be surprised if others are critical of us when our backs are turned! But we may also receive God's judgement as a form of discipline.

In Corinth, Paul has to take the church to task about their divisions and the way they were conducting the Lord's Supper. At this shared meal, some were eating without waiting for others to join them, some were going hungry, and some were even getting drunk! Paul challenges them about despising the church of God and humiliating those who had nothing. But more seriously, he warns them that those who eat the bread or drink the cup of the Lord in an unworthy manner, will become guilty of sinning against the body and blood of the Lord. In doing so, they will bring judgement on themselves. He makes the point that God's judgement had fallen on some of them already, and this was why a number of them were weak and sick, and why others had even died. He makes it clear to them they should examine themselves before they eat and drink, and if they judged *themselves* rightly, they would not come under God's judgement (see 1 Corinthians 11 v 17 - 34):

> But if we were more discerning with regard to ourselves, we would not come under such judgement. Nevertheless, when we are judged in this way by the Lord, we are being disciplined so that we will not be finally condemned with the world.
> (1 Corinthians 11 v 31 - 32)

Should we be surprised at this? The writer to the Hebrews provides context by reminding us that a loving heavenly Father is committed to the discipline of the children he loves:

> Because the Lord disciplines the one he loves, and he chastens everyone he accepts as his son.
> (Hebrews 12 v 6)

While the Lord has every right to judge and discipline his children right now, it is important that we ourselves do not engage in judging others by speaking of them in a condemnatory and derogatory manner, passing sentence on their lives, and creating an environment of judgmentalism, rather than grace.

Jesus states the way we judge others will set the standard of our own judgement. Commentators differ on whether this refers to the way others in turn will criticise and judge us, or the way God himself will judge us. Regardless, the way we must position our hearts on the matter is clear:

> "For in the same way you judge others, you will be judged, and with the measure you use, it will be measured to you." (Matthew 7 v 2)

Have you ever thought about the standard you apply to others? When you criticise, do you ever express an opinion without a full knowledge of the facts, or without taking the time to find out about them first? Do you take the trouble to examine or understand the wider circumstances surrounding someone's life?

We're talking about an enduring problem. Harold Macmillan, a former Prime Minister of the United Kingdom, once said:

> *I have found in a long experience of politics that criticism is never inhibited by ignorance.*[2]

Or do you readily excuse or show mercy, rather than immediately rejecting every explanation put before you? Do you listen to people's arguments because you have an open mind and are ready to give others the benefit of the doubt? Can it be said of you that you are forgiving, understanding and loving?

The measure you use, will be that measured to you.

When speaking of criticism, American lawyer and politician, Frank A Clark, said:

> *Criticism, like rain, should be gentle enough to nourish a man's growth without destroying his roots.*[3]

This thought is more than just a beautiful image; it's clearly an approach we'd all benefit from.

Beware Of Hypocrisy

An important help in the battle to overcome our inclination to judge others, is to remember that we ourselves are not perfect. In fact,

Jesus says we may have a plank in our own eye, compared to the speck of sawdust or straw we're focusing on in our brother's (see Matthew 7 v 3).

Paul makes a similar point when he writes to the believers in Rome:

> You, therefore, have no excuse, you who pass judgement on someone else, for at whatever point you judge another, you are condemning yourself, because you who pass judgement do the same things.
> (Romans 2 v 1)

When Jesus talks of planks and specks, you may have noticed he uses the word *"hypocrite"* (see Matthew 7 v 5). I take that to mean there is a gap between what we can show on the outside, compared to what we know is true on the inside. What we criticise in others is also true about ourselves, and perhaps our motive in speaking ill of others is simply to build up our own reputation and standing! Or maybe again, to justify our own lives so we might feel a little better.

If we are going to be of any help or value to our brothers and sisters in Christ who may be struggling, we must first clean up our act and cultivate a fresh attitude. The late John Stott provides helpful advice when he says:

> *We need to be as critical of ourselves as we often are of others, and as generous to others as we always are to ourselves.*[4]

Then, and only then, will we see clearly to help others tackle their faults, sins and weaknesses. For while it is only God with the right to judge others, we do have a God-given responsibility to help each other become more like Jesus! When we have cleaned up our own act and dealt with our plank, we will be able to see clearly to perform a most delicate operation, the removal of the speck from our brother's eye. Of course, this is an operation that must be performed with the utmost care, sensitivity and love.

How do we do that? Once again, Paul comes to our aid.

Restoration

> Brothers and sisters, if someone is caught in a sin, you who live by the Spirit should restore that person gently. But watch yourselves, or you also may be tempted. Carry each other's burdens, and in this way you will fulfil the law of Christ.
> (Galatians 6 v 1 - 2)

You will note the situation here is that, *"someone is caught in a sin"*. Perhaps a better translation would be 'even if someone is caught in a sin,' for it seems Paul's expectation of believers is that they will live transformed lives to the glory of God.

In the previous chapter, he had encouraged the community of God's people to walk in the Spirit. But Paul was a realist. He knew there would be times when believers would give way to temptation; exceptional times when they would fall into sin and foolishly cross the line of what they knew to be right. The indication is they have been 'caught or overtaken in a sin,' when they may have either relaxed their guard and given way to an impulse, stepped off the main path and taken the wrong turning, or been caught in the act of doing something wrong.

He says when this happens, they are not to let people stew in their own juice and give way to a 'serves them right,' or 'they should have listened to me' attitude. They are certainly not to gossip with others about their downfall, for they are to always seek healing and the good of others. For as the writer in Proverbs points out:

> Whoever would foster love covers over an offense, but whoever repeats the matter separates close friends.
> (Proverbs 17 v 9)

Paul's heart is for the brother or sister to be restored, put back into their proper condition, and made useful again. It's like a stone-mason repairing a broken wall, or a doctor resetting a broken bone. We can picture it like fishermen overhauling their nets or repairing their boat after a storm, allowing them to take to the sea once more.

Restoration sees people returning to the place where, once again, they can do what they were made for – live to the praise of his glory!

And, in line with Paul's teaching, restoring a fellow believer must be done with the right heart attitude, led by the Spirit with meekness and gentleness, while remembering:

- There can be no place for condemnation and attack – 'How could you possibly have done that, what were you thinking?'
- There's no place for superiority – 'You would never catch me doing a thing like that or behaving in that manner.'
- There's no place for the voice of condescension – 'If you had only listened to me!'

Instead, restoration must take place in a spirit of gentleness and grace, being aware of one's own human limitations, weaknesses or failures, and remaining fully conscious of one's own vulnerability to sin.

On Your Guard

> So, if you think you are standing firm, be careful that you don't fall!
> (1 Corinthians 10 v 12)

Note that Paul says, *"watch yourself"* and be careful, or *"you also may be tempted"* (see Galatians 6 v 1). Fully aware of our old nature, which we can't afford to give any power to, he's warning believers not to fall into the same trap. It's been said, 'In this life we continually walk through the devil's red-light district, where sin is always waiting on the street corner to entice us to taste her wares.' Genesis puts it this way:

> "But if you do not do what is right, sin is crouching at your door; it desires to have you, but you must rule over it."
> (Genesis 4 v 7)

Keep In Step With The Spirit

When it comes to the question of who should engage in the restoration process, Paul's answer is, *"you who live by the Spirit,"* or we could say, *"a spiritual person"* (see Galatians 6 v 1). At first sight, this instruction might lead us to think of church leaders or those experienced in pastoral care. We might even conclude it should be spiritually mature Christians, or those who have been Christians for a long time. But the context shows Paul was addressing the whole church.

By a spiritual person, I would suggest from the surrounding verses that Paul is probably thinking of anyone who is walking and keeping in step with the Spirit - someone alive, alert and in tune with the Spirit's leading. This should be a person who is not grieving the Spirit by sin in their own lives or quenching the Spirit by not being obedient to his prompting. We can, therefore, look to those exercising their spiritual gifts on behalf of others (see Galatians 5 v 25; Ephesians 4 v 30; 1 Thessalonians 5 v 19; 1 Peter 4 v 10).

The context would also suggest he is thinking of those with a right view of themselves - those who are not conceited, exhibiting an air of superiority, or envious of others, but those who are secure in their identity in God. We can think of people able to make a sober judgement of their God-given faith in Christ.

> ...Do not think of yourself more highly than you ought, but rather think of yourself with sober judgement, in accordance with the faith God has distributed to each of you.
> (Romans 12 v 3; see also Galatians 5 v 26)

But above all, Paul is looking for people who love their brothers and sisters, and who have accepted responsibility for the welfare of their church family. We can think of those who, unlike Cain, happily admit to being their *"brother's keeper,"* (Genesis 4 v 9) and count it a joy and privilege to fulfil their family obligations. Or those ready to carry another brother's or sister's burden, sharing and shouldering with them their heavy load of weakness and shame. Or people who demonstrate being 'for' others and who consistently: want to shore up, not show up; raise up, not rub it in; restore, not write off; and point others to Jesus as the hope to receive cleansing and renewal.

The outcome of carrying each other's burdens within church communities will see us fulfil the law of Christ to love one another as Christ loved us. Paul's words to the Roman church can then become a reality:

> Let no debt remain outstanding, except the continuing debt to love one another, for whoever loves others has fulfilled the law.
> (Romans 13 v 8 - 10)

When someone caught in a sin is restored, serious backsliding is prevented, unkind words and gossip is avoided, and the church is built up. She advances against the forces of darkness and God is glorified in and through his people. His holiness is reflected in a holy people that bear his name.

The reason we are not to judge or write people off, is not simply so that we can live in harmony and build each other up, nor just to avoid ourselves being judged. More than that, our corporate lifestyle can magnify the wonderful truth of the mercy and grace of God. His grace can transform the most hardened sinner or the weakest saint, and we want people to see it, experience and be forever changed by it. No one is beyond the transforming power of Christ!

> For God did not send his Son into the world to condemn the world, but to save the world through him.
> (John 3 v 17)

Notes

1 Published by Longfellow in 1849 in his novel entitled "Kavanagh"

2 www.brainyquote.com/quotes/harold_macmillan_115612

3 www.brainyquote.com/quotes/frank_a_clark_105689

4 www.accessinspiration.org/library/1156

CHAPTER TEN

On Guard

Modern living creates many challenges – potentially more than ever. From money, to what we watch, to what we eat, potential trappings and temptations are never too far away. Although the specific battles we face will be individual, every one of us needs to make sure we are 'on guard' and alert.

According to a recent NHS and Government report, obesity rates among adults in the UK have almost quadrupled in the last 25 years. Around one in four now fall into this category, while a further 62% of the adult population are overweight. This means Britain has the second highest rate of obesity in the world, and the largest in Europe. As a result, £48 billion is spent each year on obesity-related healthcare and management of the problem.

In recent years there has also been a dramatic rise in the numbers of youngsters classed as overweight or obese. The reasons given are increasingly sedentary lifestyles, poor diet, and a lack of exercise across the population. If things do not change dramatically, it is predicted that by 2050, some 60% of the UK adult population will be obese.[1]

Our first response to anyone dealing with issues like this one, must always be based on care, compassion and a desire to understand. When we look to understand first, we're better placed to meaningfully support – I think of Jesus looking beyond the obvious and seeking to see the heart of a problem. Many of us may have managed to avoid wrestling with problems of obesity or being overweight. In fact, some may even feel it could never become a problem for them as they eat sensibly, exercise regularly, and maintain a balanced lifestyle. Nevertheless, if that is how you are feeling at present, I suggest the reality is any of us can be vulnerable to this kind of challenge throughout our lives. Especially so if we live in the West, where there is an abundance of food! And if it's not this specific challenge for you, other areas of vulnerability will inevitably emerge.

Let's also remember, everyone brings their own context. For example, others won't have experienced the many privileges I took for granted during my start in life. When I look back on my childhood, I remember taking every opportunity to get outdoors and kick a ball around for hours on end. School days were filled playing sports, all of which contributed to keeping me reasonably fit. It was only when I started my banking career in the City of London, working long hours and commuting by train each day, that I found it harder to maintain regular exercise. I still managed to play the occasional game of football or squash, but as work, church and family responsibilities increased, I found it harder to fit in regular sports activities. The need to be more intentional grew if I was going to stay 'on guard' in this part of life.

These days, a long walk or cycle often suffices as my fitness regime. Though if I'm honest, as I get older, making good decisions about this is harder. I find it harder to choose between staying on the sofa to read a book or watch TV, or making the effort to go for a walk. It now takes more willpower for me to take only one chocolate from the box, rather than finish off the whole lot in one sitting. And, of course, there's also the battle to refuse an extra helping of my wife's amazing cooking (although, maybe there's kindness in doing so semi-regularly)!

This specific lifestyle example serves to show the wider challenge of our ongoing need to rely on God's strength, across all aspects of our lives.

Sloppy Living

As followers of Jesus, we know we are called to show self-control and self-discipline, remembering that our bodies are the temple of the Holy Spirit. However, we also know of the temptation to drift into 'sloppy' living, where we don't keep our bodies and minds in top condition to serve the purposes of God.

Paul was well aware of this danger too. In his first letter to the Corinthians, he uses an athletic metaphor to illustrate his single-minded goal of bringing as many people as possible to faith through the gospel:

> Do you not know that in a race all the runners run, but only one gets the prize? Run in such a way as to get the prize. Everyone who competes in the games goes into strict training. They do it to get a crown that will not last, but we do it to get a crown that will last forever. Therefore, I do not run like someone running aimlessly; I do not fight like a boxer beating the air. No, I strike a blow to my body and make it my slave so that after I have preached to others, I myself will not be disqualified for the prize.
> (1 Corinthians 9 v 24 - 27)

Eugene Peterson paraphrases the same passage in The Message:

> You've all been to the stadium and seen the athletes race. Everyone runs; one wins. All good athletes train hard. They do it for a gold medal that tarnishes and fades. You're after one that's gold eternally.
>
> I don't know about you, but I'm running hard for the finish line. I'm giving it everything I've got. No sloppy living for me! I'm staying alert and in top condition. I'm not going to get caught napping, telling everyone else about it and then missing out myself.

False Security

None of us want to miss out on God's best for our lives. Paul continues by explaining this danger to the Corinthians, listing a number of temptations they were not to yield to. He also warns of the subtle danger of having a false sense of security and thinking they were somehow immune to such urges:

> So, if you think you are standing firm, be careful that you don't fall!
> (1 Corinthians 10 v 12)

The danger the Corinthians faced was to assume their newfound freedom and status in Christ would automatically protect them from spiritual harm. We learn of their attendance at cultic meals in the pagan temples, even though it was an expression of idolatry. We can deduce they felt it would not harm their spiritual lives or affect their relationship with God to engage in these practices. In their minds, the grace of God in Christ had set them free from the demands and expectations of others, so they no longer needed to be unduly influenced by other people's thinking. They considered themselves totally free to adopt and implement their own fresh, self-determined outlook on life.

But Paul says, 'Wait a minute, it's not that simple.' He reminds them clearly of others who enjoyed the privilege of God's provision and protection, yet still fell to all manner of temptations, before ending up honouring, serving and worshipping false gods. In full awareness of the danger to the church he loves in Corinth, Paul sounds a warning from Israel's history.

Lesson From Israel

> For I do not want you to be ignorant of the fact, brothers and sisters, that our ancestors were all under the cloud and that they all passed through the sea. They were all baptised into Moses in the cloud and in the sea. They all ate the same spiritual food and drank the same spiritual drink; for they drank from the spiritual rock that accompanied them, and that rock was Christ. Nevertheless, God was not pleased with most of them; their bodies were scattered in the wilderness.
> (1 Corinthians 10 v 1 - 5)

The Hebrews had been slaves in Egypt for 400 years when God sent them a deliverer in the person of Moses. Through a series of miracles, culminating in the death of every first-born in Egypt, they were rescued from slavery. On their journey to freedom, God's presence went with them, leading them by a pillar of cloud by day and a pillar of fire by night. When Pharaoh and his army sought to re-capture them and prevent them escaping, God parted the Red Sea to let the whole Israelite nation - men, women, children, animals and all their possessions - cross over on dry land. As they reached safety, the waters returned, killing the pursuing Pharaoh and all his army. Once and for all, the people of Israel had been cut off from their past life of slavery. They experienced unbelievable blessing and favour at this time.

Paul explains that what happened to their forefathers was a forward look to the hope they now enjoyed through their own Christian baptism, reflecting how Christ had also delivered and rescued them, from slavery to their sin. Baptism marked the end of their previous way of living, and by the power of God's Spirit they were now living a new life. They were free - they too had been cut off from their past.

Throughout Israel's journey to the land God promised as an inheritance, he provided supernaturally for them, giving them food from heaven (Manna) and water from a rock. As Paul says, Christ himself (The Rock) was present with them throughout their journey. This mirrored the privilege the Corinthians were experiencing as they journeyed to their own promised inheritance of a new heaven and new earth. God's supernatural provision and presence was also with them. He was fulfilling his promise to meet all their needs according to his glorious riches in Christ Jesus, and his presence was dwelling in them in the person of the Holy Spirit.

Yet, despite all the wonderful blessings and privileges Israel enjoyed, God was not pleased with most of them and they failed to make it to the promised land. Paul describes God's displeasure with them in the awful and graphic description, *"their bodies were scattered in the wilderness"* (verse 5).

How could this be the follow-up to God's rescue and blessing? Why did they not respond to their freedom with obedience and devotion?

Paul did not want the Corinthians to end up in the same position and miss out on God's promises by being disqualified from the prize. He was adamant that what happened to the Israelites needed to be an example to them, so they would not fall into similar temptations and set their hearts on evil things. To drive his point home, he shared four occasions in Israel's history where the nation fell into temptation, sinned, and failed to honour their God.

Four Examples Of Failure

> Now these things occurred as examples to keep us from setting our hearts on evil things as they did. Do not be idolaters, as some of them were; as it is written: "The people sat down to eat and drink and got up to indulge in revelry." We should not commit sexual immorality, as some of them did—and in one day twenty-three thousand of them died. We should not test Christ, as some of them did—and were killed by snakes. And do not grumble, as some of them did—and were killed by the destroying angel.
> (1 Corinthians 10 v 6 - 10)

The first incident Paul mentions in Israel's history was them falling into the sin of idolatry. Moses had gone up the mountain to receive the Ten Commandments from God, and when he came back he found the people had made an idol, a golden calf. They worshipped the statue as their God and ascribed to it a place of honour for bringing them out of Egypt.

As Paul says, it was written that, *"the people sat down to eat and drink and got up to indulge in revelry"* (verse 7). This description probably indicates some form of sexual impropriety, often associated with heathen feasts and cultic worship, such that Moses spoke of them as, *"running wild,"* and being *"out of control"* (Exodus 32 v 25).

God's judgement on their sin resulted in 3,000 people dying that day by the hands of the Levites, and him inflicting a plague on the people.

The second incident was one of sexual immorality. Some of the Israelite men began to indulge in sexual relationships with Moabite women, who in turn encouraged them to worship their own gods. Sadly, the men ended up worshipping a false god, the Baal of Peor, and drew down God's judgement on their sin. This time some 24,000 Israelites died from a plague.[2]

The third incident was one of impatience. Having forgotten God's past deliverance and provision, Israel wanted what God had promised them *immediately* and without further delay! Their impatience boiled over into grumbling and complaining against God and Moses. The result of their response was that, once again, God's judgement fell on the people. Many of them began to die from venomous snake bites. However, God heard Moses' intercession on behalf of the people and showed mercy. He instructed him to make a bronze snake and put it up on a pole, so that anyone bitten could look at the snake and live.[3]

The final incident was one of insurrection or rebellion (see Numbers 13 - 14). The twelve men sent out to explore the promised land brought back a report to Moses, Aaron and the whole Israelite community. All of them agreed it was a good land but ten of them gave a fearful report, saying it was impossible for them to take hold of it. Only Joshua and Caleb responded with faith, declaring that, with God's help, they could undoubtedly possess the land.

Sadly, the people believed the ten, forgetting all the miraculous signs God had performed among them in their history. They even wanted to choose another leader to take them back to Egypt and slavery! Joshua and Caleb encouraged the people that God was with them and that the land *could* be taken. Their response to the encouragement was to talk of stoning them, such was their fear and unbelief. Warnings to the people not to rebel against the Lord fell on deaf ears and ignited God's judgement. God decreed that what they feared most would come upon them, and they would die in the desert... and die they did!

> In this wilderness your bodies will fall – every one of you twenty years old or more who was counted in the census and who grumbled against me. Not one of you will enter the land I swore with uplifted hand to make your home, except Caleb son of Jephunneh and Joshua son of Nun.
> (Numbers 14 v 29 - 30)

Having looked at the four incidents, the question arises as to why Paul used these serious, solemn and sobering examples? Having already said it was to keep them from setting their hearts on evil things as the Israelites did, he expands his explanation in the next few verses:

> These things happened to them as examples and were written down as warnings for us, on whom the culmination of the ages has come. So, if you think you are standing firm, be careful that you don't fall! No temptation has overtaken you except what is common to mankind. And God is faithful; he will not let you be tempted beyond what you can bear. But when you are tempted he will also provide a way out so that you can endure it.
> (1 Corinthians 10 v 11 - 13)

These incidents provided a warning. What happened to the Israelites could so easily happen to the Corinthians. Followers of Jesus could similarly fall prey to idolatry, immorality, impatience and insurrection. Indeed, these very things were already beginning to surface in the lives of believers at Corinth. Sloppy living, characterised by careless, undisciplined and sinful lives would have grave consequences, disqualifying them from receiving the prize. As well, Paul knew there was no space for complacency and misplaced self-assuredness; reliance must be placed squarely on Christ. If they were considering themselves as *"standing firm"* (verse 12), and somehow immune to these issues, they too must be careful they don't fall!

Idolatry

As followers of Jesus today, we do well to heed Paul's warning and examine our own lives. Are we falling for the enemy's temptations? We may feel that literal idols forged in bronze have no place in our lives, but we do need to ask ourselves what else we may be placing above God:

- Is there a good thing we have elevated to a 'God thing' in our life?
- What is the most important thing in our life?
- What is the object of our allegiance, love, devotion, time, energies and money?
- What or whom do we worship, honour and serve?

John Calvin is reputed to have said, 'The human heart is an idol factory.' Elsewhere it's been commented, 'Idolatry is the default mode of the heart, if we are not loving and worshipping God then we will worship something or someone else!'

In his book, "Counterfeit Gods," Tim Keller defines an idol as:

> *Anything more important to you than God, anything that absorbs your heart and imagination more than God, anything you seek to give you what only God can give.*
>
> *An idol is whatever you look at and say, in your heart of hearts, "If I have that, then I'll feel my life has meaning, then I'll know I have value, then I'll feel significant and secure." There are many ways to describe that kind of relationship to something, but perhaps the best one is worship.*[4]

It is no coincidence that during the time of temptation, when Satan offered Jesus all the kingdoms of the world and their splendour, the one condition Satan attached was for Jesus to, *"bow down and worship him."* Note that Jesus' rebuke to Satan came straight from God's own command, *"For it is written: Worship the Lord your God, and serve him only"* (see Matthew 4 v 8 - 10; Deuteronomy 6 v 13).

Immorality

Turning to the question of immorality, the Bible is quite clear we are called to, *"flee from sexual immorality"* (1 Corinthians 6 v 18). Sometimes this act can be quite literal, like when Joseph fled after being propositioned by Potiphar's wife (see Genesis 39 v 12). Whether married or single, it is imperative to recognise we live in a society where sexual temptation is always close. The French Catholic, Francois Mauriac, aptly reminds us that, "*...the sexual act has no resemblance to any other act... It is a tidal wave able to cover everything and bear away everything.*"[5]

While grace *"teaches us to say 'No' to ungodliness and worldly passions"* (Titus 2 v 12), we nevertheless need to maintain integrity and purity in every aspect of our human relationships. It may help to regularly ask ourselves questions like: 'Is my mind truly fixed on what is true, noble, right, pure, lovely and admirable?' 'Am I comfortable that my watching, reading, and listening material is acceptable to my heavenly Father?' 'Do I remain captivated only by the love of my spouse, safeguarding that God-ordained bond?' 'Do I treat the opposite sex, both in my thoughts and actions, with honour and respect?' (see Philippians 4 v 8)?

People often say that prevention is better than cure. This may be true, so if we are to really help ourselves maintain sexual purity, we need to be wise and proactive. We must not only learn to say 'No!' to certain behaviours, but also to build positive attitudes, actions and rhythms into our lives.

One of the greatest blights on modern society at present is the increasing availability of, and addiction to, pornography. The internet and our devices have, quite literally, put this damaging material in our pockets and right in front of our eyes. The temptation is far reaching, extending to both men and women. And conversation with those working with children in schools will tell you, a growing number of our young people are experiencing this too. Devastatingly, this includes those younger than ten years old. Make no mistake, Christians are certainly not immune from falling into this snare. In fact, where struggles with this type of behaviour need bringing into the light to be dealt with supportively, Christians can experience a double hit. Believers battling with this will often feel a weight of shame and remain silenced by the lies of the enemy, which commonly attack their identity in Christ.

As well as helping those caught in this sin, we need to ask how we promote positive practices in our homes. How do we give our children a good foundation to meet the sexual challenge of pornography as they grow up? One thing we can't do is close our ears, pretend it's not there, or hope it'll go away. One Christian organisation working in this field has suggested a number of positive ways to help:

1. By mum and dad **modelling romantic love in the home.** There needs to be a lot of hugging and kissing between the husband and wife, as children need to see marital romantic affection.
2. By **avoiding a climate of instant gratification.** When children run the home by easily persuading their parents to give them what they want, when they want it, with no regard for right or wrong, the wrong message is given. This environment makes it more likely for them to seek the instant gratification of pornography when the opportunity arises.
3. By modelling **good verbal communication.** Children need to see their parents value each other by consistently giving their best words to each other - words which build up, cherish and nourish. Teaching young ones to talk in ways which build up another person is not only a demonstration of the value of that individual, but a way of exalting the use of words and building a rhythm of honouring others. In doing this, we contrast the lack of value placed on relationships in pornography, shining a light on its darkness and emptiness.
4. By ensuring there are **consequences for wrong actions,** preventing the development of false confidence through risk-free relationships. A child who does not have to pay for what they've done wrong will learn they can get away with

anything. Children must have a comprehensive view of love, which means being appropriately disciplined when they do wrong.

5. By ensuring **your home is not a critical community.** The most common ways we devalue others is through criticism and anger towards them. Therefore, we must make sure there is more encouragement, praise, affirmation and love in the home, than frustration, impatience, criticalness, and self-centeredness.[6]

It is not enough to simply address temptation when it confronts us directly, although we must stand strong when it does. Rather, we must seek to build a holistic walk with God, allowing him to direct and guide every area of our day-to-day lives. From this position of strength, we will be better equipped to face temptations when they come, seeing how poor they are in comparison to the richness of knowing God's love and blessing.

Impatience

They say it is easy to be patient when you are on your own. The addition of other people into your life is the real test of your patience! Impatience is often revealed by the things we complain about most, or the frustrations we repeat to ourselves or others.

The impatience Paul centres on is an impatience with God, particularly if a promise appears slow in being fulfilled. Scripture says, *"Hope deferred makes the heart sick"* (Proverbs 13 v 12). It can also make us angry at times, especially when something we have wanted or thought God had promised seems a long time in coming. It is then we can begin to doubt the goodness of God and we can question whether he truly has our best interests at heart. Like Israel, we can quickly forget the many blessings we have already received by his hand.

Think back to the garden of Eden when Satan whispered to Eve, *"Did God really say...?"* (Genesis 3 v 1). He continues to assault us today with similar doubts. We must not be caught off guard by him but must put our total confidence in our faithful God, whose every word proves true and whose mercy and grace follows us all our lives (see Psalm 23 v 6). Our God can be trusted:

> God is not human, that he should lie, not a human being, that he should change his mind. Does he speak and then not act? Does he promise and not fulfil?
> (Numbers 23 v 19)

> He who is the Glory of Israel does not lie or change his mind; for he is not a human being, that he should change his mind.
> (1 Samuel 15 v 29)

When we search Scripture, we find many people whose heart's desire was delayed or who had to wait for the fulfilment of something God had promised. Sometimes, the wait continued for many years - Abraham, Joseph, Hannah, David, Zechariah and Elizabeth... the list goes on. Yet in each story, God proved himself to be true to his word. In this era of instant gratification, we need to hold even more tightly to the truth of Scripture and the testimony of God's blessing in our lives:

> Every word of God proves true. He is a shield to all who come to him for protection.
> (Proverbs 30 v 5 NLT)

Insurrection

The last area of insurrection may be the one we might quickly pass over, because we don't easily see ourselves as being rebels against God's plans and purposes. After all, in our response to God's call to salvation, we confessed with our mouth that 'Jesus is Lord.' We are those who have been rescued from the dominion of darkness and been brought into the kingdom of the Son he loves. Jesus is our Master and King.

Nevertheless, if we examine ourselves, we know the truthful answer to the question of whether we have areas of our life where we are fearful and not trusting God? We could also ask whether we are seeking to retain control over an area of our life we should be submitting to God's rule? Or do we always honour and respect those who the Lord has put over us in his church? And are we willing to submit plans for our life to fatherly shepherds and respond to their godly wisdom and input? Obedience in these areas is important and is highly valued by God (see Romans 10 v 9; Colossians 1 v 13):

> Have confidence in your leaders and submit to their authority, because they keep watch over you as those who must give an account. Do this so that their work will be a joy, not a burden, for that would be of no benefit to you.
> (Hebrews 13 v 17)

God's Path

Having finished his warning to the Corinthians (and us), Paul ends with a word of encouragement, reminding them God is fully trustworthy. Be assured, God is able to help us in times of temptation. Not only is he Almighty God, but he became man and experienced every temptation we will ever face ourselves, as we're wonderfully reminded in the letter to the Hebrews:

> Therefore, since we have a great high priest who has ascended into heaven, Jesus the Son of God, let us hold firmly to the faith we profess. For we do not have a high priest who is unable to empathise with our weaknesses, but we have one who has been tempted in every way, just as we are—yet he did not sin. Let us then approach God's throne of grace with confidence, so that we may receive mercy and find grace to help us in our time of need.
> (Hebrews 4 v 14 - 16)

Paul reminds the Corinthians that all their temptations are common to man, faced by others, and conquered by Jesus himself. He says God won't allow them to be overwhelmed (pushed past their limit) by any temptation and he will make it possible for them to overcome. God will also provide a way out, so they won't be defeated, but can stand up in the face of temptation (see 1 Corinthians 10 v

11 - 13). Of course, they were responsible for not ignoring the escape route God will provide, just as we must take ours today.

For many of us, the way out or exit enabling us to overcome temptation may be immediate and clear, as it was for Joseph when confronted by Potiphar's wife. But, at other times, although God will show us the way of escape, it will require patience, perseverance and discipline on our part.

We could think of overcoming temptation like being stranded in a lonely hostile place with no means of escape, before help arrives and we are airlifted to safety by a helicopter – all we have to do is passively surrender to the rescue from above! God is, of course, able to deliver the helpless, and his eyes always remain on those who fear him (see Psalm 33 v 18). Indeed, Christ's salvation is the ultimate demonstration of his compassion for the lost and his heart to help those who can't help themselves.

However, experience tells us that overcoming temptation is more like being enclosed in a dense jungle, surrounded by mountains with seemingly no way out – energy depleted, light failing, all alone, and hope fading. You then become aware of, or are prompted to recall, a hidden path leading out of the jungle through a small pass in the mountains. From here, you find strength and resolve to walk the path to safety.

The key is, we are active participants in overcoming temptation. God's plan for the believer is to cultivate a relationship that sees us grow in strength and mature in faith. He is committed, through the work of the Holy Spirit, to seeing our character and innermost desires changed and shaped to match the new identity of righteousness Christ has secured in us. While we become increasingly reliant on the Holy Spirit, this growth moves us to a position of strength, not passivity, weakness and helplessness.

In our lives there is always a route for us to walk to overcome temptation and stand strong against it. Throughout, we're able to lean on wise safeguards we've put in place ahead of time. These include godly friendships, routines of devotion, and knowledge of Scripture, which give us strength to yield to God's best for us, not the temptation to satisfy the desires of our old self. God promises to reveal that path to us, provide power for the journey, and to walk with us until we are safe. We must, therefore, confidently call out to God during these times, for we're not alone. The God who is faithful will travel with us as we fight temptation, because he has walked the road before us and overcame it.

His faithfulness makes this part of the Lord's Prayer all the more important, even though it's the part we can often forget to pray:

> "And lead us not into temptation, but deliver us from the evil one."
> (Matthew 6 v 13)

The temptation to sin and for sloppy living is real. However, we can know victory in our lives by finding mercy and grace as we confidently approach God's throne in our times of need (see Hebrews 4 v 16). Paul's emphasis is always on the faithfulness of God, not on our own ability and strength.

Asking the Lord not to lead us into circumstances where we could be easily tempted, and where we would be liable to fall, is right and wise. In fact, asking to be delivered from evil in every shape and form shows our reliance on and faith in him. It is also reflective of a healthy, sober judgement of our own frailty and vulnerability. Be in no doubt, answering these prayers meets God's desire for us to honour him, and for him to maintain unbroken fellowship with us.

Notes

1 www.healthexpress.co.uk/obesity/uk-statistics

2 Numbers 25

3 Numbers 21

4 Counterfeit Gods: The Empty Promises of Money, Sex and Power, and the Only Hope that Matters by Tim Keller. Copyright © Tim Keller 2009. Published by Hodder and Stoughton Ltd. Introduction - Pages 16 and 17. Reproduced with permission of the Licensor through PLSclear

5 What I believe, by Francois Mauriac, Farrer Straus, New York, 1963, Page 50

6 5 Sure-Fire Ways to Motivate Your Child to Use Pornography by Rick Thomas. Covenant Eyes, E Magazine – Pure Minds Online - dated 20th March 2013

CHAPTER ELEVEN

Facing Trials

"Why does God allow 'bad' things to happen to 'good' people?"

Throughout my many years of church leadership, this is easily one of the most frequently asked questions relating to life, faith, God and the universe. It's a question that arises in both Christian and secular settings, and it's a natural thought for those searching for meaning when facing or seeing hurt and difficulty. You won't be surprised to know, it's given rise to a plethora of answers.

You may recognise some of the common responses given to Christians experiencing 'bad' things, namely: that God allows them to teach believers lessons they might not learn in any other way; to discipline them; to improve their character; or to encourage them to depend on him more.

Others focus on the 'economy of God,' where so-called 'bad' things experienced by Christians can bring about good results in our lives. As such, one of the more popular answers often heard in church is that God allows 'bad' things because he is more interested in our character than our comfort!

Wherever you land on this issue, there is no denying that as followers of Jesus, we all encounter similar troubles and trials to others around us. We live in a broken world, meaning we all face the many consequences of man's continued rebellion against God. Nobody is immune to sorrow or sadness and we all encounter unanticipated and unplanned difficulties – there's no surprise in the unexpected.

More than this, as disciples of Jesus, we can expect to face the world's hostility. Shortly before his death Jesus warned his disciples of the cost of following him – their new life meant they no longer belonged to the world:

> "If the world hates you, keep in mind that it hated me first. If you belonged to the world, it would love you as its own. As it is, you do not belong to the world, but I have chosen you out of the world. That is why the world hates you. Remember what I told you: 'A servant is not greater than his master'. If they persecuted me, they will persecute you also. If they obeyed my teaching, they will obey yours also. They will treat you this way because of my name, for they do not know the one who sent me."
> (John 15 v 18 - 21)

We see this truth worked out further in Paul's writing to Timothy. He reminds him of the ongoing suffering and persecution he had endured himself, making the bold statement that, *"In fact, everyone who wants to live a godly life in Christ Jesus will be persecuted, while evildoers and imposters will go from bad to worse, deceiving and being deceived"* (2 Timothy 3 v 12 - 13).

Earlier in the same chapter, he points out that the surrounding godlessness of the last days would make things difficult for those seeking to follow Jesus:

> Don't be naïve. There are difficult times ahead. As the end approaches, people are going to be self-absorbed, money-hungry, self-promoting, stuck-up, profane, contemptuous of parents, crude, coarse, dog-eat-dog, unbending, slanderers, impulsively wild, savage, cynical, treacherous, ruthless, bloated windbags, addicted to lust, and allergic to God. They'll make a show of religion, but behind the scenes they're animals. Stay clear of those people.
> (2 Timothy 3 v 1 - 5 MSG)

Life is hard, and days are difficult for both Christians and non-believers. The challenge (and hope) for those who know Jesus is to seek him amid hurt and confusion, trusting in something bigger than the immediately consuming and painful.

Handling Difficult Days

As those who desire to become more like Jesus and live lives that bring glory to God, how are we to handle the difficult days in which we are living? What should be our attitude to the everyday trials of life we face, or the hostility and persecution we may encounter as followers of Jesus?

One place we can turn for answers is James' letter, where he was writing to believers facing the challenge of being scattered and dispersed. He wanted to encourage them in the face of their difficulties and address the practical aspects of their faith and everyday living. James knew they needed sustaining, so starts his pastoral letter by instructing them on how to have a right attitude towards the trials they are facing:

> Consider it pure joy, my brothers and sisters, whenever you face trials of many kinds, because you know that the testing of your faith produces perseverance. Let perseverance finish its work so that you may be mature and complete, not lacking anything. If any of you lacks wisdom, you should ask God, who gives generously to all without finding fault, and it will be given to you. But when you ask, you must believe and not doubt, because the one who doubts is like a wave of the sea, blown and tossed by the wind. That person should not expect to receive anything from the Lord. Such a person is double-minded and unstable in all they do.
> (James 1 v 2 - 8)

External Trials

The first thing to note is James does not specify the nature of the trials they will face, but simply talks of *"trials of many kinds"* (verse 2). In this context, he is probably referencing trials that would tempt them to lose their faith, to lose hope, or to become resentful.

The challenge faced was real, especially when we consider their experience of displacement from their homeland, social ostracism, economic boycott, and the loss of loved ones through persecution.

When talking of trials, the original wording translates as, 'to meet,' or 'to face,' meaning to come across or encounter unexpectedly. Interestingly, it's the same word used in the parable of the good Samaritan. Here, we are told the man *"was attacked by robbers"* (Luke 10 v 30), showing a clear example of a trial that was sudden, unexpected, and certainly not of his choosing!

James is speaking of similar trials; ones we have not chosen or created, but suddenly appear and stare us in the face. When things are thrust upon us in this way, it's easy to focus on the circumstance being 'unfair or unjust.' It is naturally hard to understand why God allows these external trials to come into our lives. After all, passages like Psalm 91 seem to indicate that if we make the Most High our dwelling and the Lord our refuge then, *"no harm will overtake you, no disaster will come near your tent"* (verse 10). Yet things like illness, hardship or tragedy can feel much like a disaster coming near, so dwelling on the unfairness of a situation is a real temptation... and it often seems logical and justified! However, James knows believers must strongly resist this if we are to maintain our focus on our greater hope and joy.

Test Of Faith

The answer James gives, is that such trials prove the validity of our belief, speaking specifically of a *"testing of our faith"* (verse 3). The original word translated as 'testing' refers to a proof or a crucible, the container used to hold materials being melted and worked on under extreme temperatures. As such, we see how our faith is put in the fire to prove its genuineness. External trials prove the reality, substance and power of our faith, revealing us as true followers of Jesus. The Message paraphrase puts it this way:

> You know that under pressure, your faith-life is forced into the open and shows its true colours.
> (James 1 v 3 MSG)

Peter says a very similar thing in his first letter. After reminding the believers they have been born again, given a living hope, and promised an eternal inheritance, he states that *"through faith they are shielded by God's power until the coming of the salvation that is ready to be revealed in the last time"* (1 Peter 1 v 5). Yet, he also talks of them as having suffered grief in all kinds of trials, and gives the reason:

> These have come so that the proven genuineness of your faith—of greater worth than gold, which perishes even though refined by fire—may result in praise, glory and honour when Jesus Christ is revealed.
> (From 1 Peter 1 v 3 - 7)

Trouble, loss or grief hurts, blindsides and confuses, but we will face it in this life. We are certainly not to be unsympathetic to the emotional pain of others, but we must maintain a sure hope in the growth that comes through it. The challenge for every follower of Jesus is whether we will let our trials define us or *refine* us.

The truth is, we are all called to a life of faithful endurance amid our troubles and afflictions. Where we feel anguish, how do we hold fast to our eternal hope and encourage others to do the same?

Development Of Christlikeness

James' encouragement is that, handled well, the testing of our faith will produce a mature Christian character and a greater likeness to Christ. For the testing of our faith develops perseverance in us, and perseverance when it finishes its work, results in a mature character that is complete and lacks nothing (verses 3 - 4).

I once heard this process likened to fruit ripening - it stayed with me: *Trials are like the sun ripening immature fruit, ripening it in such a way that the fruit is without spot or blemish and becomes the perfect fruit!*

Paul gives further confirmation of the blessing that arises when trials are handled well:

> Suffering produces perseverance; perseverance character; and character hope.
> (Romans 5 v 3 - 4)

The word 'perseverance' means, 'to abide under, to last, to stay put, to endure.' God's goal is not that we should sink under the weight of our trials, nor be blown around by them spiritually, mentally or emotionally. Rather, we should hold our ground undefeated by our circumstances, no matter how hard they become. As a result of God's abundant grace, our trials become an opportunity for us to grow up and become stronger in Christ, allowing us to exhibit more of his character.

Paul suffered countless trials in his lifetime and sets us an example of how to stand firm through difficult times, trusting in the all-surpassing power of God. Listen to the way he expresses his own experience, not airbrushing the pain, but pointing to our greater hope and strength:

> We are pressed on every side by troubles, but we are not crushed. We are perplexed, but not driven to despair. We are hunted down, but never abandoned by God. We get knocked down, but we are not destroyed.
> (2 Corinthians 4 v 7 - 10 NLT; see also 2 Corinthians 11 v 23 - 28)

The big question for us is whether we are following in Paul's footsteps, just as he walked in the footsteps of Jesus? Or do our reactions to life's troubles and trials fall short of what is expected of us, or what we would hope for in ourselves? (see 1 Corinthians 11 v 1)

Right Response

For some of us, a natural response might be one of confusion, as we think these kinds of testing and trial should not happen to a Christian. Others might respond in anger, feeling a sense of injustice that we don't deserve all the current hassle and trauma in our life. This response can be amplified if we feel we've been living an exemplary life of late! Some find their trials eliciting an overwhelming sense of despair, coupled with a feeling of not being able to cope with the situation or find the right solution.

Whatever our response may be, we need to look again at James' instruction on how to engage well when we face troubles and trials:

> Consider it pure joy, my brothers and sisters, whenever you face trials of many kinds.
> (James 1 v 2)

The right reaction is to respond with joy! This is also the reaction Paul exhibits when he writes to the church in Rome. Not only does Paul say he rejoices in the hope of the glory of God, but he is also able to rejoice in his sufferings (see Romans 5 v 3 - 4).

At first sight, this kind of response might appear to be utter madness. How can God's people possibly react with joy in the face of the most difficult, trying and demanding of circumstances?

Both James and Paul had known God's faithfulness in their lives and they provide us with an answer. From experience, they knew their God was able to turn trials into blessing, and that trials are an opportunity to mature in our faith in Christ. God had repeatedly revealed his glory and strength in their lives despite their own weakness, so they held onto this when new troubles confronted them. We also need to readily recall God's faithfulness in our lives.

James does not give us a detailed description of the kind of joy, rejoicing or happiness with which we should respond. Perhaps the joyful reaction he is looking for could be likened to the response when, at long last, the postman arrives and a student discovers they have got those all-important exam passes they need to open the door to an exciting future. Or maybe it's like the time when, after plucking up the courage and rehearsing the words a million times, a man finally asks the girl of his dreams to marry him and she says 'Yes!' Or imagine, after all those months of discomfort and a seemingly unending experience of pain, the midwife places a baby in a mother's arms for the first time, and those little fingers curl around hers. Do you notice something? In each of these examples, endurance and courage comes from having our hope and focus on the future promise.

In case you think I'm going over the top with these illustrations, I want to show you that James uses the same word for *"joy"* found elsewhere in the Bible. For example, in the Christmas story when the angels appear to the shepherds, we read:

> Do not be afraid. I bring you good news that will cause great **joy** for all the people. Today in the town of David a Saviour has been born to you; he is the Messiah, the Lord.
> (Luke 2 v 10 - 11; emphasis added)

Can you imagine the joy of the shepherds, when after hundreds of years of waiting for the coming of God's Messiah, they are the ones chosen to receive the message of the Saviour of the world being born?

Paul also uses the same word when he expresses deep affection for the church in Philippi:

> Therefore, my brothers and sisters, you whom I love and long for, my **joy** and crown.
> (Philippians 4 v 1; emphasis added)

Similarly, the word is used in relation to Jesus' death and resurrection:

> And let us run with perseverance the race marked out for us, fixing our eyes on Jesus, the pioneer and perfecter of faith. For the **joy** set before him he endured the cross, scorning its shame, and sat down at the right hand of the throne of God.
> (Hebrews 12 v 2 ; emphasis added)

Future promise, future hope, and future joy set before Jesus enabled him to endure the suffering of the cross and overcome.

Be reassured, James is not talking here of meeting life's trials by mustering a faint or false smile, or even a stoic resolution to simply accept whatever may come our way. Nor is he advocating the fatalistic approach to life we find in some other religions. James speaks of "pure joy," or as some versions translate it, "all joy." We should meet our trials with a joy that is not temporary, but enduring. We can find strength by maintaining joy in the Lord who is sovereign over all things, including all the trials that come into our lives.

Promise Of Wisdom

Now you may ask, 'This is all very fine in theory, but surely it's impossible in practice?' Such an approach is contrary to the climate and culture of society as we know it today. But this is no surprise, for we are called to live counter-culturally; the world is no longer home! Our hope in Christ goes beyond the very best comforts this world can offer. With God's help, we are called to live according to our new God-given nature, not according to our old nature. This means following in the footsteps of Jesus and living out the values of the kingdom of God.

The world is in desperate need of (and is looking for) a people who will model a different approach to life, a different way to live, and a different way to handle the pressures and complexities of twenty-first century society. As a community of the Spirit, we are called to be that people and be a blessing to those around us.

If we are to demonstrate a Jesus way of living, we must not give way to defeatist thoughts in our own life, checking ourselves for unhealthy outlooks including: life is just too complicated today; the pressures are too great; the world is in too much of a mess; my personal circumstances are just too complicated; I wouldn't know how to get started, how to act, what to do; or I am just not wise enough to tackle the things life throws at me and my family!

Do you recognise any of these? If we're honest, we'll all recall times where we've given these thoughts more time than we should - where your attention goes, your energy flows. But let me ask you a question. Do you think God expects us to rely on our own wisdom and resources when facing trials?

King David tells us:

> As a father has compassion on his children, so the Lord has compassion on those who fear him; for he knows how we are formed, he remembers that we are dust.
> (Psalm 103 v 13 - 14)

God knows our weaknesses and has made provision for us. He is committed to supplying us with the necessary wisdom we need to tackle the trials of life.

Look again at James' encouragement to us:

> If any of you lacks wisdom, you should ask God, who gives generously to all without finding fault, and it will be given to you.
> (James 1 v 5)

When we are confused about the way forward and don't know what to do, he will guide us. If we're concerned we may not react in the right way, he will come alongside us. So, if we sense we are being motivated by fear rather than by faith, then we need to respond to God's amazing invitation.

James says God will answer our request by giving us wisdom generously, liberally, bountifully and without reserve. He will not find fault with us, which means he will not blame us for asking, nor look at us disapprovingly because we did not come up with our own answer. God does not want us to hesitate in coming to him in prayer and asking for wisdom.

Nobody is excluded or disqualified from asking and receiving his wisdom. James is referring to the God-given ability to apply spiritual insight into the true nature of things, and to outwork his truth in the practical issues of our everyday lives. Outworking of truth and spiritual insight sound like high callings! But be reassured, James says God gives this wisdom to *"all,"* not just some. To be very clear, this includes you!

Centrality Of Faith

However, there is a condition attached. James says that when we ask, we must ask in faith with a settled confidence in God, based on his character and his promises revealed in Scripture (see James 1 v 6). We need to have a firm conviction and be fully persuaded that God will be true to his promises and keep his word.

There can be no room for doubt, where we waver between trusting God and trusting the world or our own natural abilities. Doubt not only dishonours God but calls into question his generosity. Rather, we should be set on the firm expectation of receiving wisdom from him. Otherwise, we will be like a wave of the sea, blown and tossed by the wind, vulnerable to every changing circumstance or pressure. Not only will we discount ourselves from receiving the wisdom from the Lord we desperately need, but we could easily end up swamped and overwhelmed by life itself. Doubt breeds the confused state of being in two minds, which James calls double-mindedness, making us unstable and uncertain in everything we do. It's that important! We must come to God in faith, ready to battle and dismiss thoughts that might tell us anything other than, 'My God is good, he can be trusted, and he is for me!'

God's desire for his church and for believers is different and Paul speaks of believers as being, *"more than conquerors through him who loved us"* (Romans 8 v 38); even persecution, suffering and death are turned into good for followers of Christ. Just as sure as trouble and trials will come (see John 16 v 33), followers of Christ should be those that overcome them with God's provision of a loving church community, and the help of the Holy Spirit.

Trials, adverse circumstances, external threats and dangers are the stuff of life in a fallen world. They test our faith and trust in God, but by his grace we don't have to meet them with grumbling and complaining... still less with fear, anger or resentment. In contrast, God's power working within us can help us meet them with *"pure joy"* (James 1 v 2).

Therefore, we need to remember Paul's encouragements, which have sustained countless people met with the harsh reality of this broken world in their lives. For those of us who have been brought into an intimate and loving relationship with God, he is committed in his sovereignty to using everything we experience for our ultimate good. The trials we face, in God's providence, are not random or meaningless but have divine purpose. However loud our immediate circumstances may shout, or whatever our emotions may try to convince us, the truth of God's faithfulness remains:

> And we know that God causes everything to work together for the good of those who love God and are called according to his purpose for them. For God knew his people in advance, and he chose them to become like his Son, so that his Son would be the firstborn among many brothers.
> (Romans 8 v 28 - 29 NLT)

The *"good"* Paul speaks of in this verse is not earthly comforts, but is about us being conformed more and more into the likeness of his Son, Jesus. We must let go of our desires for a comfortable life and instead embrace and welcome a life of purpose, even when that includes hardship and suffering.

Trials will always be an opportunity to prove the genuineness of our faith and a means of deepening it for the future. They promote faithfulness so that we remain strong in our faith, and they help us to cultivate perseverance that lets us mature in Christ. Trials are common to Christians and non-believers, so handling our trials in a godly manner demonstrates to others that the eternal kingdom of God is breaking in on this age! The aim is not for the world to be in awe of our faith (although they may be), or to see some kind of emotionless stoicism, but rather to see and be invited into the hope that sustains us beyond the immediate:

> Blessed is the one who perseveres under trial because, having stood the test, that person will receive the crown of life that the Lord has promised to those who love him.
> (James 1 v 12)

CHAPTER TWELVE

We Are Family

One summer, while visiting family in the USA, we had the joy of walking through a forest of giant California redwood trees. These are the world's tallest trees, growing to over 300 feet tall and 30 feet across. Many live for hundreds of years.

Unlike many other trees, they do not have a tap root to anchor them deep into the ground. Their roots are shallow, only going down around ten or so feet. Instead, they are held up by lateral roots that intertwine with those of the other redwoods. They work together in an intricate network that travels for miles beyond each starting point, forming a sophisticated root system to sustain them all. As each tree indelibly connects with the roots of others, they form something like a felt mat which anchors and supports the collective.

I find this lesson from nature a helpful picture of God's intention for us as his children. In the same way, we are not meant to live solitary Christian lives! Rather, we are designed to be knitted into a community of believers from whom we can draw strength and encouragement, allowing all to grow together into the full stature of Christ. But it goes beyond just connectedness. In this community, all can find love, acceptance, help, forgiveness, hope and purpose. In a world of individuals, often too pre-occupied to care and experiencing unprecedented levels of loneliness, we're to enjoy being known within a caring church family. Here, we can be supported, be sustained, be anchored, and can grow alongside a diverse community of all ages, social backgrounds and ethnicities, who are united as one in Christ:

> So, in Christ Jesus you are all children of God through faith, for all of you who were baptized into Christ have clothed yourselves with Christ. There is neither Jew nor Gentile, neither slave nor free, nor is there male and female, for you are all one in Christ Jesus.
> (Galatians 3 v 26 - 28)

God's Household, Where His Family Are

When you become a Christian, you become part of a wider community. You become part of God's church, likened in the New Testament, to a household or family:

> Consequently, you are no longer foreigners and strangers, but fellow citizens with God's people and also members of his **household.**
> (Ephesians 2 v 19; emphasis added)

> Although I hope to come to you soon, I am writing you these instructions so that, if I am delayed, you will know how people ought to conduct themselves in God's **household,** which is the church of the living God, the pillar and foundation of the truth.
> (1 Timothy 3 v 14 - 15; emphasis added)

> Therefore, as we have opportunity, let us do good to all people, especially to those who belong to the **family of believers.**
> (Galatians 6 v 10; emphasis added)

These verses are a clear reminder that church life is essentially relational, to be conducted with the same care we should place on our family relationships. As such, we're meant to treat each other with love, as Paul shares when he instructs Timothy:

> Don't be harsh or impatient with an older man. Talk to him as you would your own father, and to the younger men as your brothers. Reverently honour an older woman as you would your mother, and younger women as sisters.
> (1 Timothy 5 v 1 - 2 MSG)

In these verses, Paul speaks of treating family members with honour, respect and reverence, telling us that our attitude should be one of gentleness, patience and grace. Of course, as we read this, we may see we have some work to do on our own family connections. Or perhaps, this picture of love is not something you have ever experienced in the earthly family you grew up in.

In many families today we see a very different picture to the honour Paul speaks of. In fact, human brokenness is often magnified in this context and it's not uncommon to see family members frequently put each other down, or being abusive to each other. In many cases, we see earthly families uninterested in each other's welfare and well-being, or readily looking for something to criticise. It doesn't sit right, it's not what we or God want to see, but it is all around. From my years as a church leader, I know the hurts of these family experiences run deep and this will resonate with many. If this is you, God does care deeply about where you've been placed, and he is committed to walking with you as you navigate your earthly relationships. He is also set on using his church to rewrite your experience of family and restore what has been lost.

As members of God's family and across our church communities, we are called to live very differently, by loving each other as Christ loves us (see John 13 v 34 - 35; John 15 v 12).

In Romans, Chapter 15, Paul describes the kind of caring family God is seeking to build. He is looking for a family where the strong lend a hand to those struggling to live out their faith, and where each family member looks out for the good of others around them. Here, brothers and sisters will spot need and consistently ask, 'How can I help you?' People will encourage and build one another up, and a spirit of unity and togetherness should pervade everything.

However, from our own experience of church life, we know any church family also brings challenges. There are people we naturally gel with or find easy to get on with, and others we find 'hard work.' It's why so many of us discover Paul's words to be a real challenge!

> Accept one another, then, just as Christ accepted you, in order to bring praise to God.
> (Romans 15 v 7)

Acceptance

Maintaining a right view of ourselves is crucial. When we think seriously about Christ's abundant love for us, we're quickly reminded how we were accepted 'just as we were,' with all our faults, failings, selfishness and sinfulness. Our complete acceptance came at a time when we were hostile in mind and deed towards him, completely powerless to help ourselves. Yet here we now stand - forgiven, accepted, fully known and fully loved.

Thankfully, we know his acceptance did not rely on us first making major changes to our behaviour, or on our initial compliance with God's instructions for right living. Nor did we have to attain to some high level of understanding of spiritual truths. It wasn't even dependent upon any expression of love towards him on our part. Rather, our unconditional acceptance rested solely on God's mercy and grace, revealed in Jesus' death for us on the cross:

> But God demonstrates his own love for us in this: While we were still sinners, Christ died for us.
> (Romans 5 v 8)

It is only by our union with Jesus, and the power of the Holy Spirit, that we can truly learn to accept one another... warts and all!

But what does this mean in practical terms?

The original word Paul uses for "accept" is rich in meaning, and translates as 'to welcome, or to take to oneself.' The central idea is to receive someone into one's own society or friendship group, treating them with the utmost kindness and actively showing them that they belong. Let me offer a few illustrations to convey the kind of response Paul is looking for from the family of God.

Paul wants us to welcome one another with a genuine warmth, just as in the story of the prodigal son, where the father has been waiting for his lost son to return home. When he does return, the father runs to meet him and embraces him. In the same way, the family of God are called to joyfully embrace all who come home to our Heavenly Father.

He also wants us to build genuine relationships with one another. I liken it to the way a special delivery by post has to be signed for before the gift package can be received. There must be an intentional act of the will, with a deliberate choosing to accept others as God's gift to us, and to the whole church family. There is to be no room for reluctance or any attitude of, 'OK I will welcome them if I *have* to!'

What Paul is looking for can be seen in a marriage ceremony, where both bride and groom are asked separately, 'Will you take this person to be your husband or wife?' Not only is a deliberate act of the will required, but an earnest commitment is made to share life together, through the good times and the bad. This decision must be accompanied by a sincere vow to take responsibility for each other's welfare. Similarly, for Paul, the family ethos in the community of believers is to be one where people don't look to their own interests but to the interests of the others (see Philippians 2 v 4).

Do we really have to accept everyone in this way? Is this too much to ask? I think not, particularly when we consider the call to love others in relation to our own complete and underserved acceptance. Think about these questions, which I ask because they've challenged me over the years:

- Do I avoid conversations with some people after a service on a Sunday?
- How do I feel seeing a new Christian, whose life is still outwardly 'messy,' worshipping wholeheartedly?
- What about when a new person joins my settled house group, which is full of close friends I like spending quality time with? How do I feel then?

Paul also makes it clear that the purpose of our acceptance and heartfelt welcome of others is not primarily for our own blessing, but is a way *"to bring praise to God"* (Romans 15 v 7). The goal of church family relationships is to bring God honour and proclaim him as Lord to the world. We need to choose (and learn) to acknowledge each other's value and unique contribution to church life, to willingly take responsibility for each other's well-being, and work towards living together in harmony and unity. From here, the world can see God's wisdom manifested before their eyes.

Wouldn't this be wonderful, not least because it is so very needed! However, the current state of the Church, or your own experience, might discourage you from thinking this could ever be a reality. If so, let us remember what Jesus prayed to his Father:

> "I do not ask for these only, but also for those who will believe in me through their word, that they may all be one, just as you, Father, are in me, and I in you, that they also may be in us, so that the world may believe that you have sent me. The glory that you have given me I have given to them, that they may be one even as we are one, I in them and you in me, that they may become perfectly one, so that the world may know that you sent me and loved them even as you loved me."
> (John 17 v 20 - 23 ESV)

Jesus prayed it, and so must we.

Dear church! With God's help, we can see this happen. There are many stories of people finding faith after looking in, joining in, and then experiencing church family as different to anything they've known before. We can not only have confidence that Jesus' prayer will be answered, but Scripture tells us the ascended Jesus has given gifts to his church to help bring this about:

> Now these are the gifts Christ gave to the church: the apostles, the prophets, the evangelists, and the pastors and teachers. Their responsibility is to equip God's people to do his work and build up the church, the body of Christ. This will continue until we all come to such unity in our faith and knowledge of God's Son that we will be mature in the Lord, measuring up to the full and complete standard of Christ.
> (Ephesians 4 v 11 - 13 NLT)

Unity and maturity are the objectives Jesus has for his church. He wants to see a united community, where every person is growing in spiritual maturity to become more and more like him. Paul reflects this goal when he writes to the believers at Colossae:

> He is the one we proclaim, admonishing and teaching everyone with all wisdom, so that we may present everyone fully mature in Christ. To this end I strenuously contend with all the energy Christ so powerfully works in me.
> (Colossians 1 v 28 - 29)

Context Of Community

It is important we are clear on the best context and environment for our growth into maturity – where this development is designed to take place. Both Paul and other New Testament writers are clear that growth occurs in the context of the family of God. Here, we should find relationships where each person is seeking to help others move further along the path towards maturity in Christ. We should experience a safe space, where people are open to the encouragement and wisdom of others, as well as to their loving admonition and correction.

It is interesting how frequently the phrase, 'one another,' is used in the New Testament when addressing believers' attitudes and actions within their community. You will see the phrase used to highlight positive encouragement for people to:

> *care for; pray; encourage; teach; warn; comfort; be devoted to; honour; be kind and compassionate; forgive; serve; and offer hospitality.*

At other times, we see it used in relation to damaging negative characteristics we should not show, including:

> *do not bite and devour; pass judgement; grumble against; slander; lie to; provoke; or envy.*

These are all issues that centre on our relationships with 'one another.' How we think about our church community and how we act and behave here matters. I remember hearing a Christian leader teaching on the challenges of this truth:

> *'I always considered myself to be an extremely patient man when I was on my own. It was only when I began to interact with other people around me that my impatience was aroused, and the true nature of my fallen humanity was exposed!'*

No man or woman is an island and able to attain spiritual maturity alone. Sharing in each other's everyday lives provides us with the opportunity to change, develop and grow more like Jesus. We need to be in meaningful relationships with other believers for this growth to happen – staying connected to other 'redwoods' in the shape of Christian brothers and sisters.

Your church community needs what you uniquely bring, for it to be at its best. We may have some sympathy with others who say, 'I love Jesus, but I don't like the church.' Of course, relationships are messy and take work but they're critical, they're worth it, and they're in need of your commitment. I love the challenge that one church leader presents on this topic:

> *If you are following Jesus, he will always lead you back to His bride. Jesus' intention is that you would be connected with other believers to sing, study the Bible, evangelise, baptise, and remember His sacrifice by taking communion.*[1]

Meeting Together

We are not the only generation that has grappled with the vital importance of God's people sharing their everyday lives together. It is a choice and an act of the will to continue to gather regularly to pray, have fellowship, break bread, and be taught God's word. Naturally, because it's a choice, there's inherently a temptation to opt for something else. In the book of Hebrews, we discover that some of the early believers had stopped meeting together. Indeed for some, not meeting had become so frequent, it had become habitual and a regular pattern of living:

> Let us hold unswervingly to the hope we profess, for he who promised is faithful. And let us consider how we may spur one another on toward love and good deeds, not giving up meeting together, as some are in the habit of doing, but encouraging one another—and all the more as you see the Day approaching.
> (Hebrews 10 v 23 - 25)

The writer uses strong language when he warns believers not to, *"give up meeting together,"* with the original translation meaning, 'to leave, forsake or abandon.' It carries the sense of deliberately walking out or away and leaving others to struggle on their own, like a parent walking away from their family responsibilities.

For the writer, this was both unacceptable and serious. Not only because it left others shouldering the work of God, but because he knew it would be detrimental to their own spiritual health and well-being. A loving community of believers is the setting where your growth happens. As such, not meeting meant they were missing their opportunity to develop and grow, as well as the chance to meet and encounter God!

Gathering together was an opportunity for them to give time and attention to working out how they could spur, stimulate, encourage, provoke, and sharpen one another towards love and doing what is good. In the same way as a rider uses his spurs to provoke their horse to action, so we are called to sharpen each other's faith, awaken each other's feelings, and stir each other to action!

Genuine Love

The love we are to exhibit should reflect God's love, which is not weak and passive, but intentional, active and powerful. One writer speaks of love in this way:

> *Christian love, whether exercised toward the brethren, or toward men generally, is not an impulse from the feelings, it does not always run with the natural inclinations, nor does it spend itself only upon those for whom some affinity is discovered. Love seeks the welfare of all.*[2]

Paul writes in a similar manner to the Galatians:

> Therefore, as we have opportunity, let us do good to all people, especially to those who belong to the family of believers.
> (Galatians 6 v 10)

Love not only takes advantage of an opportunity to do good, but it is always seeking the opportunity to do so in a way that builds up the church. Just as we saw in the passage from Hebrews, it is our responsibility to think about, ponder and reflect on how we can stir up one another to do this good.

Sadly, Christians can find themselves caricatured as negative people, known more for what they oppose or stand against, than for what they champion and promote. When people think of a Christian, they may think about what they don't do, rather than what they accomplish. Even the word, 'do gooder,' can have negative connotations of being meddlers, self-righteous, or constantly interfering with other people's business. And when it comes to matters of justice, because of our emphasis on forgiveness, we can be wrongly seen as those who let the guilty go free! Even when the intentions of believers are good, the Christian life takes wisdom and support to navigate.

The picture of believers in the New Testament is far more positive. Here, we see followers of Jesus focused on the good of others, lacking in self-interest and full of self-sacrifice. We want to see this in our churches today, with believers characterised by and known for their expressions of love, kindness and compassion. We want Christians to be seen as secure, stable and sociable, living life to the full, while caring for the sick, the disabled and the marginalised. We want our churches and those in them to reflect the character of Jesus:

> "You know what happened throughout the province of Judea, beginning in Galilee after the baptism that John preached – how God anointed Jesus of Nazareth with the Holy Spirit and power, and how **he went around doing good** and healing all who were under the power of the devil, because God was with him."
> (Acts 10 v 37 - 38; emphasis added)

Eager To Do Good

Disciples of Jesus are eager to do good. It's a natural response to his love, his sacrifice and the work of the Holy Spirit in our life:

> Jesus Christ gave himself for us to redeem us from all wickedness and to purify for himself a people that are his very own, **eager to do what is good.**
> (Titus 2 v 14; emphasis added)

> This is a trustworthy saying. And I want you to stress these things, so that those who have trusted in God may be careful to devote themselves to **doing what is good.** These things are excellent and profitable for everyone.
> (Titus 3 v 8; emphasis added)

It is right to want to make a difference and seek purpose for our lives. Such feelings are a stirring of the Holy Spirit, for we have been saved by grace to do the good works he has prepared for us to do:

> For we are God's handiwork, created in Christ Jesus **to do good works,** which God prepared in advance for us to do.
> (Ephesians 2 v 10; emphasis added)

Our gathering together and sharing of life is designed to provoke one another to do these good works! They are not beyond our capability or reserved for 'super saints,' but they become part of life for every individual believer. Sometimes doing the will of God from the heart may appear very ordinary, but however small these things appear, they are precious in God's sight. Just look at the examples

Paul gives to show the value placed on 'ordinary' behaviours in a widow's life, as she should be known and honoured for:

> ...her good deeds, such as bringing up children, showing hospitality, washing the feet of the Lord's people, helping those in trouble and devoting herself to all kinds of good deeds.
> (1 Timothy 5 v 10)

Good works are much harder when operating in isolation and outside of church community; over time they will invariably become less purposeful and less frequent. All of God's people need contexts where they can meet and be encouraged to do good. Especially, in the light of the coming *"Day"* of the Lord (Hebrews 10 v 25). Beyond worshipping together on a Sunday, meeting together regularly in a small group within church life is one such context. Indeed, these smaller group settings serve as important building blocks of authentic Christian communities - countless believers will link their personal growth to the close relationships formed here.

Meaningful Relationships

We all need a setting where we can build genuine friendships and share the full journeys of our lives together, both highs and lows.

We thrive in relationships where we hold each other accountable to obey the commands of Christ to love God, love one another and love the lost. Through friendship we can support each other in our daily work, so we each develop a sense of purpose as we seek to extend God's kingdom in our personal spheres of influence. And we need a place of challenge, where we can provoke and help each other to reach out in our networks of unchurched friends, sharing the gospel with them in word and deed.

God also knows our need for love, care and compassion. Church community provides a set of safe relationships where we can take off our masks and receive encouragement and healing for our lives. It offers the primary space where individuals and families can be looked after, and where the *"one another"* verses of the New Testament can be worked out. Relationship is the place, 'where the rubber hits the road!' It creates an environment where we can grapple together with our understanding of God's word and its application to our lives, bringing about spiritual maturity and Christlikeness.

We need to learn to live life together in such a way that we experience Christ's presence together, through the Holy Spirit. As we do, we're moved to express our love to him in worship by offering our whole lives as living sacrifices, as well as showing our passion for him in our witness.

The writer of Hebrews does not tell us why some people had stopped meeting together. Perhaps it was no longer a high priority on their personal agenda, or they saw it as being of no personal value or benefit to them. Or was it simply they had found themselves 'too busy,' or they could not be bothered? The context of the passage seems to suggest the reason may have been that they had either fallen back into a sinful lifestyle or found it too costly to identify with the people of God in an ungodly society. Perhaps some had prized material possessions over their eternal reward. Either way, none of these explanations would be out of place in our modern context – the challenge well and truly remains today.

What we do know is that we all have an enemy, out to destroy our Christian walk and witness. We also know the influence of the world is strong, with the ability to erode our trust in God in the absence of the right support. Alongside these, we also have the battle we fight against our own fleshly appetites and desires. It's not easy, and Paul seems to indicate that as *"the Day"* approaches, the more difficult it will be to stand for Christ. Hence the vital need for us to gather regularly, share our lives, and receive personal encouragement to nourish our souls:

> You should know this, Timothy, that in the last days there will be very difficult times. For people will love only themselves and their money. They will be boastful and proud, scoffing at God, disobedient to their parents, and ungrateful. They will consider nothing sacred. They will be unloving and unforgiving; they will slander others and have no self-control; they will be cruel and have no interest in what is

> good. They will betray their friends, be reckless, be puffed up with pride, and love pleasure rather than God. They will act as if they are religious, but they will reject the power that could make them godly. You must stay away from people like that.
> (2 Timothy 3 v 1 - 5 NLT)

Serious Consequences

The consequences of not meeting together regularly for worship and mutual encouragement can be serious. I've seen how it can lead us to: fall short of our full potential in God; become vulnerable to the shipwrecking of our faith; be swept along on the tide of evil that is speeding the world to destruction; and fail to make a lasting impact through the gospel in our generation.

We can take courage from the words of the writer in Hebrews about the risk of returning to a former way of ungodly living:

> Even though we speak like this, dear friends, we are convinced of better things in your case—the things that have to do with salvation. God is not unjust; he will not forget your work and the love you have shown him as you have helped his people and continue to help them. We want each of you to show this same diligence to the very end, so that what you hope for may be fully realized. We do not want you to become lazy, but to imitate those who through faith and patience inherit what has been promised.
> (Hebrews 6 v 9 - 12)

I urge us to see the vital importance of this teaching. Our involvement in a thriving church community, where we form genuine Christian relationships, safeguard us against this danger. As we examine our own lives, may we discover that meeting together with other believers does indeed have top priority. If not, may God grant us a change of heart to make the necessary adjustments to our lifestyles. By his grace, may we determine in future to be diligent in meeting together, becoming masters in the art of encouraging and provoking one another to love and good works. And let's do so all the more as we see the Day approaching!

Tuning Up – A Lesson From Music

Did you know? In modern day orchestras everybody tunes to the oboe, with the standard concert pitch being 'A' (440 hertz, or 440 vibrations a second).

The oboe is chosen because it is least affected by humidity and weather conditions and its penetrating sound stands out from other instruments, making it easy for all musicians to hear. Its pitch is steadier than the strings and is therefore a more reliable tuning source. Once each instrument is tuned with the oboe, they are naturally also in tune with each other.

If by God's grace we seek to ensure our lives are lived in tune with Jesus, we will also find ourselves increasingly in tune with each other. Imagine the potential for us, as members of God's family experiencing his abundant blessings in our loving communities, to then model unity and harmony to the world.

> How good and pleasant it is
> when God's people live together in unity!
>
> It is like precious oil poured on the head,
> running down on the beard,
> running down on Aaron's beard,
> down on the collar of his robe.
>
> It is as if the dew of Hermon
> were falling on Mount Zion.
>
> For there the Lord bestows his blessing,
> even life forevermore.
>
> (Psalm 133)

Notes

1 Rob Shepherd, 13/01/2017 - I love Jesus, But I don't like the church, www.robshep.com

2 Expository Dictionary of New Testament Words by W.E. Vine. Published by Oliphants 1975. ISBN 0 551 00282 4. Page 21 - Love

CHAPTER THIRTEEN

One New People

Equality, like tolerance, is one of the main tenets of our generation. In October 2007, the UK government set up a new department called the Government Equalities Office (GEO). This department was given lead responsibility for gender equality within the UK government and was tasked to provide advice on all other forms of equality, including age, race, sexual orientation and disability.

This action was followed closely in 2010 by the Equality Act. You may have seen, read or received training based around the following benchmarks to protect:

> *"...equal treatment in access to employment as well as private and public services, regardless of the protected characteristics of age, disability, gender reassignment, marriage and civil partnership, race, religion or belief, sex, and sexual orientation."*[1]

In the same year the Prime Minister, David Cameron, appointed a cabinet minister for Women and Equalities, showing the extent to which equality was high on the government's agenda.

Maybe part of the reason for this was that many people in our culture were sick of gender wars, class distinction, racial division, and the inequality we see between the people groups in our world. That said, there has always been a big difference in the way people respond to these issues.

British philosopher, Bertrand Russell, cynically comments:

> *In America everybody is of the opinion that he has no social superiors, since all men are equal, but he does not admit that he has no social inferiors, for, from the time of Jefferson onward, the doctrine that all men are equal applies only upwards, not downwards.*[2]

Henry Mencken, an American scholar, despairingly remarks:

> *Equality before the law is probably forever unattainable. It is a noble ideal, but it can never be realized, for what men value in this world is not "rights" but privileges.*[3]

More recently the American writer, C. JoyBell C., has shared her belief in, and optimism for, a different kind of equality:

> *The downfall of the attempts of governments and leaders to unite mankind is found in this – in the wrong message that we should see everyone as the same.*
>
> *This is the root of the failure of harmony. Because the truth is, we should not all see everyone as the same! We are not the same! We are made of different colours and we have different cultures. We are all different!*
>
> *But the key to this door is to look at these differences, respect these differences, learn from and about these differences, and grow in and with these differences. We are all different. We are not the same. But that's beautiful. And that's okay.*
>
> *In the quest for unity and peace, we cannot blind ourselves and expect to be all the same. Because in this, we all have an underlying belief that everyone should be the same as us at some point.*
>
> *We are not on a journey to become the same or to be the same. But we are on a journey to see that in all of our differences, that is what makes us beautiful as a human race, and if we are ever to grow, we ought to learn and always learn some more.*[4]

The big question of course is, *will it ever be possible for people to be united and on an equal footing*? Can there be unity while we maintain and celebrate diversity? Does the gospel have anything to say on this subject?

Faith In Christ

In his letter to the Galatians, Paul reminds them of the enormous difference Christ's coming has made to the human race, and how faith in him brings about transformation in our human relationships. He underlines that the *"new man"* or *"one people"* created by Christ, is rooted in acceptance and equality:

> Before the way of faith in Christ was available to us, we were placed under guard by the law. We were kept in protective custody, so to speak, until the way of faith was revealed. Let me put it another way. The law was our guardian until Christ came; it protected us until we could be made right with God through faith. And now that the way of faith has come, we no longer need the law as our guardian.
>
> For you are all children of God through faith in Christ Jesus. And all who have been united with Christ in baptism have put on Christ, like putting on new clothes. There is no longer Jew or Gentile, slave or free, male and female. For you are all one in Christ Jesus. And now that you belong to Christ, you are the true children of Abraham. You are his heirs, and God's promise to Abraham belongs to you.
>
> (Galatians 3 v 24 - 29 NLT)

If you remove the burden of sin and guilt, along with the need to strive to earn acceptance, the human heart is free to love and relate radically differently. In these verses Paul explains that as followers of Jesus Christ, they were no longer under the law, which in the past had played the role of their guardian or tutor. While the law had provided some restraint on their behaviour and given them guidance on how to live and please God, it had never been able to empower them to live a pure life. But now, all that had changed. Through Jesus, *"the way of faith"* had come, and that makes all the difference.

With the coming of Jesus Christ, a new day had dawned, and a new covenant had begun. And by God's grace and mercy, great numbers (especially Gentiles) had responded to God's word in repentance and faith. People no longer trusted in themselves but put their trust in Jesus for their salvation. God fulfilled his ancient promise to give believers new hearts, and the genuineness of people's faith was expressed in their obedience to the will of God.

In this new covenant, people no longer saw God as the evaluator of their performance. Now, they experienced him as their Heavenly Father who delighted in enjoying loving intimacy and relationship with them. Paul knew the importance of the church fully grasping the amazing transformation that had taken place in their lives, now they had put their faith in Christ. The truth of their acceptance, forgiveness and new identity was unshakeable – the extent to which they took hold of it would determine their growth and maturity.

All Children Of God

What does the Bible say about people groups and equality? In the past, Israel was seen as the special, elected nation of God, while the Gentiles were viewed as outsiders:

> Don't forget that you Gentiles used to be outsiders. You were called "uncircumcised heathens" by the Jews, who were proud of their circumcision, even though it affected only their bodies and not their hearts. In those days you were living apart from Christ. You were excluded from citizenship among the people of Israel, and you did not know the covenant promises God had made to them. You lived in this world without God and without hope. But now you have been united with Christ Jesus. Once you were far away from God, but now you have been brought near to him through the blood of Christ.
> (Ephesians 2 v 11 - 13 NLT)

Paul is at pains to emphasise that all those who have put their faith in Christ are true children of God. No one *"united with Christ Jesus"* must relate to God as judge and fear his punishment like prisoners awaiting execution. Instead, as adopted, accepted and forgiven children, all can enjoy knowing him as their Father. Both Jew and Gentile were now able to find peace in the security of being loved consistently and completely, meaning they could revel in their new status. Of course, the idea of 'Jew and Gentile' extends to the heart of *any* human coming to realise their need for Jesus and putting their trust in him.

The Apostle John also comments on the amazing transformation that has taken place because of us putting our faith in Christ. What a status God's people enjoy!

> What marvellous love the Father has extended to us! Just look at it—we're called children of God! That's who we really are. But that's also why the world doesn't recognize us or takes us seriously, because it has no idea who he is or what he's up to. But friends, that's exactly who we are: children of God. And that's only the beginning. Who knows how we'll end up! What we know is that when Christ is openly revealed, we'll see him—and in seeing him, become like him. All of us who look forward to his coming stay ready, with the glistening purity of Jesus' life as a model for our own.
> (1 John 3 v 1 - 3 MSG)

United With Christ

We also see Paul reminding the Galatians of their baptism. This act was an outward and visible sign of their union with Christ, secured by their faith in Jesus' death and resurrection. Just as water cleanses, so Jesus had cleansed them from their sin. But baptism was not only a picture of what Jesus had done for them by *his own* life, death, burial and resurrection. By being immersed in water and coming up again, they demonstrated their own union with Christ's death and resurrection, in order that *they too* might live a new life!

Being united to Christ meant that all his benefits and privilege became available to them. They were enabled by this union to do the kind of things he did, including becoming more and more like him in his obedience and honouring of his Father. By getting rid of, dispensing of, or throwing off their old identity, they were empowered to live out their new identity in Him.

Put On Christ

As the old identity is taken off, so a wonderful transaction takes place. Paul reminds them, *"all who have been united with Christ in baptism have put on Christ, like putting on new clothes*" (Galatians 3 v 27). Some commentators claim this is a reference to the Toga Virilis (toga of manhood), a garment a boy of fifteen would put on as he entered manhood. It was a symbol of both manhood and citizenship, demonstrating that he had grown up and was no longer under the supervision of a tutor or guardian. He belonged somewhere new and was now a citizen of a new place, with a new identity - in this case, he had moved into adulthood. It marked the fact that he had a new status and new privileges to enjoy, belonging to grown up sons.

Here, then, is our reminder that, *"in Christ,"* the believer has a new status and new privileges. Do you notice we keep coming back to it? Your new identity, is your new identify, is your new identity - we must repeat this life-changing, peace-giving, power-releasing truth throughout our lives. Just like us, the Galatians were no longer *"in Adam"* but were *"in Christ"*(1 Corinthians 15 v 22) - the old had gone and new had come. They were sons and daughters of God, heirs of the promise made to Abraham, and inheritors of the kingdom of God.

Members Of A New People

This new status and these new privileges are shared equally by all those united to Christ through faith, no matter what their racial background, social standing or gender. Paul emphasises this oneness and unity in Christ:

> There is no longer Jew or Gentile, slave or free, male and female. For you are all one in Christ Jesus.
> (Galatians 3 v 28)

As you can imagine, this teaching and changing of deep-rooted thinking was not a 'one and done' conversation. Paul also wrote to the church at Ephesus to deal with the centuries-old hostility between Jews and non-Jews. The message was the same because the truth is the same - Christ had brought the hostility to an end through his death on the cross, creating in himself one new people:

> For Christ himself has brought peace to us. He united Jews and Gentiles into one people when, in his own body on the cross, he broke down the wall of hostility that separated us. He did this by ending the system of law with its commandments and regulations. He made peace between Jews and Gentiles by creating in himself one new people from the two groups. Together as one body, Christ reconciled both groups to God by means of his death on the cross, and our hostility toward each other was put to death.
>
> He brought this Good News of peace to you Gentiles who were far away from him, and peace to the Jews who were near. Now all of us can come to the Father through the same Holy Spirit because of what Christ has done for us.
>
> (Ephesians 2 v 14 - 18 NLT)

Look at how The Message paraphrases verses 17 and 18:

> Christ brought us together through his death on the cross. The Cross got us to embrace, and that was the end of the hostility. Christ came and preached peace to you outsiders and peace to us insiders. He treated us as equals, and so made us equals. Through him we both share the same Spirit and have equal access to the Father.

Their challenge, just like ours, was to let this truth renew their minds, change their hearts and transform what they had always (or habitually) thought on these matters.

Through faith in Christ, we all have the privilege of being part of this new people of God. We are now characterised by acceptance and equality, meaning as those who belong to God and one another, we can relate as true brothers and sisters. Relating to each other in such a way should mean we give no power to things which normally distinguish and divide mankind, such as racial, social and sexual status. We are a people who express the reality of being one in Christ Jesus, with the literal translation being, "You are all one person in Christ." Paul is crystal clear on this unity in Christ. He considers it a grave error (or an anathema) for any person to think their Jewishness, free status, maleness, or any other earthly qualification should count as the basis of their inclusion into God's family, or as something meriting them a greater share of God's inheritance.

It's so very relevant to us today! As a white, Western, educated male, I'd be foolish to think the Holy Spirit hasn't had to work hard to prompt and free me of cultural tendencies towards privileged thinking. Sadly, there are still many in our world who consider themselves better or holier than others by reason of their gender, education, racial or religious status, class or social background. Many would claim their economic standing should mean greater status and privilege for themselves and their families. Invariably they like to position themselves against others and think that they have some measure of holiness or increased virtue because of something that they are or possess.

Paul was clear that even though Israel had been entrusted with God's unique self-revelation, both Jew and Gentile stood in need of being saved. Both were equal in their inability to earn or deserve forgiveness, but were equally offered the free gift of salvation through faith in Christ. They were now both members of God's new people, so their previous hostility could be transformed into friendship and family. As fellow citizens and members of God's household, distinctions of rank and status were rendered void, as were the circumstances of birth, wealth, privilege and education.

There was also a re-defining of male and female relationships. Women, who had regularly been despised, exploited and ill-treated in society, were placed on an equal footing with men. Men and women would share together in all the benefits of being in Christ, as shown when Peter speaks of husbands and wives being *"heirs together"* of the grace of life:

> In the same way, you husbands must give honour to your wives. Treat your wife with understanding as you live together. She may be weaker than you are, but **she is your equal partner in God's gift of new life.** Treat her as you should so your prayers will not be hindered.
> (1 Peter 3 v 7 NLT; emphasis added)

Distinctions Remain

It is important at this juncture to say that racial, social and sexual distinctions are, nevertheless, not eradicated. We are not colour blind, we still notice a person's skin colour, and we are still aware that people come from different cultural and educational backgrounds. Every person belongs to a certain race and nation, having been nurtured in a particular culture. Neither do we ignore a person's sex, not treating a woman as if she was a man, or a man as if he were a woman.

New life in Christ does not mean differences don't exist; it means they no longer matter or define our relationships. While they still create barriers for many across our broken world, the Holy Spirit empowers Christ's *"one people"* to shine all the more brightly as ministers of friendship, fellowship and understanding. We are equal before him, but he is certainly not trying to make us all the same – our distinctions remain. As Christ has dealt with our inequality, we're able to view and enjoy our individuality as part of how God uniquely made us. Indeed, our differences benefit our witness because they demonstrate the power of the gospel to reach all human hearts and unite them with one truth.

I particularly like this reflection on unity, diversity and distinctiveness:

> *The aim of unity is not to supersede diversity; it is to celebrate it. Seeking togetherness by eradicating difference is not a full reflection of the community God has given us.*
>
> *By disregarding people's ethnicity or cultural background, we risk devaluing or entirely losing their contribution to the church family.*[5]

The love, grace and kindness of God our Father enables us to live together in unity and harmony. The young poor white man and the rich old black woman are friends because of Jesus. The Cambridge academic and the car mechanic are friends because of Jesus. The single mum and the businesswoman are friends because of Jesus. And the best is still to come! In Revelation, we see in the description of heaven, people from every tribe and nation gathered round God's throne, still retaining their distinctiveness, yet fully unified!

> After this I saw a vast crowd, too great to count, from every nation and tribe and people and language, standing in front of the throne and before the Lamb. They were clothed in white robes and held palm branches in their hands. And they were shouting with a great roar,
>
> "Salvation comes from our God who sits on the throne
> and from the Lamb!"
>
> (Revelation 7 v 9 - 10 NLT)

One of the reasons for the breakdown in society is that many of us separate into, and stay within, affinity groups. We only like to associate or get together with people we consider to be like us, or we perceive as being the same as us. We can feel more comfortable around people of our own race, our own gender, those who are like-minded, or those who share our own interests. But Jesus enables us to experience real community by eliminating inequality, bias and affinity, meaning we can be one. He empowers us to build genuine loving relationships with people who are totally different to us.

We still have our race, culture, ethnicity, gender, socio-economic status or financial obligations, but he makes us *"one people,"* so we can live as God's family. We are unified because each of us is loved equally by God, enabling us to love one another with changed and grateful hearts. With our distinctiveness remaining, more than ever we're to seek understanding in differences like race or culture, meaning they can be enjoyed by all. By acknowledging our differences, we can live in unity *and* celebrate our diversity.

Diversity is a sign of maturity and evidence we have come of age, leaving the guardianship of the law behind and becoming, by faith in Christ, the true children of the living God. As Abraham's seed, we are heirs according to the promise of God and can take our place in the historical succession of God's people of faith. Our lives have eternal meaning because they are centred in the unfolding purposes of God. Beautifully, this unifying meaning is shared by each individual Christian, within each church community, across all fellowships worldwide.

Time And Effort

That said, we cannot deny that working out our unity and diversity requires time and effort on our part. Our personal commitment must be intentional, for good and godly relationships do not develop overnight. We must learn to prioritise people over projects, and even our Christian service when needed. Moving from the superficial to meaningful, loving understanding requires an investment of ourselves, our time, energy, finances and emotional capacity:

> As a prisoner for the Lord, then, I urge you to live a life worthy of the calling you have received. Be completely humble and gentle; be patient, bearing with one another in love. **Make every effort to keep the unity of the Spirit through the bond of peace.** There is one body and one Spirit, just as you were called to one hope when you were called; one Lord, one faith, one baptism; one God and Father of all, who is over all and through all and in all.
> (Ephesians 4 v 1 - 6; emphasis added)

More than ever, it is a time for us to *"make every effort"* to build relationships, to honour each other, to learn from each other, to be enriched by each other, and to celebrate our oneness in Christ.

The Christian leader, Ajith Fernando, helpfully reminds us that we are called to a corporate life of togetherness in our Christian communities:

> *We are involved in church not primarily because it helps us to be good Christians but because Christianity is essentially a corporate life. You cannot have Christianity without corporate life, because you cannot have an individual part of a body, like a finger or a toe, without its connection to the body. Community living is an aspect of who we are.*
>
> *We miss the blessings of community when we try to avoid the inconveniences that come with community.*[6]

I want to leave the last word in this chapter to Yemi Adedeji, Director of the One People Commission at the Evangelical Alliance. Writing on both the importance and challenge of integration in our churches, he wonderfully helps us to see the direction in which we all need to travel:

> *There is a big difference between accepting diversity, becoming inclusive and pursuing integration. Embracing diversity is like inviting people to the party. Inclusion is inviting them to dance. But integration means we host the party together.*[7]

Notes

1 www.legislation.gov.uk/ukpga/2010/15/contents

2 www.brainyquote.com/quotes/bertrand_russell_105013

3 www.goodreads.com/quotes/130597-equality-before-the-law-is-probably-forever-unattainable-it-is

4 www.goodreads.com/quotes/362424-the-downfall-of-the-attempts-of-governments-and-leaders-to

5 The Impossible Dream – Believing for an integrated, ethnically diverse church by Steve Clifford, Yemi Adedeji and voices from the One People Commission. Copyright © Evangelical Alliance 2019. Published by the Evangelical Alliance. Pages 32 & 33

6 Ajith Fernando – Discipling in a Multicultural World, Copyright © 2019, p 60 & 63. Used by permission of Crossway, a publishing ministry of Good News Publishers, Wheaton, IL 60187, www.crossway.org

7 The Impossible Dream – Believing for an integrated, ethnically diverse church by Steve Clifford, Yemi Adedeji and voices from the One People Commission. Copyright © Evangelical Alliance 2019. Published by the Evangelical Alliance. Page 39

CHAPTER FOURTEEN

Contending As One Man

In my childhood, one of the most popular series on television was "The Three Musketeers," based on the well-known classic by Alexandre Dumas. Even if you have not read the book, you may well have come across the famous quote from it, *"All for one and one for all, united we stand, divided we fall."*

But did you know there is a similar thought to be found in the book of Philippians, where Paul urges the church at Philippi to stand together as one man?

> Whatever happens, conduct yourselves in a manner worthy of the gospel of Christ. Then, whether I come and see you or only hear about you in my absence, I will know that you stand firm in the one Spirit, striving together as one for the faith of the gospel without being frightened in any way by those who oppose you. This is a sign to them that they will be destroyed, but that you will be saved—and that by God. (Philippians 1 v 27 - 28)

Gospel Proclamation

Paul knew unity in the local church impacts the sharing of our faith, and that loving one another acts as a key witness and argument for the truth of the gospel. Our unity is critically connected to the task of gospel proclamation, which is reflected in Jesus' own prayers:

> "My prayer is not for them alone. I pray also for those who will believe in me through their message, that all of them may be one, Father, just as you are in me and I am in you.

> May they also be in us so that the world may believe that you have sent me. I have given them the glory that you gave me, that they may be one as we are one—I in them and you in me—so that they may be brought to complete unity. Then the world will know that you sent me and have loved them even as you have loved me."
> (John 17 v 20 - 23)

I have no doubt Paul would have also concurred with Ian Galloway's reflection:

> *Disciple-making is inviting your brother, your friends and your community to come and join the party. This is not a closed clique or a self-help group or a meet-my-needs session. Disciple-making is finding yourself being caught up in the mission of Jesus to save the world.*[1]

The early church was completely caught up in their focus on proclaiming the gospel to the world. We see this described clearly by pastor and author, David Mathis, when commenting on the unifying mission shared by believers:

> *The koinonia – the commonality, partnership, fellowship – which the first Christians shared wasn't a common love for pizza, drinks, and a nice clean evening of fun among fellow church members. It was their common Christ, and their common life-or-death mission together in his summons to take the faith worldwide in the face of impending persecution.*[2]

God's plan for the church today is to cultivate this same unity and impact. It is through the church, worked out in people like you and I, that God will display his manifold wisdom in its rich variety (see Ephesians 3 v 10 - 11). Across the countless communities of believers worldwide, he will make known his eternal purposes *"to bring unity to all things in heaven and on earth under Christ"* (Ephesians 1 v 10). Together, we are a living declaration to the world of the truth and power of the gospel.

Paul describes the work proclaiming Christ as spreading the fragrance of the knowledge of him everywhere. As local churches now, we are called to play our part in this same global task:

> But thanks be to God, who always leads us as captives in Christ's triumphal procession and uses us to spread the aroma of the knowledge of him everywhere. For we are to God the pleasing aroma of Christ among those who are being saved and those who are perishing. To the one we are an aroma that brings death; to the other, an aroma that brings life. And who is equal to such a task? Unlike so many, we do not peddle the word of God for profit. On the contrary, in Christ we speak before God with sincerity, as those sent from God.
> (2 Corinthians 2 v 14 - 17)

United In The Gospel Of Christ

When Paul writes to the church in Philippi, his concern for them goes beyond just demonstrating love and care for each other in accordance with Jesus' *"new commandment"* (see John 13 v 34). He is absolutely clear they must remain united around Jesus and his mission. Paul's teaching carries even more weight when we remember he was writing to them while under house arrest and awaiting trial in Rome. Despite the uncertainty of not knowing whether he will live or die, he continues to communicate his uncompromising message of unity. Let's explore what he is saying to them (see Philippians 1 v 27 - 28).

Whatever happens ...

The uncertainty of his own future and the possibility of imminent execution is shown in the opening phrase, *"whatever happens."* Whether he is released and able to visit them, or if nothing changes and he can only hear about them, he remains primarily concerned that their conduct brings glory to God.

...conduct yourselves in a manner worthy of the gospel of Christ.

Paul is encouraging and challenging their growth as a community, not just as individuals. How they live together as a local church must show them to be authentic followers of Jesus, known for living out the truth they say they believe. By reflecting the love, grace, mercy and compassion of the God they serve, their everyday lives needed to be full of integrity and purity, in order to honour the gospel of Christ.

...stand firm in one Spirit...

Paul was fully aware that following Jesus brings believers into a spiritual battle, so he remains eager to strengthen them and ensure they are secure in their faith.

Paul uses a warfare term, *"stand firm,"* because he is aware they face many enemies to their faith, each of which oppose the spread of the gospel. Therefore, it's crucial they continue to be united and strengthened by the same Spirit, who is seeking to build unity, promote courage and confidence in the gospel, produce determination and perseverance, and inspire them to contend as one man for the *"faith of the gospel"* (Philippians 1 v 27). By *"faith of the gospel,"* Paul means the Christian belief in Jesus' eternal victory over sin, and the new life for anyone who puts their trust in him. He needs the church to know it is fellowship with the Holy Spirit that unifies believers in their trust, so lives are transformed and become centred on upholding and proclaiming this truth.

He urges the church to stand firm in the face of opposition, *"without being frightened in any way by those who oppose you."* The original word Paul uses here relates to horses bolting when they are startled. The Philippians were not to bolt or run off when things got difficult... and neither should we!

In Mark's gospel, Jesus warned of a similar danger in the "Parable of the Sower." Here, he describes seed sown on rocky ground and likens it to the response of some when trouble comes:

> "Others, like seed sown on rocky places, hear the word and at once receive it with joy. But since they have no root, they last only a short time. When trouble or persecution comes because of the word, they quickly fall away."
> (Mark 4 v 16 - 17)

...contending as one man...

Paul then urges them to put all their energy and effort into fighting for the truth of the gospel. The original word, "athleo," translates to 'contend or contending together,' and is the root of our English word for athlete. It appears Paul sees the local church as a body of athletes who have trained, disciplined their bodies, and brought them to the peak of fitness so they could fully commit to the contest before them. Believers are to operate as a squad of spiritually fit athletes, actively engaged in wrestling the spiritual powers of darkness, and straining every muscle to make the gospel known. And unity is key to all this – the church is to be *"striving together"* with eternal purpose (Philippians 1 v 27).

Our thought life is critical here because contending as *"one man,"* could also be translated as contending with 'one mind.' We see this idea conveyed in the similar statement Paul uses at the beginning of the second chapter of the letter:

> ...make my joy complete by being like-minded, having the same love, being one in spirit and of one mind.
> (Philippians 2 v 2)

He is looking for a deep-seated, *"like-minded"* unity among them. Even though they are many individuals, he knows they will only make real progress in sharing the gospel if they live and move together as *"one man"*.

For many years, I have had the privilege of living in the city of Cambridge. One of the many things my home is famous for is The Boat Race between Oxford and Cambridge Universities, taking place each year on the River Thames in London. And while most of the training of the official Cambridge crew now takes place on the River Great Ouse at Ely, you can still see many university students trying out their rowing skills on the River Cam in the city.

To the observer on the riverbank (please forgive any oversimplification), it's evident that the fastest moving boats are the ones where the crew work as a unit and move together. To avoid upsetting the balance of the boat and slowing it down, they row in time, at the same rate, and with the same intensity. This image serves as an apt illustration of what Paul desires for the saints at Philippi.

Paul longs for unity and oneness in the church because he knows the world is looking on, in need of a demonstration of the kingdom of God. People will always look to find answers about a place, community, or set of beliefs they encounter. In fact, initially, there is often more curiosity and interest than we might think as they decide and assess, 'How does this impact me, or what might this mean for my life?'

What do people see when they look into our church communities? Those around us need evidence of what it means for a people to live under the loving rule of God; they need to experience a Spirit-filled community in all its unity and diversity.

The Rev. Dr Israel Olofinjana, director of the Evangelical Alliance's One People Commission, expresses it this way:

> *The church is meant to be a window into this new human community, offering a glimpse of the life of the age to come.*[3]

...for the faith of the gospel

But we must not miss the primary purpose in Paul's mind – standing firm in one spirit and contending as one man is for the sake of the faith of the gospel. He did not want them to contend for his own reputation, even though it was often under attack by false teachers who claimed he was not an authentic apostle. Neither was his concern for the reputation of the church at Antioch, who had sent him out on his church planting mission. Nor was he burdened for the reputation of the 'mother church' in Jerusalem, with its great pillars of Peter, James and John. For Paul, only one thing mattered:

> The important thing is that in every way, whether from false motives or true, Christ is preached. And because of this I rejoice.
> (Philippians 1 v 18)

Being united mattered because the gospel mattered. They needed to contend for the faith of the gospel because of the gospel's ability to reveal the way of salvation for all people. From beginning to end, salvation was a work of God – it was something he had provided for sinful humanity through the finished work of Christ, to be received by faith as a free gift. Paul was convinced of its transformative power and ability to save everyone:

> For I am not ashamed of the gospel, because it is the power of God that brings salvation to everyone who believes: first to the Jew, then to the Gentile.
> (Romans 1 v 16)

Paul lived with the revelation that the gospel of salvation in Christ was for any person, regardless of their past, gender, social class, race, or the colour of their skin. No doubt if Paul lived today, it wouldn't matter to him if a person was a respected member of society or one of the downtrodden poor, whether they were a pop-star or a prostitute, or whether they were excelling as a business executive or struggling as a heroin addict. Similarly, a person's location would not make any difference. The same need exists in the hearts of those in suburbia, downtown New York, rural villages in Africa, middle class Cambridge, or any one of the city slums across the globe.

Rich or poor, educated or uneducated, employed or unemployed, successful or utter failure, achiever or addict, healthy or sick, Paul was convinced there was no condition or situation that sat outside the transforming work of the gospel. And there was also no optimum time to hear and receive the good news! You were equally in need of Christ (and he was equally ready to welcome you) as a child, teenager, adult, or octogenarian... or as someone starting out in life, someone in a mid-life crisis, or someone much closer to 'meeting their maker!'

As far as Paul was concerned, the gospel had the power to transform lives that others wrote off! Praise God for the truth he revealed to Paul, and that this is just as true for us today. His knowledge of salvation in Christ meant he could wholeheartedly testify, *"I am not ashamed of the gospel."*

In effect, he was saying:

- I don't hang my head because of it.
- I don't make excuses for it.
- I don't have any regrets about coming into contact with it.

- I don't feel humiliated by it.
- It is one of the most wonderful and powerful things in the universe!

No doubt he would also remind us of his encouragement to the church at Colossae that, *"In the same way, the gospel is bearing fruit and growing throughout the whole world—just as it has been doing among you since the day you heard it and truly understood God's grace"* (Colossians 1 v 6).

Paul's heart cry from prison was for the church in Philippi to live their lives in a manner worthy of the gospel of Christ, standing firm without being frightened by the opposition. If they did, then Paul knew they would contend together, united in one mind for this life changing gospel.

Facing Opposition

The nature of opposition faced by most today may not be exactly the same as in Paul's time. However, in many parts of the world, brothers and sisters do still experience similar persecution and harassment with beatings, imprisonment and death. They deserve not only our prayers, but our practical and financial support as they hold out the word of life in the communities where God has placed them.

What might this opposition look like for others, such as those in the Western world? In many places today, there is increasing pressure to remove Christianity from the public square. Followers of Jesus can often be portrayed in popular culture as bigoted, intolerant and out of touch with mainstream society. At other times, they may be presented as intellectual dinosaurs who hold on to irrational or outdated beliefs and myths. In each case, this popular view sits very easily with the world, however untrue it is, meaning Christians can find themselves living, working and relating in a difficult climate.

We might, therefore, want to ask ourselves how we respond to such challenges to our faith. Is our response to them to stand firm, or do we tend to back away or back down when religious, moral or ethical issues are being discussed? Do we find it easier to keep quiet, rather than to be considered a religious bigot? Do we show a willingness to face the stigma of becoming identified and involved with the broken and marginalised in our society?

Just as important, is the need to ask if we hold any attitudes that would grieve the Holy Spirit and be destructive to the unity and well-being of our local church? Or on the corporate spectrum, is there anything in us hindering the community of God, of which we are a part, from contending as one man for the faith of the gospel?

Battle For Unity

It is interesting that in Chapter 4 of Philippians, Paul addresses a case of disunity in the church. Considering the verses we have just been looking at, does this appear strange? I think not. Like all of us, Paul had to deal with the realities of life, and his teaching here matches the guidance he gives to all the churches. The need to encourage and protect unity is common to all groups of believers:

> Make every effort to keep the unity of the Spirit through the bond of peace.
> (Ephesians 4 v 3)

> If it is possible, as far as it depends on you, live at peace with everyone.
> (Romans 12 v 18)

Unity needs to be worked for and secured - it doesn't just happen. Look at how Paul makes a personal appeal to two specific women in the church, who appear to have fallen out badly with each other:

> I plead with Euodia and I plead with Syntyche to be of the same mind in the Lord. Yes, and I ask you, my true companion, help these women since they have contended at my side in the cause of the gospel, along with Clement and the rest of my co-workers, whose names are in the book of life.
> (Philippians 4 v 2 - 3)

The Message paraphrases it this way:

> I urge Euodia and Syntyche to iron out their differences and make up. God doesn't want his children holding grudges.

Wow, that's a challenge today! Are you, or I, holding any grudges?

We know their names, but we don't know who these women were or why they had fallen out. However, we do know that in Philippi historically, there were many prominent women known for their social and religious devotion. There is a high probability that both were Gentile followers of Jesus, and women of prominence and influence in the life and ministry of the church.

Paul values them highly. He says of them both that they *"contended at my side in the cause of the gospel,"* using the same Greek word for *"contend"* that we looked at earlier. They had made every effort for the sake of the gospel, striving alongside Paul to see the good news of salvation in Jesus Christ spread across the world.

There is also a helpful reminder here that Paul was a team player. He speaks in these verses of *"Clement and the rest of my co-workers,"* and we know he was often accompanied on his journeys by people from different ethnic backgrounds (see Acts 20 v 4). As with Jesus' ministry, women were thoroughly involved with Paul in God's mission to make disciples of all nations. In Romans, Paul lists some of the women whom he greatly valued, and Euodia and Syntyche would also have been regarded in this way. The wonderful faith of these women will have made the situation in Philippi all the more painful for him, and it serves as a challenge for us to make sure we're looking after this part of our own Christian walk (see Acts 20 v 4; Luke 8 v 2; Matthew 27 v 55 - 56; Romans 16 v 1 - 16).

We don't know why these two women had fallen out or the cause of their continuing antagonism. However, we can glean some clues about the possible reasons from our own experience, and from Paul's comments in the body of his letter.

Root Of The Problem

Were their troubles the result of a clash of personalities? Did one party feel strongly about something, perhaps convinced they were right and the other person in the wrong? Had they misunderstood the other person's motives or intentions? Were their expectations of each other unrealistic? Had they reacted hastily or impatiently, ignorant of the pressures or circumstances the other person was living under?

From Paul's earlier comments in the letter, we may wish to ask whether the root of their disagreement was selfish ambition? When selfish ambition is in anyone's heart, other people can quickly become diminished in their eyes. If this happens, people can begin to consider the value of others as being inferior to their own. Such attitudes would often not be voiced openly; indeed people may try to convince themselves their bad attitude is hidden, unseen and undetected by others, or is even somehow justified. But the reality is, it will never be too long before the feelings surface in the way they talk about, and act towards, the other person.

Perhaps, the antagonism was over who should occupy the place of greatest prominence, or exercise the greatest influence in church life? Of course, there was precedent for this among Jesus' disciples in their early days (see Luke 22 v 24)! Had they begun to undermine each other by subtle negative comments to other church members? What started as musings in their hearts may have ended with them finding fault with one another, before growing into open criticism. And let's remember from our previous chapter, criticism stems from the disapproval of people, not for having faults, but for having faults different from our own!

Or could the root have been vain conceit, which is having a higher opinion of themselves than they should have had? When this flaw is present, we fail to consider the other person better (or more important) than ourselves - certainly not an uncommon situation. When urging the believers in Galatia to live by and keep in step with the Spirit, Paul reminds them not to be conceited because it can lead to provoking and envying each other (see Galatians 5 v 25 - 26).

Where does this tendency to provoke others stem from?

Provoking others can often spring from feelings of superiority and an inner desire to challenge somebody to a contest. We can be so sure of our position that we're happy when people dispute or challenge us – we want others to know and feel our superiority, so it gives us a chance to prove ourselves! On the other hand, we may feel inferior to others. In this case, our hearts and minds consider others superior to us, such that we can become envious and jealous of their gifts, achievements and personal relationships. As we feel the pain of this negative view of ourselves, we can even secretly harbour the wish to see them fail in order to bolster our own ego (see Philippians 2 v 3)!

In either case, the dangerous combination of comparison, insecurity and misplaced identity are at play, and together they stifle and harm our relationships.

Then again, maybe it was a doctrinal issue and a simple case of a clash of personalities or personal preferences? We may never know, but it was serious enough for Paul to make an impassioned plea for them to find agreement together in the Lord and reconcile. Paul knew how destructive disunity was to the church and how it would have devastating effects:

> If you bite and devour each other, watch out or you will be destroyed by each other.
> (Galatians 5 v 15)

Leith Samuel helpfully paraphrases this same verse:

> *If you attack one another's character and tear to pieces one another's reputation you may be only digging a grave to bury your church in.*[4]

This, and similar issues, were more than simply a matter of a dispute between two church members – they were a cause of serious potential damage to the church's witness, and Paul knew this. Their personal disagreement was a threat to the unity of the church and its ability to contend as one man for the faith of the gospel. So, he was making this impassioned plea to both, straight from his heart that they should end their continued antagonism for the gospel's sake.

You will notice he does not command them or seek to apportion blame. Neither does he try to identify the guilty party or give his opinion on who is right. Instead, he seeks to turn their thoughts to Jesus, addressing the real core of the matter - their hearts. Their agreement must be for the Lord's sake, for his honour and glory. They must submit their personal agendas to the larger agenda of the gospel, remembering how, by the grace and mercy of Jesus, they have both been declared equal, completely forgiven, and the beneficiaries of unmerited, unending love and acceptance. One can hear again, the echo of his words to the whole church earlier in the letter, which we also need to heed:

> Make my joy complete by being like-minded, having the same love, being one in spirit and of one mind.
> (Philippians 2 v 2)

Personal Responsibility

But notice one last thing of importance in relation to the dispute Paul is resolving in Philippi. In some translations, the friend Paul asks for help with the matter is referred to as Syzygus, meaning loyal yoke-fellow. As is often the case in the Bible, this name is significant. He knows his trusted friend will, like an ox yoked together with him, pull them in the same direction and be committed to the same outcome of reconciliation. This is instructive, for it reminds us we all have a personal responsibility for the well-being and witness of God's church. It also challenges us about how willing we are to deal with any unhealthy or broken relationships we see threatening the unity of the church, which will affect the honour and glory being given to our Lord Jesus Christ.

Sadly, it is too easy for us to try and sidestep or abdicate our responsibility towards other brothers and sisters in the body of Christ. We may know people are at odds with each other and in need of guidance, but leave it to them to sort things out. It's understandable to feel out of your depth, unsure of where to start, or that it's best to leave it to someone else. Perhaps, we don't want to be known as a busybody or fear that if we intervene, we may make things worse. Maybe we fear ending up in the middle and being attacked by both parties – none of us want to be on the receiving end of harsh words or given the cold shoulder. But do we understand the gravity of the damage to the church's witness that may occur if things are left unresolved? We, too, must submit our own personal comfort to the larger agenda of the gospel and God's kingdom. We have a personal responsibility to actively seek peace and unity.

Remember, the role of peacemaker is a blessed position, and God's provision of wisdom is at hand for us if we ask (see Matthew 5 v 9; James 1 v 5). As followers of Jesus, we remember he paid the ultimate price to reconcile us to the Father and bring us peace with God. At the same time, he made it possible for us to live in peace and harmony with one another, for at the cross he created in himself one new man, a united people. In the letter to the Ephesians, the same unifying message is shared to address and heal the deep-rooted hostilities between Jews and Gentiles – we can point our brothers and sisters to this truth as we encounter division:

> Christ brought us together through his death on the cross. The Cross got us to embrace, and that was the end of the hostility. Christ came and preached peace to you outsiders and peace to us insiders. He treated us as equals, and so made us equals. Through him we both share the same Spirit and have equal access to the Father.
> (Ephesians 2 v 16 - 18 MSG)

Ministry Of Reconciliation

Paul was not only conscious of being reconciled to God through Christ, but also that God had given him the ministry of reconciliation. Christ's death and resurrection achieved the ultimate healing by mending the relationship between God and man, which then re-wrote how we can love and relate to each other. As Christ's ambassador, Paul had been entrusted with this message of reconciliation - God was making his appeal through him as he implored others to be reconciled to their Heavenly Father. Paul carried quite a calling, but in similar fashion, we too are to proclaim this message of reconciliation to the world. The challenge is, how can we do this if we are at odds with each other, fighting for position, status and recognition? And how can we show Christ to be the hope for eternal healing and reconciliation of all human hearts, if we remain determined to put our own personal ambitions first (see 2 Corinthians 5 v 16 - 21)?

Thank God for grace! The grace of God that saved us, is the grace that daily sustains us and makes it possible for us to live together in complete unity. We continue to remind ourselves that our brothers and sisters are also those for whom Christ shed his blood. Just like you and I, from helpless sinners, they were rescued from hell and restored to relationship with God, the Father. As such, they are precious, valued and dearly loved authentic children of the living God, worthy of our wholehearted love, devotion and support. And crucially, the same applies to you - you, too, are precious, valued and dearly loved. When we have a right view of God, a right view of salvation, and a right view of ourselves, we are secure enough to learn to consider others more important than ourselves. Do this, and *then* the world will begin to sit up and take notice!

The church can do this - just look at Paul's words of encouragement to the church at Ephesus:

> In light of all this, here's what I want you to do. While I'm locked up here, a prisoner for the Master, I want you to get out there and walk—better yet, run!—on the road God called you to travel. I don't want any of you sitting around on your hands. I don't want anyone strolling off, down some path that goes nowhere. And mark that you do this with humility and discipline—not in fits and starts, but steadily, pouring yourselves out for each other in acts of love, **alert at noticing differences and quick at mending fences.**
>
> You were all called to travel on the same road and in the same direction, so stay together, both outwardly and inwardly. You have one Master, one faith, one baptism, one

> God and Father of all, who rules over all, works through all, and is present in all. Everything you are and think and do is permeated with Oneness.
>
> (Ephesians 4 v 1 - 6 MSG; emphasis added)

Make no mistake, you're called to minister reconciliation to the world like Paul was... but not alone. The world doesn't need *you* as one, it needs *us* as one, together. So, to finish this chapter, read this true story. The account is a sobering challenge and illustration of the importance of the church's unity, as we continue to seek the lost by revealing Christ in our world:

> *There is a tragic story of a little boy who had gone outside to play in the snow. Suddenly the snowfall reached blizzard dimensions and the little boy was lost in a gigantic snowdrift. Alarmed, both parents ran outside through the large field next to their home, searching for their son. They even telephoned neighbours to come and assist in looking for the lost child. Independently and intensely, many continued to look for the little boy, but to no avail. Finally, it was determined that all of the volunteers in the field should take hands and walk across the field together. Only then could they rescue the lost boy. Resolutely, they determined to lock arms and walk the field together. They did find the lost little boy – but it was too late. He had frozen to death, as many people were frantically, yet independently, looking for him.*[5]

Notes

1 Called To Be Friends – Unlocking the heart of John's Gospel by Ian Galloway. Copyright © Ian Galloway 2022. Published by Hodder and Stoughton, ISBN 9781529356830, Page 91. Reproduced with permission of the Licensor through PLSclear

2 Habits of Grace by David Mathis. Copyright © David Mathis 2016. Published by IVP, ISBN 9781783594177, Chapter (13) Page 145. Reproduced with permission of the Licensor through PLSclear

3 Idea Magazine of the Evangelical Alliance, September/October 2021, Page 4

4 Stand Firm! Studies in the Epistle to the Galatians by Leith Samuel, 1965. Published by HarperCollins Distribution Services

5 Once in a Lifetime by David Shibley. Copyright © David Shibley 1998. Published by Sovereign World Ltd, ISBN 9781852402204, Page 93

CHAPTER FIFTEEN

Self-Care

Have you noticed the massive increase in self-care books available to buy in recent years? Or the rising number of online influencers advising on well-being across social media or on podcasts?

Self-care, of course, means different things to different people. When we first hear the word, we sometimes think of small acts like getting a massage or treating oneself to a really nice dinner. Other times, our minds jump to essential habits and life rhythms we can develop to make sure we relax, recharge and take care of ourselves. It's an important topic and it has become big business!

Recently, looking at the reviews of eight new self-care books on the market, I came across this description of the content of one book:

> *Through her own personal stories, it builds a path you can follow to change how you see yourself and build emotional strength in order to deal with all of the stressors that life throws your way, as well as how to overcome hurtful things in your past and stop letting them define who you are. This kind of self-care is the real work, but it also has the most lasting benefits for your mental health.*

Quite an endorsement! It all sounds very good, and no doubt people will glean helpful insights from such content, especially when personal stories are involved. But big business creates big amounts of noise, and inevitably leads to some big promises. So we must not forget that the Bible also has some very important things to say about self-care - and we need to be ready to talk about and share their relevance. As we consider these, we shouldn't sideline, minimise or undervalue the weight the Bible puts on caring for one another. The Christian life is often described as one of interdependence rather than independence, and we have an enduring call to encourage and build one another up. Nevertheless, it is vital for us to learn how to care for ourselves and build ourselves up in the faith. As we'll see, doing so also has a positive impact on those around us.

As we look at the topic, let's remember the promises we put our hope in as Christians. Jesus is the healer of hearts and the promise of rest for weary souls, and we have been given the Holy Spirit as our advocate and counsellor to help bring this reality into our lives (see Matthew 8 v 2; Matthew 11 v 28; John 14 v 16). We can celebrate the increased profile given to well-being, mental health and self-care in the world. But humbly, and with gentleness and wisdom, we are to realise we also have an important voice in this important area of life, both in and outside the church. So, in this chapter I want to help us think about a key factor in Christian self-care, the critical importance of learning how to encourage oneself in God.

When Trouble Comes – Lessons From David

A good illustration is found from the life of King David in the first book of Samuel (see 1 Samuel 30 v 1 - 30). It demonstrates the clear value and benefit of knowing how to encourage and strengthen yourself in God when facing adverse circumstances.

King Saul's jealousy and desire to kill David resulted in him living as a fugitive in the land of the Philistines. There, he joined and allied with the King of Gath, working as a bodyguard for his son, Achish. At David's request, he was given the town of Ziklag to live in with his 600 men and their families. After settling here, David served the king *"reliably,"* and without *"fault,"* for over one year (see 1 Samuel 29 v 1 - 6).

However, during a time when the Philistines went out to fight against Israel, David's integrity was brought into question by the commanders of the Philistine army. Fearing that David and his men might switch sides in the battle, they were sent home to Ziklag. Upon their arrival, they found the town burned to the ground, with their wives and children captured by Israel's bitter enemy, the Amalekites:

> David and his men reached Ziklag on the third day. Now the Amalekites had raided the Negev and Ziklag. They had attacked Ziklag and burned it, and had taken captive the women and everyone else in it, both young and old. They killed none of them, but carried them off as they went on their way.
>
> When David and his men reached Ziklag, they found it destroyed by fire and their wives and sons and daughters taken captive. So, David and his men wept aloud until they had no strength left to weep. David's two wives had been captured—Ahinoam of Jezreel and Abigail, the widow of Nabal of Carmel. David was greatly distressed because the men were talking of stoning him; each one was bitter in spirit because of his sons and daughters. But David found strength in the LORD his God.
>
> (1 Samuel 30 v 1 - 6)

It is not hard to imagine the fears and anxieties racing through the minds of David and his men on that day. Perhaps uppermost, was the chilling thought they had little prospect of finding their wives and children alive. What we do know for certain is that they were utterly distraught, *"So, David and his men wept aloud until they had no strength left to weep"* (verse 4).

Let's remember David's men were strong, seasoned warriors, which offers a lesson for us in terms of processing and expressing our own grief, emotions and vulnerability. Stoicism is not the answer, and they were understandably broken, but what people do with these feelings is hugely important.

What was alarming, and what compounded David's personal distress, was that his men were talking of stoning him as they became consumed by bitterness.

Have you ever noticed this response to a crisis striking? We want someone to blame. Sometimes, anyone will do. When we feel unable to cope, or when we find ourselves overwhelmed by feelings of hopelessness and despair, we quickly forget the journey we've been on and the experiences we've enjoyed in the past. More than that, we also fail to value the genuine friendships and loving relationships we enjoy in the present. In the face of an uncertain future or outcome, we can begin to look for a scapegoat for the adverse circumstances we find ourselves in!

We can imagine how David must have felt in this moment. His integrity and leadership were being called into question and he was struggling with the loss of his own family. He was also surrounded by grieving friends, whose anguish was etched on their faces and evident in the tears running down their cheeks. And now, these same friends who were previously willing to lay down their lives for him in battle, were now acting towards him with hostile aggression.

As the situation developed, consider the painful questions that may have been assaulting David's mind. Where was God in all of this? Why had he allowed this to happen? Is God truly faithful, or had he made a mistake? What should he now do to try and turn things around himself?

Self-Care, But Not From Your Self

How would you or I react if we were in his shoes? David's response is telling. We're told he *"found strength in the Lord his God,"* or, as the King James Version says, he *"encouraged himself in the Lord his God"* (1 Samuel 30 v 6). When everybody and everything seemed to be against him, he knew where to place his confidence and trust. He didn't look to a principle, a system or technique, but instead trusted in a person... the living God. He knew he was looking to and leaning on the sovereign ruler over all the affairs of humanity, yet still knew him personally and was the shepherd of his life.

When David felt down, confused, desperate, and backed up against the wall, he knew how to approach God's throne to receive mercy and find grace to help him in his time of need. Like many saints of old, he knew that those who wait for the Lord, who expect, look for, and hope in him, will renew their strength and power (see Hebrews 4 v 14 - 16; Isaiah 40 v 29 - 31).

As circumstances challenged what he knew of the nature and character of his loving God, David had a choice. We can see how he chose to believe that God was still his shepherd and that he would not want for anything. Even if he were to pass through the valley of the shadow of death, his God would be with him, and he would have nothing to fear. David strengthened himself with the truths God had revealed about himself through his words, works and wonders (see Psalm 23).

Out of this strengthening, he was enabled to seek God's help and guidance with renewed confidence that his needs, and those of his people, would be met. As he looked to God, he was empowered by a promise of success, and looked forward in faith to see its fulfilment. He found courage to lead his men on, motivating them to pursue the enemy and engage in battle for a sustained period of over 24 hours. This act of positive defiance saw them secure an astonishing victory, recovering everything the Amalekites had taken.

David experienced, once again, that God truly was the faithful protector and deliverer of his chosen people. But I think it would be wrong to assume that David's ability to strengthen himself in God was learnt on that one day at Ziklag. I'm convinced his response didn't just come from having no other option available to him as he stared into the abyss of adverse circumstances. I would suggest David had learnt this vital lesson through his daily walk with God over many years, where he had taken time to build this relationship. So, like the wise man in Jesus' parable of the wise and foolish builders, he had sought to build his life on obedience to God's word (see Matthew 7 v 24 - 27). It is in life's challenges, or when facing imminent disaster, that our true character and colours show; when his trial came, David knew what to do. He knew leaning on his own strength and understanding was not the path to take (see Proverbs 3 v 5 - 6). I imagine this experience of God's faithfulness then saw him treasure and cement these truths even more.

David had learnt to make God the primary source of care in his life; he knew the Lord as his shepherd who fed, guided and protected him. But more than this, he speaks of God as his light and salvation, calling him the stronghold of his life. He had confidence that even if his father and mother should forsake him, the Lord would faithfully receive him (see Psalm 27 v 1 - 10). His relationship with God had become part of his innermost being, which we see when he speaks of his heart prompting him to seek the Lord:

> My heart says of you, "Seek his face!"
> Your face, Lord, I will seek.
> (Psalm 27 v 8; see also Psalm 23)

As followers of Jesus today, we need to think about how our own hearts direct us when we face the rigours and challenges of everyday life? Do we push the panic button or tend towards emotional collapse? Do we immediately phone a friend or try to contact a church leader for help? Do we just try to "hang on in there" until the next meeting of our small group, hoping someone might be able to offer some words of wisdom? Do we simply work harder to "fix" the problem, or do we bury our head in the sand?

To be clear, seeking support is entirely appropriate; we saw previously that we are called to lives of interdependence in the body of Christ. But David had trained his heart to seek God first and foremost, not as a last resort. His primary inclination was to immediately turn to God for help and, aided by the Holy Spirit, he found his heart urging him into God's presence. As David put his connection with God ahead of anything else, all his men and their families became the beneficiaries of the relationship he had cultivated and the impact this had on his life and leadership.

Training Ground For Trust

By God's grace, despite the many pressures of modern life, it is possible for us to train our hearts to seek God as our primary source of care. But we need to be aware of the kind of things, the type or experiences, and the different contexts God uses to speak to us and build our confidence and trust in his faithfulness.

Nature And The World Around Us

David's younger life was spent as a shepherd looking after his father's sheep, providing him with a rich opportunity to appreciate the created world. In many of David's psalms, we find him extolling the creator God as he admires the majesty of all he has made. Lots of what he learnt about God may have come through these observations and his meditations on the natural world. In the same way, we can expect to learn about God by 'taking in' the world around us. Look at how Paul encourages believers in the book of Romans – God's invisible qualities are revealed in what has been made:

> For since the creation of the world God's invisible qualities – his eternal power and divine nature – have been clearly seen, being understood from what has been made, so that men are without excuse.
> (Romans 1 v 18 - 20; see also Psalm 8)

We live in a fast-paced world with seemingly little or no time to stop and contemplate the natural world around us. Perhaps, our knowledge of God would deepen if we took more time to contemplate the wonders of creation. Interestingly, in the same way we can access the Bible on our phones whenever we need it, using technology well can help us. There has never been more easily available resources to allow us to examine in depth the wonders of the natural world.

Jesus valued nature. When teaching about worry and anxiety, he uses common observations of nature to drive home spiritual truth. In one example, he asks his listeners to, *"See how the flowers of the field grow"* (see Matthew 6 v 25 - 34). The word translated here as, *"See,"* means to notice carefully, consider closely, observe thoroughly, consider accurately and diligently, and to contemplate. I wonder if you've noticed how readily children learn like this, by looking closely at and absorbing the world around them? As adults, are we making contemplation of the created world a feature of our Christian walk?

A few years ago, my wife and I had the privilege of taking a holiday in the north of Scotland. During our two weeks, we immersed ourselves every day in the beautiful countryside, seeing giant hares, magnificent stags and eagles. We also walked through a number of forests of tall trees and along pathways by the side of beautiful lochs glistening in the sunshine. Each day, my wife would ask God to speak to her through our encounters with the natural world, and each day something new would be entered in her journal to record the words and thoughts that came to her. We returned home with fresh insights and appreciation of the God who made us, and who cares for us and all his creation.

Law And The Prophets

God is a speaking God who reveals himself to us today. He has consistently spoken to humanity through his prophets at many times and in various ways, and supremely through his son, Jesus Christ. God *has* spoken, and we do well to learn to put our confidence and trust in whom he reveals himself to be, the Sovereign Lord of heaven and earth (see Hebrews 1 v 1 - 4).

David is an example to us, in that his life was built on a knowledge of God's law, a love for that law, and an obedience to God's commandments. In Psalm 19, David not only recognises that God speaks through his creation, but also through this law, which he declares perfect and trustworthy. Look at the experience described in Psalm 1 for someone who meditates on and delights in God's commands:

> Blessed is the one who does not walk in step with the wicked or stand in the way that sinners take or sit in the company of mockers, but whose delight is in the law of the Lord, and who meditates on his law, day and night. That person is like a tree planted by streams of water, which yields its fruit in season and whose leaf does not wither - whatever they do prospers.
> (Psalm 1 v 1 - 3)

As we make time in our busy schedules to read, study and meditate on God's word, we will increasingly see our confidence and trust in God's nature, character and ways grow. Not only will we delight in the truth revealed to us, but we will develop delight in God himself. From here, the more we learn to speak the truth to ourselves, the more we'll be able to encourage ourselves in God, enabling his strength in our lives in times of need.

Our Responsibility In The New Covenant

Like all of us, David had his down times. Yet he had learnt how to speak to his own soul, encouraging himself to put his hope in God. His knowledge of God's character, drawn from times of meditation on God's word, helped nurture in him an authentic hope. Speaking to oneself is not, as some say, 'the first sign of madness.' For the believer, it's a sign of trust and a source of strength! For when we consistently speak God's truth to ourselves, it strengthens our hope and trust in him, who is willing:

> Why, my soul, are you downcast?
>   Why so disturbed within me?
> Put your hope in God,
>   for I will yet praise him,
>   my Saviour and my God.
> (Psalm 42 v 11; see also Psalm 43 v 5)

It's also true that we're never actually without an internal monologue or conversation; the difference is the focus or direction of it. Rather than talking ourselves into a positive mindset or being held back by a negative focus on ourselves, we can look to a different hope. Like David, we have the responsibility to play our part in training our hearts to instinctively prompt us to look to God in all situations. And we can be confident, and must not forget, that in Christ we live under a different covenant than David - the New Covenant founded on better promises:

> But in fact the ministry Jesus has received is as superior to theirs as the covenant of which he is mediator is superior to the old one, since the new covenant is established on better promises.
> (Hebrews 8 v 6)

Under the Old Covenant, the Holy Spirit would come upon certain individuals at specific times, to perform specific tasks, and to fulfil the specific purposes of God. David was keenly aware of his own anointing from God. In fact, after his sin with Bathsheba, David pleaded with God not to take his Holy Spirit from him:

> Create in me a pure heart, O God, and renew a steadfast spirit within me. Do not cast me from your presence or take your Holy Spirit from me.
> (Psalm 51 v 10 - 11)

But the Old Testament prophets like Joel, spoke of a day when God's Spirit would be poured out on all people, irrespective of their age, gender or social status:

> "Then, after doing all those things,
> I will pour out my Spirit upon all people.
> Your sons and daughters will prophesy.
> Your old men will dream dreams,
> and your young men will see visions.
> In those days I will pour out my Spirit
> even on servants—men and women alike."
> (Joel 2 v 28 - 29 NLT)

We live in this very time! This scripture was fulfilled on the day of Pentecost when the risen Jesus, having made a New Covenant through his death on the cross and having been exalted to the right hand of God, poured out the Holy Spirit on the church:

> "God has raised this Jesus to life, and we are all witnesses of it. Exalted to the right hand of God, he has received from the Father the promised Holy Spirit and has poured out what you now see and hear."
> (Acts 2 v 32 - 33)

Under the New Covenant, the promise Jesus gave to his disciples was fulfilled – the Holy Spirit was given to live and reside in every believer:

> "And I will ask the Father, and he will give you another advocate to help you and be with you forever - the Spirit of truth. The world cannot accept him, because it neither sees him nor knows him. But you know him, for he lives with you and will be in you."
> (John 14 v 16 - 17)

Later, Jesus speaks of the Father giving another counsellor to the disciples after he had gone (see John 16 v 13). The promise of a 'counsellor' from heaven is wonderful when we consider that the word means, 'one called or sent to assist another, an advocate, intercessor, helper, or one who encourages and comforts.' Jesus promised someone who would come alongside to help and guide them into all truth, and the Holy Spirit is that person.

Empowered By The Spirit In You

Paul reminds the church in Rome that if anyone does not have the Spirit of Christ, they do not belong to him. But note, he is quick to underline the truth. The Spirit of him who raised Jesus from the dead *does live* in every true believer, and the Spirit himself testifies with our spirit that we are God's children. Indeed, our bodies are the temple of the Holy Spirit who lives in us, and we must be confident in this (see Romans 8 v 9 - 17; 1 Corinthians 6 v 19).

One of the reasons the Spirit resides within us is to prompt, provoke and motivate us to do the will of God. Jesus said he would be sent to help, so it follows that we can experience him working alongside, encouraging, strengthening and empowering us to fulfil God's good purposes for our lives:

> ...continue to work out your salvation with fear and trembling, for it is God who works in you to will and to act in order to fulfil his good purpose.
> (Philippians 2 v 12 - 13; see also Ezekiel 36 v 26 - 27)

Like a top athletics coach or personal trainer, the Holy Spirit works with us to train our hearts to trust God at all times and in all circumstances. His role is to bring us constant encouragement by reminding us how loved we are by our heavenly Father, and how committed he is to supply all we need. He jogs our memory and reminds us of the *"better promises"* and benefits for us written in Scripture. We need to tune in, which means quietening the noise of doubt and distractions around us, letting us hear the truth of what is ours through our union with Christ in the New Covenant.

What a blessing when facing hard times to have the Holy Spirit alongside us, reminding our hearts of God's unchanging provision for our lives, and what he has spoken to us. We need to place this truth at the centre of our thought life. What if God's word and his truth made up the soundtrack of our thinking? What if the truth of God's sovereignty in *"all things"* and his unchanging willingness to meet our need was more easily recalled?

With the Spirit's help, imagine these thoughts being our instinctive response to hard times and trials:

> We know that **in all things** God works for the good of those who love him, who have been called according to his purpose.
> (Romans 8 v 28; emphasis added)

> How will he not also, along with him (Jesus), graciously give us **all things.**
> (Romans 8 v 32; emphasis added)

> No, **in all these things** we are more than conquerors through him who loved us.
> (Romans 8 v 37; emphasis added)

> And God is able to bless you abundantly, so that **in all things at all times,** having all that you need, you will abound in every good work.
> (2 Corinthians 9 v 8; emphasis added)

> And my God will **meet all your needs** according to the riches of his glory in Christ Jesus.
> (Philippians 4 v 19; emphasis added)

Take The Help!

In an earlier chapter, we looked at Peter's teaching of how God's *"divine power has given us everything we need for a godly life through our knowledge of him who called us by his own glory and goodness"* (2 Peter 1 v 3 - 4). We have been given very great and precious promises so that through them, we may participate in the divine nature and escape the corruption in the world caused by evil desires. We must use those resources in times of trouble and testing, encouraging ourselves to trust our loving heavenly Father.

How foolish we are when in these times of trouble, hardship or crisis we don't look to God as our primary source of love, care and affection. Or when we don't turn to him to gain from his wisdom, understanding and insight, failing to ask for his guidance, protection, strength and empowerment in our time of need.

Think for a moment how you might feel if you encountered someone in desperate trouble and you had the time, know-how, skill, money, and resources to help them. Now imagine they either refused, ignored or belittled the help you offered. As they battled on in their own strength, you see them damaging or hurting themselves even more, digging themselves into a deeper pit they can't get out of!

How do you think your heavenly Father feels when you and I do exactly the same?

Prayer Opens The Door

Prayer plays an important role in encouraging ourselves to look to God in times of difficulty, conflict and challenge. Be reassured that prayer in the middle of hardship doesn't always look pretty – it will be messy, confused and even desperate, but God hears these cries all the same. The key is to do it.

It is perhaps difficult to imagine Jesus himself needing encouragement, but we must remember in his earthly life he faced many setbacks that could have so easily led to doubt. Consider the rejection in his hometown or his own disciples' lack of belief and understanding. There was ongoing hostility from the religious leaders of the faith he grew up with. People repeatedly turned back from following him, while others demanded he prove himself through signs and miracles. He was betrayed by one close to him, there was misunderstanding of his teaching, he was accused of being in league with the devil, and his disciples were vying for position and greatness as he preached a message of loving others. Potential for discouragement? Absolutely... and all while the burden of the cross and humanity's sin drew closer and closer. Jesus knew everything about looking to God, and prayer was central to it.

I remember reading in John, Chapter 10, of the time the Jews sought to stone Jesus for blasphemy, *"because he a mere man claimed to be God"* (verse 33). I found myself intrigued by the way he escaped their grasp and went back to the other side of the Jordan, to the place where John had been baptising in the early days. I wondered to myself, if the reason was because it was the very place where John had declared him to be both the Lamb of God and the Son of God. It was where Jesus had heard the words of his Father, *"This is my Son, whom I love; with him I am well pleased"* (Matthew 3 v 17). Following the period of hostility and rejection, did Jesus need fresh encouragement and affirmation? By returning to the place that held such memories for him, are we seeing how he continued to look to God, the Father, in all circumstances? Remember, Jesus knows all about and is sympathetic to our weaknesses, yet never sinned, so he must understand the need for reassurance, encouragement and affirmation (see Hebrews 4 v 14).

It's important to note, we do not read of Jesus being in any way discouraged by the course of events. Perhaps, this was because he had cultivated this lifestyle of connection in prayer, meaning he continually turned to his Father as his primary source of help. Prayer was his pattern and life's rhythm. Following the feeding of the five thousand, when Jesus knew the people intended to come and make him king by force, we are told, *"he withdrew again to a mountain by himself"* (John 16 v 15; see also Matthew 14 v 23; Mark 6 v 46). Similarly, we see when news of him spread and crowds of people came to hear him and be healed of their sicknesses, *"Jesus often withdrew to lonely places and prayed"* (Luke 5 v 16).

The Gospels make it clear he wanted to devote time to prayer, as fixing his heart on God and his mission was the priority. Another time, the whole town gathered at sunset to the house where Jesus was staying and he healed many who had various diseases and drove out demons. There was a clamour for Jesus, and after this we read, *"Very early in the morning while it was still dark, Jesus got up, left the house and went off to a solitary place, where he prayed"* (Mark 1 v 35 - 37). Jesus prioritised and protected these times. He was clearly mindful of both his needs and the needs of the people, for when Simon and his companions came searching for him and found him, they exclaimed, *"Everyone is looking for you!"* Was it these moments alone with his Father that encouraged and strengthened him to face the growing pressure of people's expectations?

It's also clear to see how prayer guided Jesus at key moments in his life. When it came to choosing his twelve disciples, Luke tells us *"Jesus went out to a mountainside to pray, and spent the whole night praying to God"* (Luke 6 v 12). And, in the garden of Gethsemane as Jesus faced the horrors of his impending death, we see the same pattern. As his soul became overwhelmed with sorrow, we find him separating from his three disciples so he could pray to his Father (see Matthew 26 v 36).

When we examine Jesus' life, we see again and again how he made praying a priority. It was this fellowship with the Father in prayer that enabled him to say, *"The one who sent me is with me, he has not left me alone, for I always do what pleases him"* (John 8 v 29). And, at the raising of Lazarus Jesus looks upward and said, *"Father, thank you that you have heard me. I knew that you always hear me..."* (John 11 v 41 - 42). Prayer opened the door to absolute certainty of God's goodness in all circumstances. If only we could learn to cultivate the same intimacy and confidence as we bring our own prayers to our heavenly Father.

Look at the description of Jesus' prayer life in this passage:

> During the days of Jesus' life on earth, he offered up prayers and petitions with fervent cries and tears to the one who could save him from death, and he was heard because of his reverent submission.
> (Hebrews 5 v 7)

Prayer shows our dependency on the Father, and is the pathway to finding personal encouragement and strength in God as our primary care giver. So just like the disciples who recognised the life-giving role of prayer in Jesus' life, I urge us to ask of him again, *"Lord, teach us to pray"* (Luke 11 v 1).

CHAPTER SIXTEEN

Standing In The Gap

Prayer.

You'll have heard, many times, the value of taking our eyes from ourselves and looking to God in regular quiet times, reflections, devotions and intercession. You'll have heard the value of putting prayer at the heart of your own Christian life, with these patterns backed up in the Bible. Indeed, we highlighted the centrality of prayer in Jesus' life at the end of the last chapter. It's my experience that believers want to build these same rhythms into their own lives. They acknowledge the value of doing so. However, many of us can find prayer to be hard work and may experience discouragement when trying to build a consistent routine. In response, I've seen many earnest believers try to convince themselves prayer is the domain of church leaders or a few gifted people – the spiritual elite with a hotline to heaven!

But Scripture is clear. Prayer is both the privilege and responsibility of every believer. It is true that some people develop an ability to pray for extended periods of time and do so on a regular basis, seeing frequent and specific answers to their prayers. Nevertheless, prayer is still a key responsibility for all of us, both personally and as a corporate body. It's a spiritual discipline rather than a spiritual gift, so our spiritual health depends on us not giving up.

Rule yourself in, not out

Still, many struggle on for years without knitting prayer into their everyday lives, either finding reasons not to, or resigning themselves to never getting it right. Neither feeling is God's best for us. The excuse of not having the right kind of personality simply will not do. Some may consider themselves extroverts, go-getters, or action-types, thinking that being 'stuck in a room for an hour to pray' would somehow stifle them. But let's remember, activity without God's direction is always a fruitless route. So, bring your unique personality and energy into your prayer life. You're needed! Similarly, the idea of 'just not having enough time' sounds hollow when our lives show we always find time to do things of great importance to us. The question is really one of priority, rooted in a proper understanding of our deep, ongoing spiritual need to connect with God.

The Bible shows us all types of people praying, and also that we need to be intentional about making time to do it. Trying to wriggle out of prayer by saying, 'I'm just an ordinary believer and lack the ability,' is countered by James' comment on the 'normality' and humanity of the prophet Elijah:

> The prayer of a righteous person is powerful and effective. Elijah was a human being, even as we are. He prayed earnestly that it would not rain, and it did not rain on the land for three and a half years. Again he prayed, and the heavens gave rain, and the earth produced its crops.
> (James 5 v 16 - 18)

From 'normality' Elijah developed quite the prayer pedigree, which provides a challenge to us. As God's people, there is always more to discover and more of his great power to see when ordinary believers give themselves to praying. We will experience this truth when believers and churches cultivate, not simply a schedule of prayer meetings, but a culture and lifestyle of prayer.

Responsibility, Regularity And Relationship

I will always be grateful for my church youth leaders, who in my early teens, encouraged me to start praying regularly by using a prayer list. Taking the seven days of the week, each day I would write in the people and things I wanted to pray for. I remember being motivated by a popular saying of the time, "Seven prayerless days makes one weak!" The only danger was that such a format could easily turn prayer into a kind of duty, rather than a delight - it's always important not to attach guilt to responsibility. But what it achieved for me, was to cement the habit of a daily time of intentional prayer into my young life, proving of great benefit throughout the years.

It was not long before I came to understand that prayer was not simply bringing my requests to God, even if I accompanied them with thanksgiving. I learnt my prayer life was much more, having everything to do with developing my relationship with my heavenly Father. When the disciples asked Jesus to teach them how to pray, I don't think they were looking for a set of religious rules, methodology or techniques. Rather, they wanted to learn how to cultivate something like the rich relationship with God they saw in the life of Jesus. They'd seen enough to know his connection to the Father was deeply linked to his devotion to prayer. How could they also see prayer permeate every aspect of their lives? How could they know ongoing communion with God throughout the normal activities of the day?

Again, being assured of our new identity in Christ is key - we can come to God confident of our fixed position as dearly loved children. We are praying to a Father who is interested in every aspect of our lives, meaning prayer can become a delight, rather than a duty. Through Jesus, we have been restored to fellowship with the Father and can come boldly to him. We don't need to hide or pretend, and we can tell him everything because we know he cares for us and wants us to enjoy all his many blessings. Rather than hard work, prayer becomes a natural and enjoyable experience. No wonder Paul instructs the early church to always pray, whatever the occasion:

> Rejoice always, **pray continually,** give thanks in all circumstances; for this is God's will for you in Christ Jesus.
> (1 Thessalonians 5 v 16 - 18; emphasis added)

It has been a great encouragement in recent years to see a fresh emphasis on prayer in church life. There have been many excellent books and courses written to help God's people pray, both as individuals and corporately in our churches. Prayer movements are springing up all over the globe, with many believers uniting from diverse church backgrounds to pray as one. It seems that God is bringing a fresh season of intercession into the body of Christ.

'The Gap' And God's Heart Of Compassion

There's good reason to be encouraged. The power of prayer has been integral to moves of God across the church's history - look here at the words of the theologian, Jonathan Edwards (1703—1758). When describing great outpourings of the Holy Spirit as the spontaneous work of God, he comments that such events are often proceeded by or fuelled by prayer:

> *When God has something very great to accomplish for His church, it is His will that there should precede it, the extraordinary prayers of His people. And it is revealed that when God is about to accomplish great things for His Church, He will begin by remarkably pouring out the spirit of grace and supplication.*[1]

For the Apostle Paul, praying was of first importance for the church. Not only was prayer key for the strengthening of its life and witness, but also for the completion of God's mission to save all people and bring them to a knowledge of the truth:

> I urge, then, first of all, that petitions, prayers, intercession and thanksgiving be made for all people - for kings and all those in authority, that we may live peaceful and quiet lives in all godliness and holiness. This is good, and pleases God our Saviour, who wants all people to be saved and to come to a knowledge of the truth.
> (1 Timothy 2 v 1 - 4)

The link between prayer and the salvation of people is also reflected in the book of Ezekiel. In Chapter 22, we pick up the continuing story of Israel and their relationship with God, reading a vivid description of the desperate state they found themselves in. It was a real mess, as seen in the misuse of power, disrespect of parents, oppression of foreigners, mistreatment of orphans and widows, and the despising and flouting of God's laws. It's fair to say the foundations of the community had crumbled, as Scripture details the prevalence of false accusation and verbal assassination of people's character, ongoing violence, pagan and occult practices, gross sexual immorality and indecency, and financial corruption (see Ezekiel 22 v 6 - 12). Not pretty, to say the least.

Who or what could possibly begin turning this around?

The tide can always turn with God. Even at this time, as Israel turned away and had forsaken him, God was looking for someone to stand in the gap so he would not have to pour out judgement on the land. Someone who would intercede before him for the salvation of the nation. Someone who would pray for God's mercy and forgiveness to fall upon and heal his chosen people.

He looked for such a person among four groups:

- The priests - the spiritual leaders of the nation
- The princes - the leaders in the political and social spheres of life
- The prophets - those who made God's word known
- The people - the ordinary members of society

We can see how he looked among the whole nation, searching people's hearts. But the tragedy was, he could not find anyone!

> I looked for a someone among them who would build up the wall and stand before me in the gap on behalf of the land so I would not have to destroy it, but I found none.
> (Ezekiel 22 v 23 - 30)

Why was God looking for someone to stand in the gap? The answer reflects his enduring, eternal character - it was (and is) his desire to forgive his people despite their sinful rebellion. Earlier in Ezekiel, we see this truth expressed:

> "Do I take pleasure in the death of the wicked? declares the Sovereign Lord. Rather am I not pleased when they turn from their ways and live?"

> "...For I take no pleasure in the death of anyone, declares the Sovereign Lord. Repent and live!"
> (Ezekiel 18 v 23, 32)

God's overwhelming desire was to forgive his people, despite the great pain their sin had caused him. Indeed, forgiveness is central to the revelation of who he is. When God proclaims his name to Moses, he reveals himself as the one who forgives sin:

> "The LORD, the LORD, the compassionate and gracious God, slow to anger, abounding in love and faithfulness, maintaining love to thousands, and forgiving wickedness, rebellion and sin."
> (Exodus 34 v 6 - 7)

We see the same on a personal level in King David's life, a man after God's own heart. From his own experience of God's character, he speaks of the Lord's compassion towards sinful humanity:

> The Lord is compassionate and gracious, slow to anger, abounding in love. He will not always accuse, nor will he harbour his anger forever; he does not treat us as our sins deserve or repay us according to our iniquities.
> (Psalm 103 v 8 - 10)

Of course, we subsequently see God's heart and plan for forgiveness revealed fully in the New Testament. God sent Jesus to save the world through him by giving his life as a ransom for many. In him, we find the hope of our salvation, the forgiveness of our sins, and our adoption into God's family. Jesus is the one standing in the gap for you, me, and all humanity, fulfilling God's longing to see people brought back to him:

> For God did not send his Son into the world to condemn the world, but to save the world through him.
> (John 3 v 17)

> "For even the Son of Man did not come to be served, but to serve, and to give his life as a ransom for many."
> (Mark 10 v 45)

> They tell how you turned to God from idols to serve the living and true God, and to wait for his Son from heaven, whom he raised from the dead - Jesus, who rescues us from the coming wrath.
> (1 Thessalonians 1 v 9 - 10)

God is a forgiving God, and he has a plan for salvation. He will ensure the message of repentance and forgiveness of sin will be preached to all people across all nations, in Jesus' name. Amazingly, he has included frail and flawed mankind in the process! We have been given a vital role in taking his purposes forward, both by bold proclamation of the gospel and through our prayers (see Luke 24 v 46 - 49).

The key question for us as individuals is whether or not our hearts are fully committed to his purposes? Are we truly aware of the role, the position, and power we've been given? Are we willing and prepared to be that man or woman who 'stands in the gap?'

As churches, will we do the same by collectively giving ourselves to pray for our nation and the nations? Think about the need around us. Consider our governments and civic leaders, the crime and violence in our cities, the care for the elderly and vulnerable in our society, or the broken lives and broken families desperate for hope. We've barely scratched the surface, of course, but will we be moved to actively seek healing and restoration where it's needed? Will we then look to Jesus and proclaim the gospel, declaring him as the one who has the power to change the hearts and minds of the lost?

Breaking Barriers

We've circled back.

Prayer is important... but are we doing it? And if not, why not?

I've found the work of Wayne Grudem helpful when thinking about the reasons why we might lack focus, intention and discipline in prayer:

> *If we pray little, it is probably because we do not really believe that prayer accomplishes much at all.* [2]

This barrier is linked to a right faith, trust and knowledge of God's character and willingness to intervene. Our mindset here may be conscious or hidden, but I know many can relate to it.

Another obstacle is thinking our own shortcomings somehow disqualify us from bringing our requests to God. This barrier comes from a focus on 'us who can't, not him who can.' Be reassured... it's not a new problem! It's a common deception. Here, we can consistently remind ourselves of what Daniel understood so clearly in the Old Testament. We bring our requests to God in prayer, not because of our own goodness, but because of God's great mercy and love:

> "We do not make requests of you because we are righteous, but because of your great mercy."
> (Daniel 9 v 18)

God, in his love, always hopes for the best in us, persevering despite our weakness (see 1 Corinthians 13 v 4 - 8). Take encouragement from the warm response the disciples received from Jesus when they asked him to teach them to pray. We, too, can be confident of God teaching us and strengthening us as we fully set our hearts on him:

> "For the eyes of the Lord range throughout the earth, to strengthen those whose hearts are fully committed to him."
> (2 Chronicles 16 v 9)

Praying Our Way Into The Gap

I have found the narrative of Scripture so helpful in its instruction on different kinds of prayer. I've come a long way myself, but I have had a few more years to work on it than most! Context, need and purpose of prayer all differ under the one umbrella of fixing our eyes and hearts on Father God. As such, I want to share five types of prayer we can use to develop our own prayer lives.

1. Bold And Persistent Prayer

In my leadership role, I've had the privilege of working with many churches and believers across other countries and cultures. One of the things I have learnt from my brothers and sisters in other parts of the world is to pray big and bold prayers, full of faith in us having an equally 'big' God who is eager to provide for our needs!

Think about the well-known story of Sodom and Gomorrah, where God shares with Abraham about his imminent judgement of the two cities (see Genesis 18 v 16 - 33). To all intents, the judgement seemed fully justifiable when we consider their arrogance, neglect of the poor and needy, sexual immorality and perversion. But look at the following series of events.

In Scripture, Abraham is recognised as God's friend by others and by God himself (see 2 Chronicles 20 v 7; James 2 v 23; Isaiah 41 v 8). As Jesus points out when talking to his disciples, friends share all things in trust and confidence (see John 15 v 14 - 15). So, we find God sharing his plan, at which point Abraham begins to plead with God to have mercy on the cities and to 'stay' his hand of judgement:

> "What if there are fifty righteous people in the city? Will you really sweep it away and not spare the place for the sake of the fifty righteous people in it?"
> (Genesis 18 v 24)

The Lord replies, *"I will spare the whole place for their sake,"* which itself seems incredible (Genesis 18 v 26). However, if you know the story, you'll recall Abraham coming back to the Lord with increasing boldness, reducing the number of *"righteous"* people with each request. And 45? 40? 30? How about twenty? Finally, he lands on ten *"righteous"* people. On each occasion, the Lord replies he will not destroy the cities for their *"sake"*.

Can you imagine doing this? Does it not seem like he is 'seriously pushing his luck' by entering into a negotiation with Almighty God? I'm always amazed by this exchange! The important thing to note is the way Abraham describes the manner of his request:

> "...Now that I have been so **bold** as to speak to the Lord, though I am nothing but dust and ashes..."
>
> "...Now that I have been so **bold** as to speak to the Lord."
>
> (Genesis 18 v 27, 31; emphasis added)

Where did this boldness spring from? Was it simply the result of his personality type? Was it his active and authentic friendship with God? Was it linked to the remarkable promise of blessing he had just received (see Genesis 18 v 10). Did it spring from the revelation he had experienced about the character of God? Abraham had clearly captured something special, so let's look closely at the appeal Abraham makes to God, centred on his character, integrity and uprightness:

> "Far be it from you to do such a thing – to kill the righteous with the wicked, treating the righteous and the wicked alike. Far be it from you! Will not the Judge of all the earth do right?"
> (Genesis 18 v 25)

I want to suggest that to pray with boldness like Abraham, first requires us to cultivate intimacy and friendship with God. However, we must remember we're cultivating friendship, not *earning* it. Our identity in Christ is secure; Jesus has already called us *"friends"* (see John 15 v 15). Secondly, we must intercede based on what the Holy Spirit has revealed to us about the nature and character of God.

Remember the encouragement given by the writer of Hebrews. We are to come before God with boldness and confidence, trusting in all Jesus has accomplished for us through his life, death and resurrection:

> Therefore, since we have a great high priest who has ascended into heaven, Jesus the Son of God, let us hold firmly to the faith we profess. For we do not have a high priest who is unable to empathize with our weaknesses, but we have one who has been tempted in every way, just as we are—yet he did not sin. Let us then approach God's throne of grace with **confidence (boldness of speech),** so that we may receive mercy and find grace to help us in our time of need.
> (Hebrews 4 v 14 - 16; emphasis and parentheses added)

> Therefore, brothers and sisters, since **we have confidence** to enter the Most Holy Place by the blood of Jesus, by a new and living way opened for us through the curtain, that is, his body...
> (Hebrews 10 v 19 - 20; emphasis added)

After the disciples ask Jesus to teach them to pray, he underlines the theme of boldness by telling a parable (see Luke 11 v 5 - 8). In the story, a man has a friend on a journey who turns up at his door late in the evening. To his embarrassment, the man finds he has no food to set before the friend. In the honour culture of the day, hospitality was considered to be of utmost importance, so not providing for his guest would have brought shame on his family and on the whole village. We read of the man hurrying to his neighbour and trying to obtain provisions to set before his guest.

By this time it is midnight, and as you can imagine, his request did not receive a very positive response. A polite summary might be, 'Shut that noise up, we are all locked up for the night, the kids are fast asleep - go away!'

But the man persisted, and the neighbour eventually gets up and gives him all he needs. Jesus says the reason the neighbour met the man's need was not because he was the man's friend, but because of the man's boldness. The man maintained the conviction that his neighbour would not allow shame or dishonour to fall on him or the village.

Jesus then teaches us how this interaction should guide our own confidence when praying to God. If the man had confidence that his neighbour would uphold the honour of the village, how much more should we have confidence that God, the Father, will maintain the honour of his name when we boldly bring our requests to him? God is no reluctant neighbour, but fully trustworthy and true to all his promises.

Some interpreters feel the word *"boldness"* could mean 'persistence.' While there's no evidence of the word being used in this way elsewhere, it would certainly fit the context of the following few verses. Here, we find Jesus saying we are to ask and keep on asking, and our prayers will be answered. Seek and keep on seeking, and we will find what we are looking for. Knock and keep on knocking, and the door will be opened to us (see Luke 11 v 9 - 10). All three verbs are present imperatives, encouraging prayer as a continual habit in our lives. Put simply, we are to pray *now*... and keep going. God wants us to learn how to develop bold, persistent prayer, where we come to him fully assured of his unchanging character until we receive what we ask for in his name.

An incredible example of boldness in prayer is found in the life of Basilea Schlink of the Evangelical Sisterhood of Mary, Darmstadt, Germany. In her book, "The Miracles of God Experienced Today," she writes about a time of need in 1958. After a period of ten years and ten months of experiencing God's amazing provision of money and goods for the sisters' work, the provision began to dry up. It coincided with a time when a major building project was nearing completion, and the sisters suddenly found themselves $4,000 short each month (US equivalent). In March that year, Basilea was scheduled to complete a lecture tour of Israel. In the middle of the trip, she rowed a boat out onto Lake Galilee alone, finding the spot many people believe is where the disciples received their miraculous catch of fish. She recalls her bold praying:

> *And so, I confronted Jesus on this spot where He had so wonderfully met the need of His disciples. I asked Him whether He is the same today, never disappointing the faith of His own and standing back of His word, "If you ask anything in my name, I will do it."*[3]

The idea of "confronting" Jesus feels rather uncomfortable, doesn't it? Except, this act was one of hope, reliance and bold submission. Aware of her need, she was leaning into her complete faith in God's character and goodness, much like Abraham did. After this humble confrontation on the lake, the very next day, large sums of money began arriving at the sisters' property back in Germany. Not only were all the bills on the new building paid and the project completed, but an abundance of funding made it possible for them to start an even bigger building project. In fact, they were also able to purchase twenty acres of high-priced urban land for their future work!

2. Humble Prayer

The position of our heart is important - God looks at it. The Bible describes Moses as a very humble man, humbler than anyone else on the face of the earth (see Numbers 12 v 3). Therefore, he points forward to Jesus, who later spoke of himself as being gentle and humble in heart (see Matthew 11 v 28 - 30). Humility always encourages growth in our walk with God, and we can look to an event in the book of Exodus showing the trait in Moses' prayer life (see Exodus 32 v 7 - 14).

The background to the story is that after escaping from Egypt, the Israelites had made an idol of a golden calf to worship. They had quickly forgotten God's rescue. In his anger, God wanted to destroy them, but Moses stepped in to intercede on their behalf:

> So he said he would destroy them—
>   had not Moses, his chosen one,
> stood in the breach before him
>   to keep his wrath from destroying them.
> (Psalm 106 v 23)

Moses reminds the people of the incident with the golden calf just before they are due to cross over the Jordan and enter the promised land. Speaking of his intercession on their behalf, he talks of how he fell face down before the Lord:

> Then once again I fell prostrate before the Lord for forty days and forty nights; I ate no bread and drank no water, because of all the sin you had committed, doing what was evil in the Lord's sight and so arousing his anger. I feared the anger and wrath of the Lord, for he was angry enough with you to destroy you. But again, the Lord listened to me. (Deuteronomy 9 v 18 - 19)

Moses not only humbled his body by lying prostrate and fasting but humbled his heart before God as he prayed. His faithfulness was pleasing to God, and he wanted to destroy the people and make Moses into a great nation. But Moses would hear nothing of it, and in his prayer, he showed his passion for God's glory rather than his own.

The greater concern for Moses was what the Egyptians might say in response, and how God's name would be defamed. So, he reminds God of the promises he made to Abraham, Isaac and Israel - how their descendants would be as numerous as the stars in the sky, and that the promised land would be their inheritance forever. The result of his prayer saw mercy triumph over judgement. The Lord relented and spared his people; the first of many occasions when God would forgive them!

Our knowledge of who God is fixes the direction of our confidence on him, not us. Do you see the beautiful marriage of boldness and humility here?

Although we are called to be friends of God, we must be careful not to become over familiar with Him. We are encouraged to be bold in our praying, but not bossy! God is not at our beck and call, and we do well to remember this advice:

> Do not be quick with your mouth,
> do not be hasty in your heart
> to utter anything before God.
> God is in heaven
> and you are on earth,
> so let your words be few.
> (Ecclesiastes 5 v 2)

Humility helps us maintain a right perspective on ourselves, and more importantly focuses our attention on the greatness of our almighty God and Father. It helps us to develop a passion for His glory, giving us confidence in him not only hearing our prayers, but also answering them:

> "These are the ones I look on with favor:
> those who are humble and contrite in spirit,
> and who tremble at my word."
> (Isaiah 66 v 2)

3. Passionate Prayer

The familiar story of Nehemiah and the rebuilding of the walls of Jerusalem, is one that has encouraged and challenged believers for centuries. It starts with Nehemiah serving in the court of King Artaxerxes in Susa, the Persian capital. Here, he receives a troubling report from his brother Hanani. The exiles that had returned to the province of Judah were in great trouble and disgrace; the walls of Jerusalem were broken down, and its gates burned with fire.

The news affects Nehemiah deeply and he prays to God, confessing both his own sin and the sins of the Israelites. He asks God to be true to the covenant he made with his people, and that he would know God's favour and have a part to play in the restoration of Jerusalem.

There is much to learn from his prayer in the first chapter of the book. Specifically, I want to focus on his outpouring of emotion after receiving news of the disgrace and distress of God's people. It's clear Nehemiah was moved by their plight, touched by their distress, and grieved by their disobedience:

> When I heard these things, I sat down and wept. For some days I mourned and fasted and prayed before the God of heaven.
> (Nehemiah 1 v 4)

His emotions were stirred, he was moved in the depths of his being, and his aroused passions became fuel for his prayers. Praying out of the intensity of his feelings, along with fasting, he found God waiting to meet and answer him. Sadly, today many of us seem wary of our emotions and feelings, with stoicism seen as a sign of strength. But our emotions are God-given and wholesome; recall how we saw a similar outpouring push David towards God in our previous chapter. Emotions are meant to stir us to action, turn our hope towards God, and like Nehemiah, fuel our praying.

We have permission to feel. We are moved when we hear of the killing of innocent children in areas of conflict throughout the world. We feel pain when we learn of thousands of babies being aborted each year. When children in our care systems are sexually abused or children trafficked, it is right we should feel outraged. When we receive news of yet another marriage that has fallen apart, we empathise. Where trust has been broken and children's lives torn apart, it is right for our hearts to be filled with sadness and hurt. News of more sleaze and corruption in government circles will leave us disillusioned at the lack of justice and integrity. When youngsters are killed needlessly by drunk driving or a drug overdose, we grieve wasted lives. Or when a young mother dies of cancer and leaves a baby or toddler behind, it is right to cry, mourn and weep.

It begs the question, 'How do you possibly see God when all this pain surrounds?'

It's an understandable one, but I'm left asking in response, 'How do you *not* look to him in all this?'

Our hope in Jesus and a new heaven and new earth, should make us even more sensitive to the painful evidence of this world being broken, and certainly not our home. So, when we are confronted with increasing deaths through knife crime in our cities, or hear of old ladies being raped in their homes, we should be moved to act. It is right to feel let-down, disgusted, appalled and horrified. But for believers, even these feelings are not meant to overwhelm us. Rather they are to be like a spur, driving us into the presence of God to seek his solutions. Like Nehemiah, we have a hope which lets us passionately cry out to God for mercy on our land, even amidst the despair and confusion.

One of the difficulties facing us today is how we have become de-sensitised to pain, violence, suffering and death. So often, the portrayal of suffering in its many forms has become a soundbite in a media news bulletin, before the real entertainment of the night begins. The need of the hour, and call on believers, is to ask our heavenly Father to restore our humanity and soften our hearts where they have become callous. We need to learn to be angry all over again and bring back the feelings of an aching heart, letting our tears flow down as rivers of compassion as we pray.

Jesus modelled this heart of passionate care. We are told when Jesus saw the crowds, he had *"compassion"* (was moved with pity) for them because they were harassed and helpless, like sheep without a shepherd. And it was in this context he told his disciples, *"The harvest is plentiful but the workers are few."* He prompted them to action, instructing them to *"pray earnestly"* to the Lord who is in charge of the harvest, and to ask him to send more workers into his fields (see Matthew 9 v 35 - 38).

Jesus' compassion shaped his prayers. He knew time spent with his Heavenly Father was the restorative, sustaining and encouraging outlet he needed for all he felt:

> During the days of Jesus' life on earth, he offered up prayers and petitions with fervent cries and tears to the one who could save him from death, and he was heard because of his reverent submission.
> (Hebrews 5 v 7)

The phrase, *"fervent cries"* can be translated as powerful, strong cries or shouting out! Nothing was held back, I imagine because Jesus knew the danger of not bringing his emotions into the light before God. Jesus' prayers during his entire life were constantly heartfelt, earnest, and often accompanied by tears. So, let us not be afraid of our hearts and emotions being stirred by the Holy Spirit. Let's not shy away from, or discourage, the increase in intensity of our personal and corporate prayers as we seek to follow Jesus' example when bringing our requests and petitions to God.

4. Informed Prayer

As the well-known phrase goes, 'knowledge is power.' Although our own knowledge must never replace reliance on our all-knowing Father God, we have certainly been given minds to reason and understand. We must bring this part of our design into our prayers. In the Old Testament, we find Daniel praying for the restoration of Jerusalem and for God's favour to return to his people. These prayers were triggered by his knowledge of the Scriptures, and we can see how God's word informed his understanding:

> ...I, Daniel, understood from the Scriptures, according to the word of the Lord given to Jeremiah the prophet, that the desolation of Jerusalem would last seventy years. So, I turned to the Lord God and pleaded with Him in prayer and petition, in fasting and in sackcloth and ashes.
> (Daniel 9 v 2 - 3)

We can see how Daniel's understanding motivated him to pray. His knowledge empowered and emboldened him, as having understood, he didn't remain passive and wait for events to unfold. Understanding prompted action; he set himself to pray and seek God, asking the Lord to fulfil the prophetic word given to his people.

Like Daniel, we need to learn to be people who think as well as feel, as passionate prayer combined with understanding is powerful. We, too, will be empowered as we commit to read, study and meditate on the Scriptures, asking God for insight, revelation and understanding of his word. And do you see the links? Seeking God more in Scripture reflects our reliance on him, it builds confidence in his character, moving our spirit to feel compassion for the people and circumstances we encounter. More time immersed in the Bible helps build humble, bold, passionate prayer, grounded powerfully in truth.

The same principle is true of prophetic words that come to God's people when gathered together, and to those given to individual people. Scripture says it is essential to weigh and consider the prophetic (see 1 Corinthians 14 v 29). Seeking God in prayer helps us to discern and understand what God is saying. But in turn, our understanding allows us to pray for the right response to see those prophetic words outworked in our lives and the local church.

In the Old Testament, we read about the sons of Issachar who were able to discern the times and knew what Israel should do (see 1 Chronicles 12 v 32). This brought about an understanding that King Saul's kingdom was ending, and that God was establishing David to be king. They had insight into what God was doing and when he was doing it. From here, we read how their understanding caused them to act and join David at Hebron, armed for battle. It appears they had both a spiritual and political understanding of the times -godly wisdom applied powerfully in our worldly context. We are not told how they developed their discernment, but certainly in our own day, we need to similarly understand the times in which we are living and consider carefully what God is doing.

Notice how Jesus rebuked the Pharisees and Sadducees when they came to him to test him and ask for a sign from heaven:

> "...You know how to interpret the appearance of the sky, but you cannot interpret the signs of the times."
> (Matthew 16 v 3)

Recognising what God is doing, when he's doing it, and what this means for us, doesn't just happen. We, too, won't interpret the *"signs of the times,"* unless we immerse ourselves in the Scriptures and ask the Holy Spirit to give us understanding and revelation. Seeking God in prayer is vital to this endeavour:

> For the Lord gives wisdom;
> from his mouth come knowledge and understanding.
> (Proverbs 2 v 6)

It was John Stott who said a follower of Christ should have a Bible in one hand and a newspaper in the other. I love this! Without both, he is unarmed. With the newspaper only, you have the calamity and depravity in the world with no hope to offer. With only the Scripture, you have hope but no sense of where to apply it. In other words, our faith needs to be present and engaged in the issues confronting our world.

Practical as ever, Stott also talked about "double listening."[4] By this, he meant being able to discern two voices at the same time, the voice of God through Scripture and the voices of men and women around us. Informed prayer helps us understand what we hear, before applying God's wisdom to the world around us.

5. Urgent Prayer

There are also times when a situation or a set of circumstances jump straight to the top of the list of priorities. You may recall times in your life when there has been a need to petition God for immediate intervention. In the book of Numbers, we read of a rebellion against Moses and Aaron's leadership (see Numbers 16 v 41 - 50). It starts with a complaint from a group of Levites, Reubenites and 250 well-known community leaders who formed part of the council. The rebels accused them of being out for personal gain, of lording it over the people, and not fulfilling their promise to lead them into the promised land. They also questioned the appointment of Aaron to the priesthood.

Central to their many complaints was that Aaron and Moses had put themselves above the assembly, arguing God's people were equally as holy as them, and that the Lord himself was with the people. In response, Moses accused them of wanting the priesthood for themselves, despite already being appointed to a high position of serving in the Lord's tabernacle and ministering to the community.

After warning the people to move away from the tents of the rebels, the sad result saw God judge the leaders of the rebellion. Their rebellion ended in them and their families dying an unnatural death, with them going down alive into the grave:

> As soon as he finished saying all this, the ground under them split apart and the earth opened its mouth and swallowed them and their households, and all those associated with Korah, together with their possessions.
> (Numbers 16 v 31 - 32)

Fire then came out from the Lord and consumed the 250 complicit community leaders. But worse was to come! The next day, the whole Israelite community grumbled against Moses and Aaron, rising up in opposition to them and accusing them of killing the Lord's people. At this point the glory of the Lord appeared over the Tent of Meeting. Moses and Aaron were told by God to get away from the Tent where they were standing so he could consume them in a moment. In response, Moses and Aaron fell on their faces.

Then came an extraordinary intervention from Moses! Moses tells Aaron to take a censer and fill it with incense along with fire from the altar. A plague from the Lord had started to take the lives of the people, and there was urgent need to speedily make atonement for them. We then read of Aaron running into the midst of the assembly, offering incense and making atonement. Note here, Moses' heart was not bitter towards the community but remained focused on the well-being of those he served. As Aaron stands between the living and the dead, the plague stops, but not before some 14,700 people had died.

Can you see how this act brings us back to where we started the chapter in the book of Ezekiel? God is looking for a people, who like Aaron, will stand in prayer between the living and the dead. He seeks those who will offer prayer for gospel success among the perishing, regardless of opposition. His ear is turned to those who will give themselves to prayer and intercession, with a sense of urgency to see the fulfilment of God's purposes. He will respond to ordinary followers of Jesus, like you and I, who are convinced their prayers will affect the eternal destiny of thousands.

Will we respond to the pressing challenge of the Apostle Paul?

> Now, brothers and sisters about times and dates we do not need to write to you. For you know very well that the day of the Lord will come like a thief in the night. While people are saying "peace and safety" destruction will come upon them suddenly, as labour pains on a pregnant woman, and they will not escape.
> (1 Thessalonians 5 v 1 - 3)

> The night is nearly over; the day is almost here. So let us put aside the deeds of darkness and put on the armour of light.
> (Romans 13 v 12)

The situation before us is acute, compelling, pressing and a top priority. It's a matter of life and death.

Will we be numbered among those who, together, stand in the gap? By God's grace and the indwelling power of the Holy Spirit, will we give ourselves to learn how to pray bold, persistent, humble, passionate, informed and urgent prayers.

Notes

1 Jonathan Edwards, from his Thoughts on Revival, Part 5: www.azquotes.com/author/4377-Jonathan_Edwards/tag/prayer

2 Systematic Theology: An Introduction to Biblical Doctrine by Wayne Grudem. Published by IVP 1994, Page 377. ISBN 978-0851106526

3 The Miracles of God Experienced Today by Basilea Schlink. Copyright © Basilea Schlink 1981. Published by Marshall Pickering, ISBN 9780551000087

4 The Contemporary Christian by John Stott. Copyright © John Stott 1992. Published by IVP, ISBN 9780851109732

CHAPTER SEVENTEEN

Consider Him

"The student is not above the teacher, nor a servant above his master. It is enough for students to be like their teachers, and servants like their masters."

(Matthew 10 v 24 - 25)

At the beginning of this book, we explored the goal of being a disciple of Jesus - we are to become like him. Through all the different circumstances, emotions and experiences of life, our hearts, minds and characters will be transformed into the likeness of Christ by the power of the Holy Spirit. While we've already considered many key truths to help us as we pursue this lifelong endeavour, we're now going to look at the vital importance of daily fixing our eyes on Jesus. In the busyness, in the doing, and even in 'the mission,' we need to prioritise taking time out to consider him.

Setting aside time each day with Jesus is critical to our spiritual health. Doing so shows our reliance on him and not ourselves, nourishing our souls with the truth of our new identity, and equipping us to live according to it. Look at how the writer of Hebrews encourages followers of Jesus to throw off everything that hinders them, including sin, so they can run with perseverance the race marked out for them:

> ...let us throw off everything that hinders and the sin that so easily entangles. And let us run with perseverance the race marked out for us, **fixing our eyes on Jesus,** the pioneer

> and perfecter of faith. For the joy set before him he endured the cross, scorning its shame, and sat down at the right hand of the throne of God. **Consider him** who endured such opposition from sinners, so that you will not grow weary and lose heart.
> (Hebrews 12 v 1 - 3; emphasis added)

"Fixing our eyes" means to consider attentively and look away from all others to gaze on a single object. Similarly, the word *"consider,"* means to be attentive and to think carefully. But this part of our walk is hard to maintain and is easily sidelined. Lives and minds are busy things, with endless noise and distraction fighting for our focus and attention. As work, family, love, calling, and the rest shout, 'Pick me! Pick me!' we are to pick Jesus first and trust him for everything else. Let's begin by capturing something of the wonderful saviour and friend we are to fix our eyes on.

Servant Song

In the second section of the book of Isaiah, we find four passages which have been designated, "Servant Songs." In fact, the theme of *"the servant of the Lord"* appears some twenty times within the second section of the book, suggesting it's worth us taking note!

The title, *"Servant of God (the Lord),"* is given to many men of God in the Scriptures. You won't be surprised to know this list includes Moses, Joshua and David; this seems to fit nicely with the calling on their lives. But it is also given to others we might not expect, like the pagan King Nebuchadnezzar. As such, many people think the title speaks more of a person's function than a reflection of a person's character. However, the description of the *"servant"* in Isaiah seems to suggest something far greater than function and role. There is clearly godly calling and godly character at the very core of the servant's heart:

> "Here is my servant, whom I uphold,
>   my chosen one in whom I delight;
> I will put my Spirit on him,

and he will bring justice to the nations.
He will not shout or cry out,
or raise his voice in the streets.
A bruised reed he will not break,
and a smoldering wick he will not snuff out.
In faithfulness he will bring forth justice;
he will not falter or be discouraged
till he establishes justice on earth.
In his teaching the islands will put their hope."

This is what God the Lord says—
the Creator of the heavens, who stretches them out,
who spreads out the earth with all that springs from it,
who gives breath to its people,
and life to those who walk on it:

"I, the Lord, have called you in righteousness;
I will take hold of your hand.
I will keep you and will make you
to be a covenant for the people
and a light for the Gentiles,
to open eyes that are blind,
to free captives from prison
and to release from the dungeon those who sit in darkness.

"I am the Lord; that is my name!
I will not yield my glory to another
or my praise to idols.
See, the former things have taken place,
and new things I declare;
before they spring into being
I announce them to you."

(Isaiah 42 v 1 - 9)

Consider Him, In Whom God Delights

The person in the description of the servant is not revealed. As a nation, Israel is referred to as *"servant"* on multiple occasions.

However, we are not told Israel is the focus of this first "Servant Song." Isaiah could be speaking about Israel, yet Israel's journey appears to be the very opposite of the beautiful description of unwavering faithfulness we see. Indeed, at this time we find Israel resentful, complaining, fearful, dismayed, blind, deaf and disobedient! This has led to some thinking the song is a prophetic picture of all Israel was destined to become and do; it could be reflective of the longing or enduring hope God has, in his faithfulness, for his chosen nation. After all, Israel had been chosen and elected by God to be a light to the nations, carrying the call of Abraham for all the people on earth to be blessed through her.

But we get a real sense and conviction that the servant portrayed is a real person, a real individual who embodies true servanthood. It's as if we're reading a description of the pre-eminent or perfect servant. It appears active, rather than simply hopeful.

Could this servant be anyone else but Jesus?

At the end of the previous chapter in Isaiah, God speaks to Israel of the futility of idols and their total ineffectiveness to provide counsel and guidance. Expressing the foolishness of idolatry, he pronounces idols to be nothing but *"wind and confusion"* (see Isaiah 41 v 29). Then here, in the opening verse of Chapter 42, he issues a command to Israel to look away from their idols to behold or see his servant. God is putting his servant on display, showing him off and asking them to observe him closely and carefully. There is something very special about him, for he is going to bring about significant change, both for Israel and the entire Gentile world.

The contrast between God's servant and the futility of false idols could not be clearer. Note the language God uses as he tells us how he upholds his servant by gripping him fast, signifying that it is his power strengthening and sustaining him. God describes the servant as, *"My chosen one in whom I delight"* (verse 1). Not only does the servant please God and receive his approval, but there is deep affection and delight in him. Do you recognise the same sentiment expressed by God about Jesus at both his baptism and transfiguration?

> ..."This is my Son, whom I love; with him I am well pleased." (Matthew 3 v 17)

> …"This is my dearly loved Son, who brings me great joy. Listen to him."
> (Matthew 17 v 5 NLT)

He then speaks of giving his Holy Spirit to his servant; *"I will put my Spirit on him,"* or as some versions translate it, *"I have put my Spirit upon him"* (verse 1). Both speak clearly of the promise of the personal presence and power of God, to enable his servant to complete his God-given tasks. Look at how John the Baptist gives testimony to such an endowment received by Jesus when he says that the Father gave him the Spirit without limit:

> For the one whom God has sent speaks the words of God, for God gives the Spirit without limit *(or measure).*
> (John 3 v 34; parentheses added)

Consider Him Who Brings Justice

The song records how the servant will complete God's task of bringing justice to the nations. This justice will be universal and all-inclusive in scope, reaching to earth's most remote bounds. God's justice will not be something people search for or progressively find, but something revealed and brought to them by the servant who establishes it.

It will be helpful at this point to say something about the word 'justice' (Hebrew: *mishpat*), for it has a larger meaning than our normal concept of justice. The root meaning of the word is to give an authoritative judgement or verdict, a decision at law. In the historical context it had three meanings. By exploring the meaning, we will be able to more clearly see the calling on the servant's life, and what this also means for ours.

First, it meant a judgement at law. Here, justice spoke of the trial between the Lord and the nations with their false gods and idols. The verdict was declared; there was only one true and living God, the God of Israel. So, it was the servant's task to make the truth about Israel's God known everywhere, declaring that he alone is the Sovereign Creator and Lord of history.

Second, justice referred to all which God had authoritatively settled and established. In his commentary on Isaiah, Alec Motyer says, "Justice is a summary word for God's revealed truth. The Lord's truth and truth about the Lord."[1] He also states that *"his law"* (verse 4), speaks of God's instruction and guidance, acting as a parallel expression for justice. The servant's task is, therefore, to make known this truth (law) in all its fullness, causing mankind to put their confidence, trust and hope for their future in it.

Third, it meant the righting of wrongs and the establishing of right order, which God has given to the whole universe in his sovereignty and by his creative acts. Justice meant God would reign in judging the world in righteousness and the peoples in his truth. Therefore, the calling for the servant is to establish God's kingdom, his rule and his reign (see Psalm 96 v 13).

Do we see Jesus fulfilling this call to bring justice?

Jesus' focus on justice is unwavering.

When Jesus began his earthly ministry, we are told he began to preach, *"Repent for the kingdom of heaven is near"* (Matthew 4 v 17). Matthew says, *"he went throughout Galilee, teaching in their synagogues, proclaiming the good news of the kingdom and healing every disease and sickness among the people"* (Matthew 4 v 23). Jesus knew his role in relation to God's law. He made it clear he had not come to abolish the Law and the Prophets, but to fulfil them (see Matthew 5 v 17). And when accused by the Pharisees of driving out demons by the prince of demons he answers, *"But if it is by the Spirit of God that I drive out demons, then the kingdom of God has come upon you"* (Matthew 12 v 28). Jesus tells of how the Father has entrusted all judgement to him (see John 5 v 22 - 23).

Each of these are clear expressions of how it was foretold the servant of God would bring justice to the nations. Through Jesus' words, teaching and actions, we see how he knew bringing justice was at the heart of his calling as God's servant.

Consider Him Who Is Humble

It is telling to look at how Isaiah describes the way the servant will carry out his task. We are told that, *"He will not shout, or cry out, or raise his voice in the streets"* (verse 2). We are reading of someone whose character is defined by humility. He will not try to win favour with people by ostentation or publicity. There will be no self-promotion or seeking of public attention. He will not seek to advance his cause by shouting others down or dominate others to get his voice heard. Rather, his approach will be quiet and non-threatening.

Again, we see this so very clearly in the life of Jesus when we find him performing miracles in private, and warning those he healed not to make him known. In his gospel, Matthew gives us an example of this and follows with a direct reference to Isaiah, Chapter 42:

> Aware of this, Jesus withdrew from that place. A large crowd followed him, and he healed all who were ill. He warned them not to tell others about him. This was to fulfill what was spoken through the prophet Isaiah...
> (Matthew 12 v 15 - 17)

After his transfiguration he commands his disciples to secrecy, not allowing them to publish his messianic glory which they had seen, *"until the Son of Man has been raised from the dead"* (see Matthew 17 v 9).

Jesus remained wary of unnecessary attention and how it would negatively impact how he could carry out his mission. Often this defied worldly logic, as surely everyone should see clear demonstrations of his God-given power! In his gospel, John records how Jesus rejected his brothers' encouragement to go to the Feast of Tabernacles and show himself to the world:

> After this, Jesus went around in Galilee. He did not want to go about in Judea because the Jewish leaders there were looking for a way to kill him. But when the Jewish Festival of Tabernacles was near, Jesus' brothers said to him, "Leave Galilee and go to Judea, so that your disciples there may see the works you do. No one who wants to become a public

> figure acts in secret. Since you are doing these things, show yourself to the world." For even his own brothers did not believe in him.
> (John 7 v 1 - 5)

Isn't this a timely reminder to us about the need to watch for the dangers of present-day Christian celebrity? The advance of God's kingdom does not require public platforms, great publicity and media coverage to advance its cause. Rather it grows first in small and unnoticed ways, followed by gradual and remarkable growth. We should be wary of consciously promoting others, our churches or ourselves. We don't need to elevate and raise people up more than necessary for them to fulfil God's calling; in fact, this can be a hindrance to both them and the mission. We need to lift Jesus high and become more like John the Baptist, who 'prepared the way, cleared the way and then got out of the way!' Or, as Scripture records John's words, *"He must become greater, I must become less"* (John 3 v 30).

Consider Him Who Is Gentle And Compassionate

You'll see that Isaiah shares two vivid images to reveal the understanding and compassionate way the servant treats people. Think about your own weaknesses and the areas of your life or character that leave you vulnerable. Next, read and consider the beautiful way we're told God's servant acts towards us, *"A bruised reed he will not break, and a smouldering wick he will not snuff out"* (Isaiah 42 v 3). We're reminded of the brokenness and fragility of men and women, resulting from our sin and the futility and emptiness of lives lived without God.

A bruised reed is useless as a support, or indeed for anything else, and a smouldering wick is too far gone and borders on extinction. In a natural sense, neither will recover. Yet the Lord's servant does not come with condemnation, judgement and destruction. Isaiah is adamant, he will not cause further damage or discard the bruised reed. Neither will he snuff out and extinguish the smouldering, faltering wick. Instead, he will bring the good news of salvation, and act with tenderness and compassion to bring healing and restoration.

Henry Uprichard comments beautifully on this wonderful truth:

> *The solitary reed, clipped by the wing of a bird, hangs lifeless among the other rushes, its life-giving sap restricted, its resistance to the driving wind nil. How easily it could be snapped off and forever be forgotten and lost. The servant restores it, lifts it up, replenishes its growth, heals its defects and makes it live again.*

Gentleness and compassion are seen continually in the life of Jesus. Take, for example, his conversation at the well with the woman of Samaria (see John 4). She was a woman who had gone through five marriages and was now living with a man who was not her husband. Perhaps this relationship now represented her last attempt at finding happiness? Or possibly, as she grew older and felt less and less worthy of love, she was unable to countenance life on her own? Whatever her reasons, she was lost. She was a woman with a history that assigned to her a significant social stigma, she was bruised by life and probably living on the margins of society.

Yet her encounter with Jesus transforms her life. He looks beyond the outward and obvious bruises and hurts. He gives her hope and speaks to her deepest needs, revealing that her inner longings for intimacy can only be met in God alone. But note, despite cutting to the heart of her brokenness, she feels safe in his presence and not hopeless. He shares with her the good news that God himself was ready for a relationship with her – he could give her living water to satisfy her human need for love and acceptance, leading to the promise of eternal life.

Another example is his interaction with the women caught in the act of adultery (see John 8). She has been dragged into the square of public humiliation and shame, with her accusers like a pack of wolves baying for her blood. Jesus knows fully of her sin, but he first confronts her accusers with their own hardness of heart and lack of moral integrity. When he turns to the woman, he speaks softly and tenderly to her, not with the voice of accusation or condemnation. His compassion points her to the reality of a new life, in stark contrast to her life of sin, where she can leave the brokenness behind and make a fresh start. His words, seasoned with compassion, give her back her life when it was on the brink of being snuffed out!

Consider Him Who Is Faithful

Isaiah continues by speaking of the faithfulness of the servant who will bring forth God's justice, underlining his total reliability in the discharge of all his tasks. He will persevere through to their accomplishment, unwavering in his commitment to see them finished.

We catch a glimpse of this same faithfulness as Jesus steps out boldly on his final journey to Jerusalem. Remember, at this time Jesus knew his wider journey was approaching its earthly end. He was walking towards his impending death by crucifixion, and subsequent resurrection and ascension; his steps therefore, were intentional and purpose-driven:

> As the time approached for him to be taken up to heaven,
> Jesus resolutely set out for Jerusalem.
> (Luke 9 v 51)

Some translations say *"he set his face to go to Jerusalem,"* and later in the same chapter we are told the people of a Samaritan village would not welcome or receive him *"because he was heading for Jerusalem"* (Luke 9 v 53). It's interesting to note this foretaste of the ultimate rejection Jesus was faithfully going to face for us as he continued to head towards the cross, where he would carry and conquer all sin.

When looking at these words, the well-known British preacher, C. H. Spurgeon (1834—1892), suggests the Holy Spirit may well have brought to Luke's mind the words in Isaiah Chapter 50[2]. Here, the Messiah is described as setting his face *"like a flint,"* in a similarly resolute way:

> Because the Sovereign Lord helps me,
> I will not be disgraced.
> Therefore have I set my face like flint,
> and I know I will not be put to shame.
> (Isaiah 50 v 7)

Even from the glory of eternity, Jesus resolved to save his people and nothing could keep him from the accomplishment of this purpose. There was complete determination to be fully obedient to God's will and to fulfil the calling given to him by the Father.

Isaiah next tells us how this servant of the Lord *"will not falter or be discouraged till he establishes justice on earth"* (verse 4). Here, Isaiah makes an important link to the earlier image, for *"falter"* means to grow weak or dim. In contrast to the smouldering wick, he will never burn low or faintly. *"Discouraged"* means to be crushed or broken. In contrast to the bruised reed, the servant won't let the wounds of life impact him in such a way that they cause him to run from the battle and not finish the task. Quite literally Isaiah says, "He will not flicker or break." Where we are weak, God's servant is continually strong, or as Paul describes in his revelation of Christ, *"My grace is sufficient for you, for my power is made perfect in weakness"* (2 Corinthians 12 v 9).

Consider Him Who Understands Our Humanity

We must not, for one moment, imagine the servant being immune from suffering or pressure. The difference is, it does not immobilise him from finishing what God had purposed. Jesus embodies this when he experienced and overcame the agonising weight of sin laid before him in his Father's plan. He is truly God, but he is also truly man:

> Because God's children are human beings—made of flesh and blood—the Son also became flesh and blood. For only as a human being could he die, and only by dying could he break the power of the devil, who had the power of death. Only in this way could he set free all who have lived their lives as slaves to the fear of dying.
>
> For surely it is not angels he helps, but Abraham's descendants. For this reason, he had to be made like them, fully human in every way, in order that he might become a merciful and faithful high priest in service to God, and that he might make atonement for the sins of the people.

> Because he himself suffered when he was tempted, he is able to help those who are being tempted.
>
> (Hebrews 2 v 14 – 18 NLT)

And it is in the humanity of the servant Jesus we find our own great hope:

> Therefore, since we have a great high priest who has ascended into heaven, Jesus the Son of God, let us hold firmly to the faith we profess. For we do not have a high priest who is unable to empathize with our weaknesses, but we have one who has been tempted in every way, just as we are—yet he did not sin. Let us then approach God's throne of grace with confidence, so that we may receive mercy and find grace to help us in our time of need.
> (Hebrews 4 v 15 - 16)

God's perfect servant shared the same humanity as you and I, but he never sinned, becoming like those he came to help. His internal resources and resilience allowed him to stand against the outward blows inflicted upon him.

Consider Him Who Is Filled With The Spirit

Earlier in Isaiah, we read the task of establishing justice on the earth will be the result of the Spirit of the Lord resting upon his servant, his anointed one:

> Out of the stump of David's family will grow a shoot—
> yes, a new Branch bearing fruit from the old root.
> And the Spirit of the Lord will rest on him—
> the Spirit of wisdom and understanding,
> the Spirit of counsel and might,
> the Spirit of knowledge and the fear of the Lord.
> He will delight in obeying the Lord.
> He will not judge by appearance
> nor make a decision based on hearsay.
> He will give justice to the poor
> and make fair decisions for the exploited.

The earth will shake at the force of his word,
    and one breath from his mouth will destroy the wicked
He will wear righteousness like a belt
    and truth like an undergarment.
(Isaiah 11 v 1 - 5 NLT)

Jesus was the realisation of this promise. God had put His Spirit upon Jesus without measure, meaning he could say in the synagogue at Nazareth that Isaiah's prophecy had been fulfilled in their presence. Jesus was the servant, bringing this good news and fulfilling God's salvation plan:

"The Spirit of the Lord is on me,
    because he has anointed me
    to proclaim good news to the poor.
He has sent me to proclaim freedom for the prisoners
    and recovery of sight for the blind,
to set the oppressed free,
    to proclaim the year of the Lord's favor."
(Luke 4 v 18 - 19)

Consider Him, The Revelation Of Scripture

In the remaining words of the "Servant Song" (see verses 4 - 9), God speaks to his servant, confirms his task, and pledges his support to ensure the outcome. As the Lord of history, God alone directs both the past and future. The future he has ordained will see his servant bring the whole world into freedom and obedience to him. This freedom will be achieved in such a way that God receives the glory, for his glory cannot be shared with anyone else.

These verses in Isaiah are just one example of the riches we can find when we take time to look at Jesus and consider him as the ultimate revelation of the Scriptures. This is why setting aside time to read and meditate on Scripture is so vital to our growth in Christian discipleship and Christlikeness.

Jesus knew this. He was the culmination of years of waiting, a great number of prophecies, and generation after generation of expectant hope. When talking with the Jews, he reminded them clearly that the Scriptures testify about and point directly to him and the freedom he brings:

> "You study the Scriptures diligently because you think that in them you have eternal life. These are the very Scriptures that testify about me, yet you refuse to come to me to have life."
> (John 5 v 39 - 40)

Similarly, after his resurrection, we find Jesus joining two of his followers as they walk along the road to Emmaus. Luke tells us Jesus began to share with them how the prophets writing in the Scriptures clearly predicted the Messiah would suffer and die. He then takes them through the writings of Moses and all the prophets, explaining from all the Scriptures the things concerning himself (see Luke 24 v 25 - 27).

How many of us would have loved to eavesdrop on that conversation or would love the opportunity to sit down with Jesus and have our own personal bible study with him? Yet when speaking to his disciples, Jesus encouraged them that when they received the promised Holy Spirit, he would guide them into all truth:

> "But when the Father sends the Advocate as my representative – that is the Holy Spirit – he will teach you everything and will remind you of everything I have told you."
> (John 14 v 26 NLT)

We read this knowing the Holy Spirit would come to later live in them, and also that he does the same for believers today. We, too, are recipients of God's grace and those who have the Holy Spirit within us. As such, we can have confidence the Spirit will aid us in coming to know Jesus better, granting us insight and understanding through the Scriptures. Like the Apostle Paul we can continue to pray for each other, just as he prayed for the followers of Jesus in Ephesus:

> For this reason, ever since I heard about your faith in the Lord Jesus and your love for all God's people, I have not

> stopped giving thanks for you, remembering you in my prayers. **I keep asking** that the God of our Lord Jesus Christ, the glorious Father, may give you the Spirit of wisdom and revelation, **so that you may know him better.**
> (Ephesians 1 v 15 - 17; emphasis added)

As we continue to take time to 'look' and 'behold' him, may the Holy Spirit transform us more and more into his glorious image:

> But whenever someone turns to the Lord, the veil is taken away. For the Lord is the Spirit, and wherever the Spirit of the Lord is, there is freedom. So, all of us who have had that veil removed can see and reflect the glory of the Lord. And the Lord—who is the Spirit—makes us more and more like him as we are changed into his glorious image.
> (2 Corinthians 3 v 16 - 18)

As we consider Jesus, God's servant, we can reflect his love through the power of the Holy Spirit living in us. How wonderful if the result of our own transformed lives sees us constantly reaching out, like him, to the bruised and broken lives around us. Like him, we can show compassion and understanding to those whose lives have nearly been extinguished. Like him, we can reach out in love and bring others to a knowledge of God's true servant. By God's grace, we can see the degrading effects of sin undone, with many being brought from death to life. By considering Jesus as the revelation of all hope found in Scripture, we can see others find forgiveness, healing and restoration through relationship with their heavenly Father. And as others become true sons and daughters of the living God, we will see them experience the perfect faithfulness and reliability of the servant of the Lord, who will one day establish God's justice across all the earth.

Consider Jesus, God's servant.

Notes

1 The Prophecy of Isaiah, An Introduction and Commentary by J. Alec Motyer, published by IVP

2 Charles Haddon Spurgeon, November 28, 1880. Scripture: Isaiah 51 v 7. Metropolitan Tabernacle Pulpit Volume 47

CHAPTER EIGHTEEN

Right Foundations

Why would we talk about foundations at the end of a book? A more natural and customary place would have been right at the beginning. However, I do so because I am acutely aware of one of our greatest dangers as followers of Jesus. We can accumulate knowledge, at the expense of putting what we discover into practice. Or to use biblical terminology, we have a tendency to be hearers, rather than doers, of God's word. James talked about this danger when writing to the early church:

> Don't fool yourself into thinking that you are a listener when you are nothing but, letting the Word go in one ear and out the other. Act on what you hear! Those who don't act are like those who glance in the mirror, walk away, and two minutes later have no idea who they are, what they look like. (James 1 v 22 - 24 MSG)

I'm not sure if it's encouraging or challenging to find the same human battles with faith continuing 2000 years later. It's possible to have good biblical knowledge, yet remain spiritually immature, struggling with and being dogged for years by the same habits and sins. Failing to apply God's word can result in us falling short of the fullness on offer for our lives; we can forfeit the full blessings that Christ won for us at such great personal cost. When this happens, it inevitably leads to the dishonouring of God in our lives, both as individuals and as his church. Allowing the voice of our culture to take precedence over God's voice, results in us swiftly becoming exposed to the danger of being squeezed into the world's own mould. I'm convinced this doesn't need to be your story, my story, or the story for any believer!

Going Over Old Ground

The writer to the Hebrews explains the reason for the immaturity of many believers was their slowness to learn. They were dull of hearing and needed someone to teach them the elementary truths of God's word all over again. They were still on a milk diet and not ready for solid food. However, those who had matured in their faith could cope with solid food because, by consistent use, they had trained themselves to distinguish good from evil:

> But solid food is for the mature, who by constant use have trained themselves to distinguish good from evil.
> (Hebrews 5 v 14)

Some years ago I read this statement by Neil Crosbie, who was the Director of the Bible Society at the time:

> *We believe passionately that the Bible is indispensable for the future wellbeing of our world because it reveals God's character and purpose for humankind. Not surprisingly then, we want to see a world where the inspiration, wisdom and realism of the Bible shapes and changes the way individuals, communities and nations live, where everyone everywhere has the opportunity to encounter the drama of the Bible for themselves, to bring purpose, dignity and vitality to their lives.*[1]

Most of us who count ourselves as believers would agree with those sentiments, even if others in society consider the Bible as having little relevance to our day and generation. But the prompt and challenge of the writer to the Hebrews certainly includes those actively involved in church life today. The truth is, even for many Christians, the practice of Bible reading and Bible study take a very low priority in everyday life.

Some years ago, in one of the churches I helped lead, I took the step of asking the congregation to complete an anonymous survey on their current reading and listening habits, both secular and sacred. I was not prepared for the answers!

The church was, by outward appearance, lively and thriving. However, 20% said they only read the Bible when the mood took them. 50% said they only occasionally studied the Bible, while 20% percent were honest enough to say they had never given time to serious Bible study throughout the whole of their Christian lives. Of course, I was pleased we'd created a community and context where struggles and need could be uncovered. But it was a concern; there was (and is) clearly a call to better disciple and encourage believers into establishing these life-giving rhythms.

In my experience, I feel there is something even more detrimental to a person's spiritual health and well-being, than simply a lack of reading or studying God's word. I would suggest reading, studying or hearing, without putting it into practice, is even more harmful! As we have seen, James calls this kind of behaviour self-deception or fooling ourselves. We, therefore, need to be on our guard to ensure we don't fall into the trap of assuming because we have read, studied or heard the word of God taught, we are actually doing what it asks of us.

In Ezekiel, as we read of God speaking to a prophet, we have an illustration of the dangers of not obeying the word of God:

> "As for you, son of man, your people are talking together about you by the walls and at the doors of the houses, saying to each other, 'Come and hear the message that has come from the Lord.' My people come to you, as they usually do, and sit before you to hear your words, but they do not put them into practice. Their mouths speak of love, but their hearts are greedy for unjust gain. Indeed, to them you are nothing more than one who sings love songs with a beautiful voice and plays an instrument well, for they hear your words but do not put them into practice."
> (Ezekiel 33 v 30 - 32)

The importance of listening and doing – it's a common theme and is key to the foundations we're laying in our lives. When Moses gave his farewell address to God's people before his death, he recounted God's dealings with Israel and the commands he had given to his people. As he spoke, he stressed the importance of the people, and their children, putting God's word into practice. He spoke of God's instructions as being their very *"life"* and the foundations they must build everything on:

> When Moses had finished reciting all these words to the people of Israel, he added: "Take to heart all the words of warning I have given you today. Pass them on as a command to your children so they will obey every word of these instructions. **These instructions are not empty words—they are your life!** By obeying them you will enjoy a long life in the land you will occupy when you cross the Jordan River."
> (Deuteronomy 32 v 45 - 47 NLT; emphasis added)

Similarly, the psalmist talks about the many blessings that accompany those who delight in the law of the Lord, and who meditate on it, day and night:

> That person is like a tree planted by streams of water,
> which yields its fruit in season
> and whose leaf does not wither—
> **whatever they do prospers.**
> (Psalm 1 v 3; emphasis added)

The message continues consistently all the way through to the New Testament and is underlined in the life of Jesus. During his time of temptation in the wilderness, Jesus spoke of the fundamental importance of God's words and how they are the well-spring of a person's life:

> 'Man shall not live on bread alone, but on every word that comes from the mouth of God.'
> (Matthew 4 v 4)

These verses all stress the value of God's word in our lives. It's critical for us not to miss the connection between delighting in God's law, obeying it, and seeing its outworking in our daily lives.

Lives Built On The Word

In Matthew's gospel there is a very familiar parable told by Jesus, often entitled, "The Wise and Foolish Builder." The story underlines the need for action, and is told at the end of the Sermon on the Mount, where Jesus has described the nature, character and lifestyle of his true disciples. It's as if Jesus is saying, 'You've heard what I've got to say. You've heard the truth. Now, what are you going to do with it?' Through the story, Jesus gives three very clear warnings to his listeners.

The first is that it is possible to hear about the kingdom of God, yet never enter it. The second says it is possible to be fooled by other people's appearance and abilities; the reality being that character and obedience matters more than charisma. The third shows it is possible to be self-deceived and to trust in one's own activity or good works, including one's orthodox religious beliefs, rather than in the person of Christ:

> "These words I speak to you are not incidental additions to your life, homeowner improvements to your standard of living. They are foundational words, words to build a life on. If you work these words into your life, you are like a smart carpenter who built his house on solid rock. Rain poured down, the river flooded, a tornado hit – but nothing moved that house. It was fixed to the rock.
>
> "But if you just use my words in Bible studies and don't work them into your life, you are like a stupid carpenter who built his house on the sandy beach. When a storm rolled in and the waves came up, it collapsed like a house of cards."
>
> (Matthew 7 v 24 - 27 MSG)

You will note in the story, there are a number of similarities between the two builders. They both had the same goal, which was to build a house as a place of safety, security and shelter. If we take the house to be a metaphor for their lives, then we can see how they both wanted to build a good life for themselves. Clearly, this is a relatable desire and something most people want, but we see how they try to achieve it in different ways.

This idea is completely relevant to us today. We still place universal value on peace, safety, contentment, and stability - it's either achieved, or it's longed for. We seek good relationships and happy families, however much human failings may make it difficult. We look to develop inner resources to cope with the pressures of modern living, along with wisdom and guidance to avoid constantly groping about in the dark as we navigate the stormy waters of life. These are common hopes for all. Yet there are even deeper desires which, despite being sought in different ways, also prevail. People desire a sense of internal power to live by, so they don't keep making the same mistakes over and over again. People long for freedom from guilt and shame, together with the comfort of knowing their many sins (or what they may label as 'faults') are forgiven. And crucially, there remains an enduring witness to how God has put eternity in the hearts of humanity; people not only wish for a good life now, but also look for some kind of assurance of an afterlife:

> He has made everything beautiful in its time. He has also set eternity in the human heart; yet no one can fathom what God has done from beginning to end.
> (Ecclesiastes 3 v 11)

These human aspirations are often summarised as the need for security, self-worth and significance. Security gives a sense of belonging and comes through trustworthy relationships. Self-worth is the desire to know we have value and are appreciated by others. And the need for significance is the ability to contribute, to feel a sense of purpose in your life, and to be able to make a difference. These are all worthy aspirations; they're part of how God made us. Therefore, the challenge is to give these natural desires back to the maker and creator of them, trusting him and not ourselves to meet them. For the believer, there has been the revelation of these needs being truly met by God, through a relationship with Jesus Christ and by building their lives on the solid foundation of obedience to his teaching.

In the story of the two builders, both achieved their goal. They built themselves a house, and by outward appearances, there was little to distinguish them. Built in the same locality, they looked equally complete from ground level to roof. As indeed, in certain outward aspects of daily living, there is often no difference between Christians and our neighbours. In fact, it wouldn't be uncommon to outwardly perceive non-believers as 'doing better' and achieving more by worldly measures. But there were differences; not obvious, but nonetheless vital. They had to do with the unseen realm, with the foundations, where men's eyes could not see.

One man had built on solid rock, where the other had built on sand. One man's foundation was substantial and would stand the tests of time and life's trials. The other man's foundation was superficial - we might even say non-existent - and it would fail him at the time of his greatest need. Luke's version of the story brings this out with greater clarity when he says of the first man, he *"dug down deep and laid the foundation on rock,"* while the second man, *"built a house on the ground without a foundation"* (see Luke 6 v 46 - 49).

Jesus likens the man who built on solid rock to the person who builds their life on obedience to God's word. They are someone who listens to the words of Jesus and obeys them. Their trust is shown by how they act upon his teaching, turning hearing into doing. Jesus gives them the accolade of being *"wise,"* knowing they will be able to stand strong throughout the inevitable challenges life brings.

The second man, who built on sand, is likened to the person who hears his words but disregards them. They listen to what he says but take no action, which sees them described as *"foolish."* The foolish are not simply people who live without reference to Jesus or his teaching. They are also people who hear his word but fail to act on or obey it. They fail to practise what Jesus taught and work God's truth into their lives.

It is important for us to recognise the serious consequences of lacking strong foundations in our lives. Jesus makes it clear. Building our lives and hopes on anything other than God's word will result in us not standing when the time of testing comes (pictured as rain, floods and strong winds). In fact, Matthew and Luke describe the devastating results, as we read how the house *"fell with a great crash"* (Matthew 7 v 27), *"collapsed like a house of cards"* (Luke 6 v 49 MSG), and how *"its destruction was complete"* (Luke 6 v 49).

What we do so clearly matters. Jesus had warned his listeners earlier of the grave consequences of building on a foundation of religious pretence, where outward shows of righteousness hid a lack of heart commitment and godly living. We're told the day of judgement would find such people disowned by Jesus and revealed as false disciples:

> "Not everyone who says to me, 'Lord, Lord,' will enter the kingdom of heaven, but only the one who does the will of my Father who is in heaven. Many will say to me on that day, 'Lord, Lord, did we not prophesy in your name and in your name drive out demons, and in your name perform many miracles?' Then I will tell them plainly, 'I never knew you. Away from me, you evildoers!'"
> (Matthew 7 v 21 - 23)

The Scriptures are also clear that all men will experience judgement after death. But they also speak specifically of believers having to give an account of their lives:

> People are destined to die once, and after that to face judgment...
> (Hebrews 9 v 27)

> So then, each of us will give an account of ourselves to God.
> (Romans 14 v 12)

> For we must all appear before the judgement seat of Christ, that each of us may receive what is due us for the things done while in the body, whether good or bad.
> (2 Corinthians 5 v 10)

If each one of us makes Jesus our foundation, and we build on the rock through our obedience to his teaching, then the day of judgement should hold no fear for us. When we build a lifestyle of listening and acting, so becoming doers and not mere hearers of God's word, we will increasingly bear witness to the genuineness of our faith. Lives transformed by hearing God's word and responding with our actions will bring God glory.

God's Provision For Me And You

If this all seems rather challenging and daunting, be reminded and encouraged of God's provision for me and you. He has prepared pathways for us to succeed as a follower of Jesus and he longs to see us flourishing in our walk with him. As Jesus himself said to his disciples:

> "This is to my Father's glory, that you bear much fruit, showing yourselves to be my disciples."
> (John 15 v 8)

> "You did not choose me, but I chose you and appointed you so that you might go and bear fruit—fruit that will last."
> (John 15 v 16)

Let me illustrate how God has put everything in place to help us fulfil his purpose for our lives. Or as Paul expressed it, how we might *"press on to take hold of that for which Christ Jesus took hold of me"* (Philippians 3 v 12):

Some years ago, my wife competed in the London Marathon. As she looks back, she can see that on the day, everything had been prepared and ordered for her to get across the finishing line and obtain her medal.

First, she had been accepted and named among the runners. She was given a race number, plus an electronic tracker to show her progress and current position. The course had been laid out for her, and there were marshals on route to guide her in the right direction. Along the way there were numerous water stations to refresh her and keep her hydrated.

As she ran, there were also the vast crowds cheering her on, many of them giving her personal encouragement and calling out her name! Should she trip or have an injury on her way round the course, there were first aiders to quickly come to her assistance. If flagging, she could join up with a 'buddy' for mutual encouragement and run together with them. There was also the constant verbal encouragement she could receive from fellow runners, both those she was overtaking and those shooting past her to their own finish.

Of course, she had her own part to play in wearing suitable clothing and comfortable running shoes. Also, it was important for her to identify and run 'her own race,' so she was not pulled on by other runners to a pace she hadn't trained for. When the running got tough, especially towards the end of the race, she had to dig deep and push through the pain by talking to herself. I imagine her saying, 'You're going to finish this, you're nearly there!' There were no armchairs on the route because, like the rest, she was expected to keep going and reach the finish line!

We explored previously how, by his divine power, God has given us everything we need to live a godly life, meaning we should, therefore, make every effort to respond to his promises and enlarge our faith (see 2 Peter 1 v 3 - 5). Despite the full provision he has made, it is always our responsibility to actively run the race he has set before us. But, working together with him, we can fulfil his call on our lives and receive the eternal prize.

Like the Apostle Paul, it is possible for us to discipline ourselves so we can run with purpose in every step. For us to do this, we need to daily build our lives on the firm foundation of constant application and obedience to the words of Jesus (see 1 Corinthians 9 v 24 - 27). Paul was confident the good work God had begun in the believers at Philippi, he would carry on to completion at the day of Christ Jesus (see Philippians 1 v 6). God wasn't going to change, and his faithfulness wasn't going anywhere! Yet, he speaks to them of how he himself had not already reached perfection, but was putting the past behind him, so that he could press on to reach the end of his *"race"* and receive the *"heavenly prize"* (Philippians 3 v 12 - 14). We, too, can take comfort that our growth in Christlikeness is similarly progressive and God *will* finish the work he has started in us. He will finish what he started in *you!*

Further encouragement comes from remembering how Jesus prayed for his followers, asking for his Father to, *"sanctify them by the truth; your word is truth"* (John 17 v 17). As his followers today, he is still praying for you and me. I like how authors, Andreas Kostenberger and Justin Taylor, helpfully describe the impact of this verse. God is committed to running with us throughout our entire race, seeing the finish for us when we can't, and sanctifying us bit by bit:

> *Sanctification is a lifelong process whereby believers progressively grow in holiness and purity in their thoughts, words, and actions. From Jesus's prayer, we can draw confidence that God is proactively involved in sanctifying us and that* ***God's Word will play an important part in that process.*** *The sanctification of believers enables us to engage in effective witness to a hostile world, thereby continuing Jesus's mission until his return.*[2] *[Emphasis added]*

People Of The Spirit

As we've repeatedly explored, we have not been left to battle on alone. Jesus has left us the Holy Spirit to help, guide and empower us (see John 14 v 15 - 17). As such, we are not to simply be men and women of the word of God; we are also to be people of the Spirit. If we are to progress in our likeness to Christ, we must also learn how to live by, and keep in step with, the Spirit. Believers grow when they become people of the both the 'Word *and* Spirit.'

In the past, our sinful nature governed our thinking processes, influenced our decision making, and controlled the exercise of our will. The result saw us act in ways contrary to the will of God. But now we are *"in Christ,"* we have been set free from our slavery to sin and given a new nature. We are now created to be like God in true righteousness and holiness.

Living under the control of the Holy Spirit is not automatic. It requires our active co-operation with him each day. We must actively surrender ourselves to his influence, and increasingly learn to obey his prompting and guidance. Paul reminds us of this when he says, *"So, I say, walk by the Spirit and you will not gratify the desires of the flesh"* (Galatians 5 v 16), and again when he says, *"Since we live by the Spirit, let us keep in step with the Spirit"* (Galatians 5 v 25).

Paul recognises the very real possibility of getting ourselves out of step with the Spirit and living a life that dishonours God. Hence, he speaks of both grieving the Holy Spirit and putting out the Holy Spirit's fire (see Ephesians 4 v 30; 1 Thessalonians 5 v 19). If our life is not under the influence and control of the Holy Spirit, we become vulnerable to the attacks of the enemy and the vitality of our spiritual life can begin to wane. There is a danger we become ineffective and unproductive in our knowledge of Christ. It follows, therefore, that Paul writes to the believers in Ephesus, encouraging them to continually be filled with the Holy Spirit:

> Do not get drunk on wine, which leads to debauchery. Instead, be filled (go on being filled, a continuous process) with the Spirit.
> (Ephesians 5 v 18; parentheses added)

In his letter to them, Paul uses a stark contrast to get his point across. To be drunk (literally) is to be under the influence and control of intoxicants, but he wants them instead to be under the influence, direction and control of the Holy Spirit. In a similar way to being *"drunk on wine,"* Paul knows spiritual lives can be damaged and ruined when we are not full of the Spirit – we leave space for increasing worldly influence in our lives.

It's a serious message, isn't it? Being drunk and developing an unhealthy relationship with alcohol leads to debauchery, disgrace and degradation in people's lives. To gain a greater understanding of what Paul is seeking to convey about a life that is not full of the Holy Spirit, let's consider an example we see around us. Drunk driving is considered one of the social evils of our day. For the perpetrator, the consequence can be heavy legal penalties, fines, and even imprisonment. For others, it leads to the damage of vehicles and property, and in the worst cases, injury and death of innocent bystanders. Central to this crime is the fact that, when drunk, the driver's judgement is impaired; vision is blurred, they cannot gauge distances, and their reactions are slow or inadequate.

The book of Proverbs gives us a similar description of a person drunk on wine losing their sense of judgement (see Proverbs 23 v

29 - 35). We're told they will lack clarity in their thinking as, *"Your mind will imagine confusing things"* (verse 33). As a result, character and behaviour will change, and a person will show a lack of sensitivity or care. The writer speaks of *"Needless bruises"* (verse 29), and says, *"They hit me, you will say, but I am not hurt! They beat me, but I don't feel it"* (verse 35). It's interesting to see just how pertinent this ancient writing still is today.

Spiritually, when we are not full of the Holy Spirit, our judgement also becomes impaired. We lack clarity over issues and lose the ability to distinguish right from wrong. We're not able to discern between things of primary or secondary importance, creating unnecessary divisions by getting hung up on minor issues of opinion. We fail to distinguish what is good and acceptable and can get increasingly confused about what the will of God is for our lives. The impact may start slowly and subtly. It may initially be undetectable or even considered praiseworthy to the world. But over time there is a numbing effect, with the resultant lack of sensitivity becoming a callous skin growing over our heart and conscience. We can reach a point where we are no longer pained or disturbed when we sin, leading to the danger of self-deception, where we think (or convince ourselves) everything is okay when it is not:

> If we claim to be without sin, we deceive ourselves and the truth is not in us.
> (1 John 1 v 8)

Sadly, being out of step with the Spirit also makes us unaware or indifferent to the needs of others. The impact is felt by both brothers and sisters in Christ, and those among whom we live outside the church; when the latter happens, our witness is particularly affected. Think about how someone who is drunk can be ready to fight anybody and everybody, or thinks they can walk on a narrow ledge, or scale a tall building. Similarly, we can forget our ongoing reliance on and need for God if we distance ourselves from the Spirit's influence. As we focus primarily on our own strengths, we can sideline him from even our Christian activity and think we have power to do exploits for God on our own, in effect trying to do his work for him.

A Life In Balance

We've talked about the idea of placing God in control of our lives by being open to the leading of the Holy Spirit. And we've seen how Paul contrasts this to the image of being drunk and being under the influence or at the mercy of external influences. Now consider how people who are drunk often lack a sense of balance. Think for a moment about a drunken person you may have encountered: someone laughing and joking one moment, but morose and crying the next; loud and shouting, then quiet and talking in a whisper; walking straight, but then staggering along the road from side to side; or on their feet one minute, before ending up falling over themselves the next.

It is also true that in many cases the drunken person squanders and wastes their resources. The book of Proverbs reminds us that, *"Drunkards and gluttons become poor"* (Proverbs 21 v 17), and *"Whoever loves wine and oil will never be rich"* (Proverbs 23 v 21). There is a tendency for a drunken person to waste their money on drink to the detriment of their friends and family. Their treasure is in temporary things, not on things of lasting value, courting popularity through extravagance. There is a focus on pleasure, or escapism, rather than permanence, living for the moment, with little thought for the future. While Paul uses the image of drunkenness, this all describes, albeit often more subtly, the instability of any life built on the sand of worldly wisdom and control.

In comparison, if we use the word 'balance' to positively describe a person's life, it may conjure up for us a picture of someone who demonstrates poise, calmness, composure, consistency, stability and steadiness. Or maybe, we might imagine someone who displays self-confidence, self-control and serenity in their life, being neither indifferent nor over excited. You may consider how someone seems to have found the right pace in their life; they're not impulsive and never seem to drag their heels or engage in frantic activity. You could describe a person who is equally at home with children as they are with adults, or with the poor as they are with the rich. They are able to converse with the simple, just as well as with great minds. They have become a master of themselves, able to show joy, sorrow and even anger, but never in an uncontrolled manner.

These characteristics of a life in balance are what we see demonstrated throughout the life of Jesus as he lived in continual obedience to the voice of the Spirit. Tellingly, John records that Jesus was given the Spirit without limit (see John 3 v 34). We can also live our life like this, thriving in the way God intended us to. However, if we are not full of the Holy Spirit, a lack of balance and inconsistency easily creeps into our daily living. The impact is revealed, not only in how we handle the larger events of life, but more often how we react day-to-day in the normal activities of life.

For example, the Scriptures emphasise the importance of our speech. James reminds us the same tongue we use to praise our Lord and Father can also be used to curse men, who have been made in his image (see James 3 v 9; Ephesians 4 v 29; Colossians 4 v 6).

Similarly, we might push on with Christian activity in our strength, forging our own paths, or those we think are best. These activities may even continue to look very impressive to anyone watching. We may find ourselves majoring on one of the key elements of our spiritual life, such as worship, witness, social action or prayer, while neglecting others; we may be very busy, but in activities of our own making. Instead of deepening our relationship with God through his word, we may become fascinated with listening and talking about the latest transient fad or practice to hit the Christian scene. While we know we should be focusing on the whole counsel of God's word, we can find our attention drawn to our favourite passages or doctrine, ignoring other 'hard' passages or topics. It's not uncommon to fail to remember Paul's words to Timothy, imploring us to remember the value of all Scripture:

> All Scripture is God-breathed and is useful for teaching, rebuking, correcting and training in righteousness, so that the servant of God may be thoroughly equipped for every good work.
> (2 Timothy 3 v 16)

Lives Of Purpose – Bearing Fruit

In Luke's gospel, Jesus tells the story of the prodigal son (see Luke 15 v 11 - 32). You'll recall how the younger son, having received a wonderful inheritance from his father, throws it all away! Jesus says, *"he squandered all his wealth in wild living"* (Luke 15 v 13). It is possible for us to do the same. Even if our actions don't obviously mirror those of the younger son, viewing ourselves with sober judgement (see Romans 12 v 3) should bring us to a continual realisation of the sinful nature we have been rescued from. In contrast, our new identity in Christ sees us adopted into God's family and our sin removed from our record, with an eternal inheritance assigned to us.

We are now *"heirs of God and co-heirs with Christ"* (Romans 8 v 17), and we have been blessed *"with every spiritual blessing in Christ"* (Ephesians 1 v 3). Even more than that, the Bible tells us we have an inheritance kept in heaven for us *"that can never perish, spoil or fade"* (1 Peter 1 v 4). What an amazing position to find ourselves in because of the saving work of Jesus on the cross! Yet it is still possible to squander these spiritual riches, rather than treasure them and build our lives upon them as our prized possession.

Paul tells the church at Ephesus they must be very careful how they live. Because the days are evil, Paul tells them to stay wise and make the most of every opportunity (see Ephesians 5 v 15). If we are not continually filled with the Holy Spirit, it is possible for us to waste time and miss opportunities for the gospel. We can become lazy and undisciplined, meaning we engage in pursuits that don't contribute to the building of God's kingdom. It can see us using the blessing of our finances, first and foremost, for our own comfort and well-being. Through subtle fear, we can become 'people pleasers,' seeking the world's acceptance and affection. Lines can become blurred, and we may lower our standards and values; in doing so we can lose our distinctiveness and become increasingly ineffective. All this from not staying in step with the Holy Spirit!

The Bible makes it clear. Disciples of Jesus are meant to be productive and God's intention for us is to live very fruitful lives. He chose us and appointed us with clear purposes to fulfil. Look at how Paul reminds believers in Rome of this truth:

> So, my brothers and sisters, you also died to the law through the body of Christ, that you might belong to another, to him who was raised from the dead, in order that we might bear fruit to God.
> (Romans 7 v 4 - 6)

Not being full of the Holy Spirit can result in us becoming unproductive in the work of God and the extension of his kingdom. Worse still, it leads to God our Father not being glorified in our lives. To be unproductive is a serious matter. The importance of bearing fruit is brought out in Jesus' parable of the barren fig tree, where a man who has planted a fig tree in his vineyard comes seeking fruit on it and finds none (see Luke 13 v 6 - 9). Jesus also warned Israel that the kingdom of God would be taken from them and given to a people who would produce its fruit (see Matthew 21 v 43). As he explains the teaching to his disciples, he speaks of himself as the true vine and his Father as being the vinedresser. We see how God deals with those who bear no fruit, and those who do:

> "He cuts off every branch in me that bears no fruit, while every branch that does bear fruit he prunes so that it will be even more fruitful."
> (John 15 v 2)

God not only looks for faithfulness but also for fruitfulness. And the key to being productive is to abide, or remain, in Jesus. In fact, Jesus emphasises how we simply cannot bear fruit on our own, but if we remain in him we will bear much fruit:

> "Remain in me, as I also remain in you. No branch can bear fruit by itself; it must remain in the vine. Neither can you bear fruit unless you remain in me."
> (John 15 v 4 - 5)

To remain or abide in Jesus speaks of a continuing daily personal relationship with him, characterised by trust, prayer and obedience. Jesus spoke of his abiding in the Father's love, because he had kept his Father's commandments; we ourselves will abide in his love if we obey his commandments.

As we follow him, Jesus said the Holy Spirit would glorify him by taking all he has taught and making it real to us. Indeed, the Holy Spirit lives and works within us for the express purpose of enabling us, *"to will and to act in order to fulfil his good purpose"* (Philippians 2 v 13). Fellowship, and co-operation with the Spirit of Jesus is vital to us abiding in Jesus and bearing fruit that honours God.

Ready For Battle

In Ephesians, Paul reminds the believers that the Christian life is not *like* a war. It *is* one! Therefore, he encourages them to put on the whole armour of God, so they can take their stand against the devil's schemes. They need to, *"be alert and always keep praying for all the Lord's people"* (Ephesians 6 v 18). It is plainly obvious there is no use putting the armour on and then falling asleep. Consider briefly, the picture of preparedness painted here, compared to the person who has built their life on unstable foundations, or the image of a drunk person we discussed earlier. Now, consider the builder who has built their house on the sure, solid, unchanging rock of Jesus and his teaching. We must be ready and alert for when trouble comes... because it will.

Peter speaks similarly to the believers when he writes, *"Be alert and of sober mind. Your enemy the devil prowls around like a roaring lion looking for someone to devour"* (1 Peter 5 v 8). And Paul continues the theme when writing to the church in Thessalonica, exhorting God's people to stay awake and exercise self-control in light of the coming day of the Lord:

> But you, brothers and sisters, are not in darkness so that this day should surprise you like a thief. You are all children of the light and children of the day. We do not belong to the night or to the darkness. So then, let us not be like others, who are asleep, but let us be awake and sober. For those who sleep, sleep at night, and those who get drunk, get

> drunk at night. But since we belong to the day, let us be sober, putting on faith and love as a breastplate, and the hope of salvation as a helmet.
> (1 Thessalonians 5 v 4 - 8)

If we are not being filled continually with the Spirit and living under *his* influence, we put ourselves at risk. Unless we are being guided by him and obeying his promptings, we find ourselves vulnerable to the attacks of the enemy, unprepared to engage in spiritual warfare and spiritual activity. If we're not alert, we may struggle to see or take the way of escape God provides in times of temptation. Remember how, when tempted in the desert, Jesus wielded the sword of the Spirit to defend himself. By declaring, *"It is written...,"* he rebuked the lies of the devil with the foundational truths he had built his life on (see Matthew 4 v 1 - 11). If we're not walking closely with the Spirit, these truths can be harder to reach for; we can struggle to garrison our hearts and minds with the truth of God's unconditional love.

In a broader sense, we can also miss out on playing our part in extending God's kingdom. Without our hearts and minds set firmly on the will of God for our lives and the world, we can miss the Spirit's promptings. We may find ourselves failing to take advantage of divine appointments set before us, missing the chance to witness either verbally, or by fully demonstrating God's love and compassion in practical service.

Jesus taught of the five foolish virgins who took their lamps but failed to take any oil with them. When the bridegroom unexpectedly arrived, they were not ready to meet him and so missed out on the wedding banquet (see Matthew 25 v 1 - 13). We, too, miss out on so much when we are not ready for action, having not gone on being continually filled with the Holy Spirit.

Painting A Picture – A Hope Like No Other

The contrast between Paul's image of being drunk on wine, or being filled with God's Spirit, is clear. Being continuously filled, putting him in control, and obeying his prompting transforms our individual lives. But the picture also gives us a wonderful insight into the life we may live as the people of God; what a Spirit-filled community will look like.

As we commit to growing communities that remain firmly connected to the vine, where the Spirit leads individually and corporately, we will cultivate the world-changing church God has planned. Individually and corporately, we'll see wise judgements being made in life, and about life. We'll see clarity over what is right, wrong, acceptable and unacceptable. We'll see consensus in our understanding of what is of primary importance. There'll be conviction and a keen awareness of what is harmful and what is beneficial. And where the will of God is being discerned, there'll be a sensitivity regarding sin and holiness.

With hearts and minds continually renewed, church communities will exhibit a rounded balance between the physical, material and spiritual dimensions of life. They will demonstrate stability and order, so not to be tossed around by every new trend or fashion. Yet, with the humility that comes from reliance on God, the church won't remain entrenched in its position but will continually seek to learn from, and adapt to, the whole counsel of God. As such, the church will continue to be relevant to society as it speaks into and meets the eternal needs of humanity.

Where the Spirit leads, we'll build communities where all people are welcomed and valued. People inside and outside the church will find their needs met in a caring and sensitive manner. And every vibrant emotion will be in evidence, because people have learnt to understand and celebrate their full humanity.

The practicalities of church life will also be transformed. We'll see the stewardship of time, money and talent taken seriously, with spiritual riches taking precedence over material gain and social status. Discipline, hard work, self-sacrifice and obedience will be seen as the only adequate response to God's amazing grace. In this setting, the extension of God's kingdom will become people's magnificent obsession, and people will increasingly bear fruit that honours and brings glory to him.

The power and love of God will overflow from our churches. Salt and light won't be biblical clichés, but the active reality of lives being transformed into the likeness of Christ. These lives will be characterised by their active engagement in the spiritual battle to win the nations to Jesus Christ. God's people will be committed to intercessory prayer as we wait on God, ready to catch the next breath of the Spirit to carry us nearer to the final day of the coming of the Lord.

This is the type of community I want to play my part in building! It's no wonder Paul is so emphatic about the need for them to go on being filled with the Spirit of God. Not that the filling of the Spirit is for our own aggrandisement, or to boost our reputation and massage our egos. Neither is the aim that God may simply display his power in us. Rather, it is that Jesus himself who loved the church and gave himself up for her, might have a radiant, holy and blameless church. For the will of God is our sanctification, that we may be fully restored into people ready for eternity with him (see Ephesians 5 v 25 - 27; 1 Thessalonians 4 v 3 - 8).

Look at Michael Reeves' comment on Spurgeon's view of sanctification:

> *For Spurgeon, the heart of sanctification is the sanctification of the heart. The Holy Spirit sanctifies through God's truth, but mere comprehension of new knowledge, however heavenly, is not sanctification. Spurgeon held that heartless orthodoxy is quite as bad as heartless unbelief—in fact, that it is the other side of the same coin. Equally, while the work of sanctification must involve a change of behaviour, a mere change of behaviour without a change of heart is at best but superficial and at worst rankly hypocritical. True holiness is a deep matter of those desires and loves that then drive our actions.*[3]

The heart is the heart of the matter! So it follows that Reeves is clear on the distinction between sanctification and mere morality; they are of an entirely different nature:

> *That being the case, sanctification cannot be a mechanical process. It is a matter of the Spirit wooing and turning hearts so that*

believers might not just act differently but think differently and want differently and therefore act differently.[4]

And so, we finish with my enduring hope and challenge...

We must build the transformative power of the Holy Spirit and the truth of God's word into the mortar of each brick we lay in the foundations of our lives and our churches. In doing so may we, the people of God, experience the continued infilling of the Holy Spirit, leading us to greater and greater Christlikeness as we look to his coming.

May God himself, the God of peace, sanctify you through and through. May your whole spirit, soul and body be kept blameless at the coming of our Lord Jesus Christ. The one who calls you is faithful, and he will do it.

(1 Thessalonians 5 v 23 - 24)

Notes

1 Neil Crosbie, Director, The Bible Society

2 Taken from The Final Days of Jesus by Andreas Kostenberger & Justin Taylor with Alexander Stewart, Copyright © 2014, Page 83. Used by permission of Crossway, a publishing ministry of Good News Publishers, Wheaton, IL 60187, www.crossway.org

3 Taken from Spurgeon and the Christian Life: Alive In Christ by Michael Reeves Copyright © 2018, Page 134. Used by permission of Crossway, a publishing ministry of Good News Publishers, Wheaton, IL 60187, www.crossway.org

4 Ibid, page 135.

Epilogue

Words of Oswald Chambers, Bible teacher and YMCA chaplain (1874–1917)

The reason that some of us have not entered into the experience of sanctification is that we have not realised the meaning of sanctification from God's standpoint. Sanctification means being made one with Jesus so that the disposition that ruled him will rule us. Are we prepared for what that will cost? It will cost everything that is not of God in us.

The one and only characteristic of the Holy Ghost in a man is a strong family likeness to Jesus Christ, and freedom from everything that is unlike Him. Are we prepared to set ourselves apart for the Holy Spirit's ministrations in us?[1]

Words of JC Ryle, Bishop of Liverpool (1816–1900)

There are others of the Lord's people who seem to be always advancing. They grow like grass after rain; they increase like Israel in Egypt; they press on like Gideon, though sometimes faint, yet always pursuing. They are ever adding grace to grace, and faith to faith, and strength to strength. Every time you meet them their hearts seem larger, and their spiritual stature taller and stronger. Every year they appear to see more, and know more, and believe more, and feel more in their religion. They not only have good

---

1 www.utmost.org/classic/instantaneous-and-insistent-sanctification-classic

works to prove the reality of their faith, but they are zealous of them. They not only do well, but they are unwearied in well-doing. They attempt great things, and they do great things. When they fail, they try again, and when they fail, they are soon up again. And all this time they think themselves poor, unprofitable servants, and fancy they do nothing at all. These are those who make religion lovely and beautiful in the eyes of all. They wrest praise even from the unconverted and win golden opinions even from the selfish men of the world. It does one good to see, to be with, and to hear them. When you meet them, you could believe like Moses, they had just come out from the presence of God. When you part with them you feel warmed by their company, as if your soul had been near a fire.[2]

---

2 www.monergism.com/call-prayer

THANK YOU!

I could not finish without giving sincere thanks to the many people who have given me such loving support and encouragement during my writing. They know who they are, even though I can't mention them all by name.

Thanks must first go to my wife who has travelled with me on this journey, remaining a constant source of encouragement. To say nothing of her patience, time and again, she found me seated at my laptop failing to respond to a call that the evening meal was ready!

Thanks also to those who helped with the practicalities of the book's production. Trevor Allen, who first read the manuscript, correcting its punctuation and grammar, and offering helpful suggestions. Tuuli Platner, for designing the book covers, layout, and preparing the book for printing and publication. Matthew Wood, whose excellent and sterling work editing the book ensures it flows well, stayed "reader friendly," and continues to speak to our audience.

I am also very grateful for the many spiritual fathers and mothers who taught me such wonderful biblical truth through the years, modelling what it means to live out the faith of the gospel in everyday life.

We are all shaped by what we read, listen to, and encounter in our everyday lives. But particularly, by the people God brings into our lives and the friendships which endure over many years.

My thanks go to the many friends I have journeyed with in the Newfrontiers family of churches. Being alongside people who handle the word of God with accuracy, while also embodying its truth, has been a great privilege. Like many others, I have been inspired and shaped by Terry Virgo's teaching on grace that was timely and transformational at a key time in my life.

A special thanks too, to the many brothers and sisters I have enjoyed meeting around the world. I have learnt so much from your dedication, sacrifice and passion for Jesus, while your theological insights have enriched my life. It has been such an honour and privilege to witness the grace of God in your lives and the lives of your communities.

Thank you too, to all my fellow elders and people in The Family Church, Christchurch (now GodFirst Church, Christchurch) and City Church Cambridge. Your love, prayers and support through the years, in the good and hard times, has meant so much to me and our family.

And, I could not finish without saying another big thank you to Denise and all my children. Your love, support, and many sacrifices you made to enable me to fulfil God's call on my life has been exceptional.

To him who sits on the throne and to the Lamb be praise and honour and glory and power, for ever and ever! Amen

---

Wood Writes Words - Copywriting | Content | Editing
matthew@woodwriteswords.co.uk
www.woodwriteswords.co.uk

Printed in Dunstable, United Kingdom

66997675R00188